Series in Computer Science — Vol. 18

ARRAY GRAMMARS, PATTERNS and RECOGNIZERS

Editor

P. S. P. Wang

Massachusetts Institute of Technology
Artificial Intelligence Laboratory
Cambridge, Massachusetts
USA

World Scientific
Singapore • New Jersey • London • Hong Kong

Published by

World Scientific Publishing Co. Pte. Ltd.,
P O Box 128, Farrer Road, Singapore 9128
USA office: 687 Hartwell Street, Teaneck, NJ 07666
UK office: 73 Lynton Mead, Totteridge, London N20 8DH

ARRAY GRAMMARS, PATTERNS AND RECOGNIZERS

ISBN 981-02-0083-8

Printed in Singapore by JBW Printers & Binders Pte. Ltd.

FOREWORD

The research and development of multi-dimensional pattern recognition, scene analysis, computer vision and image processing have progressed very rapidly in recent years. Among various models employed for pattern representation and analysis, the *array grammar* has attracted more and more attention because it has several advantages over others. It is a powerful pattern generative model generalized from Chomsky's phrase structure grammar; is sufficiently flexible to be extended to higher dimensionalities; has been shown to be more accurate than some other methods for two-dimensional clustering analysis; can be highly parallel and as powerful as tessellation or cellular automata; and can provide a sequential/parallel model that serves as a compromise between a purely sequential model, which takes too much time for large patterns, and a purely parallel model, which normally requires too much hardware for large digital arrays. Besides, it provides a good setting to get inside and obtain indepth views of multi-dimensional computation, automata and language theory.

This special issue, perhaps the first time ever in the literature, is a collection of fourteen papers by prominent professionals and experts mainly from France, India, Japan and USA, aimed at promoting array grammars, patterns and recognizers. They are grouped in the following four categories: (1) Array grammars and pattern generation, (2) Array pattern recognizers, (3) Coordinate grammars and L-systems, and (4) Hexagonal grids, tilings and encryption.

The first paper "Parallel generalization of finite images" by M. Nivat, A. Saoudi and V. Dare introduces image grammar and its combinatorial and language theoretical properties. The next paper "Context-sensitivity of two-dimensional regular array grammars" by Y. Yamamoto, K. Morita and K. Sugata investigates some #-sensing ability of regular array grammars (RAGs)—the lowest subclass in the Chomsky-like hierarchy of isometric array grammars, and finds that the generative power of RAGs is much greater than one can imagine. The paper "Generating rectangles using two-dimensional grammars with time and space complexity analyses" by E. Lee, S. Zhu and P. Chu explores the theoretical and practical aspects of parallel context-free array grammar and tree grammar. The fourth paper "Siromoney array grammars and applications" by K. Subramanian, L. Revathi and R. Siromoney studies a simple and elegant model called Siromoney matrix model for representing two-dimensional digital pictures, and its applications to describe tilings, polyominoes, distorted patterns and parquet deformations.

In "Two-dimensional three-way array grammars and their acceptors", K. Morita, Y. Yamamoto and K. Sugata explore three-way horizontally context-sensitive array grammar, three-way immediately terminating array grammar, their acceptors and relations with nondeterministic one-dimensional bounded cellular acceptors. The paper "Pushdown recognizers for array patterns" by H. Lin and P. Wang establishes an algorithm for constructing pushdown array automata, and the result is applied to recognize two-dimensional context-free array patterns and is implemented on VAX8650/VMS using Pascal. The next paper "The simulation of two-dimensional one-marker automata by three-way Turing machines" by A. Ito, K. Inoue and I. Takanami studies the necessary and sufficient space conditions for a three-way two-dimensional deterministic (nondeterministic) Turing machine to simulate a two-dimensional deterministic (non-deterministic) one-marker automaton. "Systolic pyramid automata, cellular automata and array languages" by K. Krithivasan and M. Mahajan shows that homogeneous and semihomogeneous pyramid automata have equal computation power though the regular pyramid automata are more powerful.

The following three papers deal with coordinate grammars and Lindenmayer systems, which have very close relations with array grammars. In "Coordinate grammars revisited: generalized isometric grammars", A. Rosenfeld shows that if we require the functions to be shift-invariant and the rules to be of bounded diameter, then coordinate grammars do have a useful hierarchy of types, and if their sentential form always remain connected, they turn out to be equivalent to "isometric grammars". A. Nakamura and K. Aizawa in "Relationships between coordinate grammars and path controlled graph grammars" show some relationships between "coordinate grammars" and node-replacement path controlled embedding (nPCE) grammars, and nPCE grammars can be extended to describe "disconnected coordinate languages". In the next paper "Finite images generated by GL-systems", A. Saoudi, K. Rangarajan and V. Dare introduce a new sequential/parallel device called GL-system (i.e. Grammar-Lindenmayer system) for generating finite images, and some closure and decidability properties are studied.

The next category consists of three papers on hexagonal grids, tilings and encryption, which deal with some variations of array grammars and related systems. In "Grammars on the hexagonal array", K. Aizawa defines array grammars on the hexagonal grid rather than on the conventional Cartesian grid, and some interesting results are found. The paper "Representation of iterative patterns" by H. Aso and N. Honda shows that the shape of a component pattern can be a rectangle for any iterative pattern, which is called a tile. Finally, in the paper "Encryption-decryption techniques for pictures" by R. Siromoney, K. Subramanian and P. Abisha, language theoretic public key cryptosystems for strings and pictures are discussed, and two methods of constructing public key cryptosystems using chain code strings and two-dimensional arrays are presented.

I would like to take this opportunity to show my appreciation to Dr. K. K. Phua and Professor Horst Bunke for their encouragement to publish this special issue. I also want to thank Professor Azriel Rosenfeld for his invaluable opinions and suggestions, and for his excellent preface, in which he skillfully gives a very concise and precise overview of array grammars. Last, but not least, I want to thank all authors for their enthusiasm and contributions, without which this special issue is impossible.

P. S. P. Wang
Massachusetts Institute of Technology AI Lab
(on leave from Northeastern University)

PREFACE

Pictorial patterns often consist of subpatterns of simple(r) types that are combined in particular ways. The subpatterns in turn may consist of still simpler sub-subpatterns, and so on. It was pointed out over 25 years ago[1] that this method of describing patterns in terms of subpatterns, sub-subpatterns, etc. is analogous to describing sentences in terms of clauses, phrases, etc. Since we can determine the syntactic structure of a sentence by parsing it in accordance with grammatical rules, this suggests that it should be possible to determine the structure of a pictorial pattern by "parsing" it in accordance with the rules of a "picture grammar".

Based on this suggestion, various types of picture grammars were introduced and investigated during the 1960s.[2] The methods of formal language theory, developed for studying languages composed of sets of strings, were extended to handle various types of picture languages. Classes of grammars analogous to those introduced by Chomsky — regular, context-free, context-sensitive — were defined. Automata that accept these classes of languages were also defined. Particular attention was paid to "array grammars", whose languages are arrays (rather than strings) of symbols, and to the corresponding types of acceptors.[3]

The literature on array grammars and acceptors, as well as other types of pattern grammars and acceptors, has grown steadily over the past two decades. The continued interest in these topics is evidenced by the fourteen papers that appear in this special issue. The first eight of these papers deal with array grammars and array pattern recognizers; the remaining six deal with closely related concepts, including "coordinate grammars", L-systems, tilings and picture encryption. It is hoped that the publication of this issue will stimulate further activity in these areas.

Azriel Rosenfeld
University of Maryland
College Park, MD

[1] M. L. Minksy, "Steps toward artificial intelligence", *Proc. IRE 49*, 1961, pp. 8–30.

[2] W. F. Miller and A. C. Shaw, "Linguistic methods in picture processing—a survey", *Procs. AFIPS 1968 Fall Joint Computer Conference*, Thompson, Washington, DC, 1968, pp. 279–290.

[3] D. L. Milgram and A. Rosenfeld, "Array automata and array grammars", *Proc. IFIP Congress 71*, North-Holland, Amsterdam, 1972, TA-2, pp. 166–173.

CONTENTS

PARALLEL GENERATION OF FINITE IMAGES

M. NIVAT, A. SAOUDI*

Université Paris VII
Laboratoire d'informatique Théorique et Programmation
2, Place de Jussieu 75221, Paris

and

V. R. DARE

Department of Mathematics
Madras Christian College, Madras, India

Received 15 January 1988
Revised 25 May 1988

We define a syntactic model for generating sets of images, where an image can be viewed as an array over finite alphabet. This model is called image grammar. Image grammar can be considered as a generalization of classical Chomsky grammar. Then we study some combinatorial and language theoretical properties such as reduction, pumping lemmas, complexity measure, closure properties and decidability results. In terms of complexity measure, we give a strict infinite hierarchy. We also characterize these families in terms of deterministic substitutions and Chomsky languages.

Keywords: Array grammars; Context-free grammars; Images; Regular grammars.

1. INTRODUCTION

The theory of formal languages, introduced by Chomsky and Schützenberger[1] has many applications such as in compiling, in parallel processing and pattern recognition. This theory has been extended by Rosenfeld,[2] Siromoney *et al.*[3-5] and Wang[6-10] to two-dimensional patterns. In Ref. 2, Rosenfeld presents various processes for generating digital pictures, such as array automata and array grammars.

In Ref. 3, Siromoney *et al.* present a model (i.e. matrix grammars) for generating matrices and use it for generating wall paper designs, Kolam patterns and some geometric patterns. Matrix grammars generate a matrix in two phases. In the first phase of derivation, a horizontal string of intermediate symbols is generated by means of any type of Chomskian grammars. During the second phase, treating each intermediate symbol as a start symbol, the vertical generation is parallel and obtained by applying a finite set of right linear rules. The vertical rewriting in each column is independent of the generation in other columns. In Ref. 4, Siromoney *et al.* generalize string rewriting rules to array rewriting rules and then obtain a more powerful model called array grammars.

* This author's research was supported by the University of Illinois at Urbana-Champaign.

1

In Ref. 6, Wang presents a new system for generating two-dimensional patterns using matrix grammars and array grammars. This model corresponds to a sequential/parallel system. In Ref. 7, Wang introduces parallel context-free array languages and studies the relationship between parallel isometric array languages and sequential isometric array languages.

The first motivation of this work is to find a process for generating two-dimensional patterns by combining sequential and parallel processing that reflects a synchronization in parallel processing. The second motivation is to extend the classical theory of Chomsky to two-dimensional patterns. For this we introduce image grammars that one might call a synchronized sequential/parallel matrix grammar. The basic difference between image grammars and matrix grammars is the concept of synchronization defined by the set of tables, where a table represents a set of rules allowed to be applied at the same time for rewriting columns. In contrast to matrix grammars,[3] the vertical rules in the tables are context-free. For rewriting columns, we apply vertical rules which are sets of rules (i.e. tables) by substituting the set of variables occurring at the top of columns, by the right sides of rules defining a table. Note that the process of rewriting columns is deterministic in the sense that two identical variables are substituted by the same thing.

The organization of this paper is as follows: In Sect. 2, we give some basic definitions. In Sect. 3, we define our model (i.e. image grammar) and we give some classification of image grammar based on the types of rules. This classification defines some families of sets of images. In Sect. 4, we extend the hierarchy of Chomsky to the above families. We study the combinatorial and theoretical language properties such as pumping lemmas, reduction, complexity measure, closure properties and some decidability results in Sect. 5. In the last section, we characterize the above families in terms of deterministic substitutions and Chomsky languages.

2. BASIC DEFINITIONS

Let Σ be a finite alphabet. Then a word is a mapping from $[n]$ to Σ where $[n] = \{1, 2, 3, \ldots, n\}$.

An image is a mapping from $[n] \times [m] \to \Sigma$. We denote by Σ^{**} the set of all images on Σ. If $x \in \Sigma^{**}$, then $\text{dom}(x) = \{(k, l) : k \in [n], l \in [m]\}$.

If $x \in \Sigma^{**}$, then the column size of x is the number of columns in x and it is denoted by $|x|_v$ and the row size of x is the number of rows in x and it is denoted by $|x|_H$.

We now define two kinds of operations on images. Let $\oplus$ be a partial operation, called a column catenation, defined from $(\Sigma^{**})^2$ to Σ^{**} by $x \oplus y = xy$ if $|x|_H = |y|_H$ undefined otherwise.

Let $\ominus$ be a partial operation called row catenation defined from $(\Sigma^{**})^2$ to Σ^{**} by

$$x \ominus y = \begin{bmatrix} x \\ y \end{bmatrix} \text{ if } |x|_v = |y|_v \text{ undefined otherwise.}$$

Let $x = \begin{bmatrix} x_1 \\ x_2 \\ \vdots \\ x_n \end{bmatrix}$ or $x = (y_1, y_2, \ldots, y_k)$ be an image such that $x_i \in \Sigma^+$ and

$y_j \in \Sigma_+$, then $x(i)_v = x_i$ and $x(i)_H = y_j$.

Let I and I' be subsets of Σ^{**}, then $I \oplus I' = \{x \oplus y : x \in I$ and $y \in I'$ and $\oplus \in \{\textcircled{1}, \ominus\}\}$. Let $I_0 = I^0 = \{\square\}$ where $\square$ is the empty image. Then $I_{n+1} = I \ominus I_n$ $(n > 0)$ and we denote by

$$I_* = \bigcup_{n \geqslant 0} I_n \text{ and } I_+ = \bigcup_{n > 0} I_n .$$

Let $I^{n+1} = I \oplus I^n$, then $I^* = \bigcup_{n \geqslant 0} I^n$ and $I^+ = \bigcup_{n > 0} I^n$.

Let Σ_n^{**} be the set of finite images having column size n and if I is a subset of Σ^{**}, then $I_{(n)}$ is the set of finite images in I of column size I.

Let $x \in \Sigma^{**}$, then x^T is the image defined as the following:

(i) $\text{dom}(x^T) = \{(j, i) : (i, j) \in \text{dom}(x)\}$.

(ii) For all $(i, j) \in \text{dom } x^T$, $x^T(i, j) = x(j, i)$.

A relabeling is a mapping from an alphabet to another alphabet. If $x \in \Sigma^{**}$ and if H is a relabeling from Σ to Σ', then $H(x)$ is defined as follows:

(i) $\text{dom}(H(x)) = \text{dom}(x)$

(ii) For all $(k, l) \in \text{dom}(x)$, if $x(k, l) = a$, then $H(x)(k, l) = H(a)$.

If I is a set of images, $H(I) = \{H(x) : x \in I\}$.

3.   GRAMMARS FOR FINITE IMAGES

We now define image grammars for generating finite images.

Definition 3.1.   An image grammar is a structure $G = (V_H, V_v, \Sigma_I, \Sigma, S, R_H, R_v)$, where

(1) V_H is a finite set of horizontal variables.

(2) V_v is a finite set of vertical variables.

(3) $\Sigma_I \subset V_v$ is a finite set of intermediates.

(4) Σ is a finite set of terminals.

(5) S is an axiom.

(6) R_H is the set of horizontal rules of the form $V \to AV_1 V_2 \ldots V_n$ where $V, V_i \in V_H$ and $A \in \Sigma_I$, and

(7) R_v is the set of vertical rules of the form $\bar{r} = (V_1 \to a_1 V_1^1 V_1^2 \ldots V_1^n;$ $V_2 \to a_2 V_2^1 \ldots V_2^n; \ldots; V_P \to a_P V_P^1 \ldots V_P^n)$ with $a_i \in \Sigma$ and $V_1^j \in V_v$ or $\bar{r} = (V_1 \to a_1, V_2 \to a_2; \ldots; V_P \to a_P)$ where $V_i \neq V_j$. Let $\bar{r} = (V_1 \to a_1 V_1^1 V_1^2 \ldots V_1^n; \ldots; V_P \to a_P V_P^1 \ldots V_P^n)$, then let $(\bar{r}) = \{V_1, V_2, \ldots, V_P\}$.

Let u be a finite word on Σ and Δ be a subset of Σ. Then we define $\underline{\text{Occ}}(u)$ inductively by

(i) $\underline{\text{Occ}}(\lambda) = \phi$ where λ is the empty word

(ii) $\text{Occ}(a) = \{a\}$ if $a \in \Sigma$

(iii) $\text{Occ}(uv) = \text{Occ}(u) \cup \text{Occ}(v)$.

Then $\text{Occ}_\Delta(u) = \text{Occ}(u) \cap \Delta$.

3

We now define the derivations in image grammars in two phases; the horizontal derivation (i.e. $\underset{H}{\overset{*}{\Rightarrow}}$) and vertical derivation (i.e. $\underset{v}{\overset{*}{\Rightarrow}}$).

Horizontal derivation:

Let u and v be two words over $V_H \cup \Sigma_I$, then v is immediately derived from u (i.e. $u \underset{H}{\Rightarrow} v$) iff

(i) $u = u_1 A u_2$ where $A \in V_H$

(ii) $v = u_1 \gamma u_2$ and

(iii) $A \rightarrow \gamma \in R_H$.

Then $\underset{H}{\overset{*}{\Rightarrow}}$ is the reflexive and transitive closure of $\underset{H}{\Rightarrow}$.

Vertical derivation:

Let $\bar{r} = (A_1 \rightarrow \alpha_1; A_2 \rightarrow \alpha_2; A_3 \rightarrow \alpha_3; \ldots A_n \rightarrow \alpha_n)$ be a vertical rule. Then we define $\sigma_{\bar{r}}$ as the partial mapping from V_V to $(V_v \cup \Sigma)_*$ by $\sigma_{\bar{r}}(A_i) = \alpha_i^T$.

Now let $\bar{\sigma}_{\bar{r}}$ be the extension of $\sigma_{\bar{r}}$ to $(V_v \cup \Sigma)$ which is defined as

(i) $\bar{\sigma}_{\bar{r}}(\alpha_1, \quad \ldots, \quad \alpha_n) = (\bar{\sigma}_{\bar{r}}(\alpha_1), \quad \ldots, \quad \bar{\sigma}_{\bar{r}}(\alpha_n))$, if $\alpha_i = u_i \ominus A_i \ominus \beta_i$, left($\bar{r}$) $= \{A_i : 1 \leqslant i \leqslant n\}$, $\beta_i \in (\Sigma \cup V)_*$, and $u_i \in \Sigma_*$. $\bar{\sigma}_{\bar{r}}(\alpha_1, \ldots, \alpha_n)$ is undefined otherwise.

(ii) $\bar{\sigma}_{\bar{r}}(u_i \ominus A_i \ominus \beta_i) = u_i \ominus \sigma_{\bar{r}}(A_i) \ominus \beta_i$.

Let u and v be two images on $\Sigma \cup V_v$, then v is immediately derived from u (i.e. $u \underset{v}{\Rightarrow} v$) iff $v = \bar{\sigma}_{\bar{r}}(u)$ for some vertical rule $\bar{r}$.

Then $\underset{v}{\overset{*}{\Rightarrow}}$ is the reflexive and transitive closure of $\underset{v}{\Rightarrow}$.

We denote $\underset{v}{\overset{*}{\Rightarrow}} \circ \underset{H}{\overset{*}{\Rightarrow}}$ by $\overset{*}{\Rightarrow}$ and $I**(G) = \{x \in \Sigma** : S \overset{*}{\Rightarrow} x\}$ and $H(G) = \{u \in \Sigma_I^* : S \underset{H}{\overset{*}{\Rightarrow}} u\}$.

We now illustrate the above definitions by a few examples.

Example 1

Let $G_1 = (V_H, V_v, \Sigma_I, \Sigma, S, R_H, R_v)$ where

$$V_H = \{S, S_1\}; \ V_v = \{A, B, A_1, B_1, C, C_1\}$$

$$\Sigma_I = \{A, B\}; \ \Sigma = \{x, \cdot\}$$

$$R_H = \{S \rightarrow ASS_1; \ S_1 \rightarrow A; \ S \rightarrow B\}$$

$$R_v = \{(A \rightarrow *C; \ B \rightarrow *C_1); \ (A_1 \rightarrow \cdot A_1; \ B_1 \rightarrow *B_1);$$
$$(C \rightarrow \cdot A_1; \ C_1 \rightarrow *B_1); \ (A_1 \rightarrow *; \ B_1 \rightarrow *)\}.$$

Then $H(G) = \{A^n B A^n \ n > 0\}$

$$u_1 = ABA \ \underset{v}{\Rightarrow} \ \begin{matrix} * & * & * \\ C & C_1 & C \end{matrix} \ \underset{v}{\Rightarrow} \ \begin{matrix} * & * & * \\ \cdot & * & \cdot \\ A_1 & B_1 & A_1 \end{matrix}$$

4

$$\underset{v}{\Rightarrow} \quad \begin{array}{ccc} * & * & * \\ \cdot & * & \cdot \\ * & * & * \end{array} \quad = I_1$$

$$u_2 = AABAA \quad \underset{v}{\Rightarrow} \quad \begin{array}{ccccc} * & * & * & * & * \\ C & C & C_1 & C & C \end{array}$$

$$\underset{v}{\Rightarrow} \quad \begin{array}{ccccc} * & * & * & * & * \\ \cdot & \cdot & * & \cdot & \cdot \\ A_1 & A_1 & B_1 & A_1 & A_1 \end{array}$$

$$\underset{v}{\Rightarrow} \quad \begin{array}{ccccc} * & * & * & * & * \\ \cdot & \cdot & * & \cdot & \cdot \\ \cdot & \cdot & * & \cdot & \cdot \\ A_1 & A_1 & B_1 & A_1 & A_1 \end{array}$$

$$\underset{v}{\Rightarrow} \quad \begin{array}{ccccc} * & * & * & * & * \\ \cdot & \cdot & * & \cdot & \cdot \\ \cdot & \cdot & * & \cdot & \cdot \\ * & * & * & * & * \end{array} \quad = I_2.$$

Thus we have

$$I^{**}(G) = \{*^{2n+1} \oplus (\cdot^n * \cdot^n) \oplus *^{2n+1} : n \geq 1\}.$$

Example 2

We define G_2 as follows:

$$H(G_2) = \{A^n B^n : n \geq 1\}$$

$$\begin{aligned} R_v = \{ & (A \rightarrow aA_1; \ B \rightarrow bB_1); \ (A_1 \rightarrow bA_1; \ B_1 \rightarrow aB_1); \\ & (A_1 \rightarrow bA_1; \ B_1 \rightarrow bB_1); \ (A \rightarrow aA_1, \ B_1 \rightarrow bB_1); \\ & (A_1 \rightarrow aA_1, \ B_1 \rightarrow aB_1); \ (A_1 \rightarrow a, \ B_1 \rightarrow a) \\ & (A_1 \rightarrow a, \ B_1 \rightarrow b); \ (A_1 \rightarrow b, \ B_1 \rightarrow a) \\ & (A_1 \rightarrow b, \ B_1 \rightarrow b)\}. \end{aligned}$$

Then $I^{**}(G_2) = \{(x^T)^n \oplus (y^T)^n : n \geq 1\}$ where $x \in a\Sigma^+$ and $y \in b\Sigma^+$. Here we note that $I^{**}(G_2)$ is not generated by the model in Ref. 3.

Definition 3.2. An image grammar G is called deterministic iff the following condition is satisfied. If $(A_1 \rightarrow a_1\alpha_1^1; \ldots A_n \rightarrow a_n\alpha_n^1)$ and $(A_1 \rightarrow a_1\alpha_1^2; \ldots A_n \rightarrow a_n\alpha_n^2)$ where $\alpha_i^j \in V_v^*$, then $\alpha_i^1 = \alpha_i^2$ for all i. ∎

We now give a connection between deterministic and nondeterministic grammars which can be given in terms of relabeling.

Proposition 3.3. The family of sets of images generated by a nondeterministic image grammar is closed under relabeling. ∎

This follows by applying relabeling to each element of each vertical rule.

Proposition 3.4. For each set I of finite images, the following conditions are equivalent:

(i) I is generated by nondeterministic image grammar, and

(ii) I is a relabeling of a set of finite images generated by a deterministic image grammar.

Proof. (ii) $\Rightarrow$ (i) follows obviously from Proposition 3.3. The part (i) $\Rightarrow$ (ii) can be verified by the following construction.

Let $G = (V_H, V_v, \Sigma_I, \Sigma, S, R_H, R_v)$ be a nondeterministic image grammar generating I. Now we shall exhibit a deterministic image grammar $G' = (V_H^1, V_v^1, \Sigma_I \Sigma^1, S^1, R_H^1, R_v^1)$ and a relabeling REL such that $\mathrm{REL}(I^{**}(G^1)) = I^{**}(G)$. Let $V_H^1 = V_H$; $V_v^1 = V_v$; $R_H^1 = R_H$; $S = S^1$ and R_v^1 is defined as follows.

Let $Y = (A_1 \rightarrow a_1\alpha_1, \ldots, A_n \rightarrow a_n\alpha_n)$, then we denote by $\mathrm{FR}(Y) = (a_1, a_2, \ldots, a_n)$ where $a_i \in \Sigma$ and $\alpha_I \in V_v^*$. Let $v \sim v^i$ iff $\mathrm{left}(v) = \mathrm{left}(v^1)$ and $\mathrm{FR}(v) = \mathrm{FR}(v^1)$. We note that $\sim$ is an equivalence relation. Let $R_v/\sim = \{\bar{R}_1, \bar{R}_2, \ldots, \bar{R}_n\}$ where

$$\bar{R}_k = \{v_{k_1}, v_{k_2}, \ldots, v_{k_p}\}.$$

Let $v_{k_j} = \{A_1 \rightarrow a_1\alpha_1^{(j)}; A_2 \rightarrow a_2\alpha_2^{(j)}, \ldots, A_m \rightarrow a_m\alpha_m^{(j)}\}$ where $j = 1, 2, \ldots, p$ we define $v_{k_j}^1 = \{A_1 \rightarrow a_1^{(j)}\alpha_1^{(j)}; A_2 \rightarrow a_2^{(j)}\alpha_2^{(j)}; \ldots; A_m \rightarrow a_m^{(j)}\alpha_m^{(j)}\}$ and $\bar{R}_k^1 = \{v_{k_1}^1, v_{k_2}^1, \ldots, v_{k_p}^1\}$. Let $\Sigma_k = \{a_i^{(j)} : j = 1, 2, \ldots, p$ and $i = 1, 2, \ldots, m\}$. Then $R_v^1 = \bigcup\limits_{k=1}^{n} \bar{R}_k^1$ and $\Sigma^1 = \Sigma \cup \left\{\bigcup\limits_{k=1}^{n} \Sigma_k\right\}$.

Let $\mathrm{REL}(a_i^j) = a_i$. Now it is easy to prove that

$$\mathrm{REL}(I^{**}(G^1)) = I^{**}(G).$$

4. CHOMSKY HIERARCHY FOR IMAGES

We now define some forms of rules that we will use.

(1) Forms of horizontal rules

$$F_1 : H \rightarrow A \text{ or } H \rightarrow A\, H_1 H_2 \ldots H_n \ (n \geqslant 1)$$
$$F_2 : H \rightarrow A \text{ or } H \rightarrow A\, H_1$$

where $H, H_i \in V_H$ and $A \in \Sigma_I$.

(2) Forms of vertical rules

$$F_3 : (V_1 \rightarrow a_1 V_1^1 \ldots V_n^1; \ldots (V_p \rightarrow a_p V_1^p \ldots V_n^p)$$
$$\text{or} \quad (V_1 \rightarrow a_1; \ldots; V_p \rightarrow a_p)$$
$$F_4 : (V_1 \rightarrow a_1 V_1^1; \ldots; V_p \rightarrow a_p V_p) \quad \text{or}$$
$$(V_1 \rightarrow a_1; \ldots; V_p \rightarrow a_p).$$

Now we define various types of image grammars depending on their nature of rules.

Type 1   CC grammar.

G is called CC grammar iff their horizontal rules are of the form F_1 and their vertical rules are of the form F_3.

Type 2   CR grammar.

G is called CR grammar iff their horizontal rules are of the form F_1 and their vertical rules are of the form F_4.

Type 3   RC grammar.

G is called RC grammar iff their horizontal rules are of the form F_2 and their vertical rules are of the form F_3.

Type 4   RR grammar.

G is called RR grammar iff their horizontal rules are of the form F_2 and their vertical rules are of the form F_4.

For each $i \in \{1, 2, 3, 4\}$, we denote $\mathcal{G}^i(\Sigma)$ (respectively $\mathcal{G}^i_{\det}(\Sigma)$) as the family of nondeterministic (respectively deterministic) image grammars of Type 1.

Remark.   The image grammars are more general than context-free grammars. Here we note that CR and RR grammars coincide with the model defined in Ref. 11.

Example 3

Let $L = \{a^n b^n : n \geqslant 1\}$
$L^T = \{x^T : x \in L\} = \{(a)_n \ominus (b)_n : n \geqslant 1\} = I_3.$

Then I_3 can be generated by the following RC grammar

$$G_3 : R_H : s \rightarrow s^1 \in \Sigma_I$$

$$R_v : \{(s^1 \rightarrow a \ s^1 B),$$
$$(s^1 \rightarrow a \ B), (B \rightarrow b)\}.$$

We note that I_3 is generated by a nondeterministic RC grammar and not a deterministic RC grammar.

Example 4

Let $L = (a^2)^* a$. Then L^T is generated by an RR grammar G such that

7

$$R_H : S \rightarrow A \text{ where } \Sigma_I = \{A\}$$

$$R_v : \{(A \rightarrow aA_1); (A_1 \rightarrow aA); (A \rightarrow a)\}.$$

Here also we note that L^T cannot be generated by deterministic RR grammar.

Proposition 4.1. For each $i \in \{1, 2, 3, 4\}$, the family $\mathcal{G}_{det}^{(i)} (\Sigma)$ is more powerful than $\mathcal{G}^{(1)}(\Sigma)$.

To prove this proposition one can use Examples 3 and 4 which cannot be generated by deterministic image grammars.

Corollary 4.2. For each $X, Y \in \{R, C\}$, the family of sets of images generated by deterministic XY grammars is not closed under relabeling.

It follows from Propositions 3.4 and 2.1.

From the last remark, it follows that classical Chomsky hierarchy is preserved and can be presented by the following diagrams.

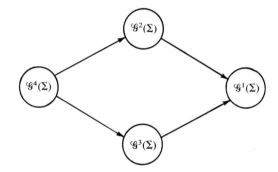

Fig. 1.

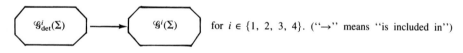

for $i \in \{1, 2, 3, 4\}$. ("$\rightarrow$" means "is included in")

Fig. 2.

5. PROPERTIES OF IMAGE GRAMMARS

In this section we will study closure properties of sets generated by image grammars and pumping lemma for image grammars. As a consequence of the pumping lemma we prove some decidability results.

If $x = (x_1 x_2 \ldots x_n) \in \Sigma^{**}$, then we define, column $(x) = \{x_1, x_2, \ldots, x_n\}$.

Lemma 5.1. For each image grammar G and each image x generated by G, we have:

$$\text{Card (Column } (x)) \leqslant \text{Card } (\Sigma_I).$$

This follows from the determinism inside each table of R_v and the parallel writings.

Definition 5.2. Let I be a set of images generated by an image grammar, then we denote by

$$\text{Index } (I) = \min \{\text{Card } (\Sigma_I) : \Sigma_I \text{ is an intermediate alphabet of image grammars generating } I\}.$$

Let $\mathscr{I}_n(\Sigma)$ be the family of sets of images of index less than or equal to n.

Theorem 5.3. (Infinite Hierarchy Theorem). For each $n \geq 0$, we have

$$\mathscr{I}_n(\Sigma) \subsetneqq \mathscr{I}_{n+1}(\Sigma).$$

Proof. $\mathscr{I}_n(\Sigma) \subseteq \mathscr{I}_{n+1}(\Sigma)$ follows directly. Let x_k be an image where

$$\text{Dom}(x_k) = \{(i, j) : 1 \leq i, j \leq k\} \text{ for each } i, j \in \{1, 2, \ldots, k\}$$

and

$$x_k(i, j) = x \text{ if } i = j$$
$$= y \text{ if } i \neq j.$$

Let $L_{n+1} = \{x_1, x_2, \ldots, x_{n+1}\}$, then we can construct an RR grammar with $n + 1$ intermediate alphabet which generates L_{n+1}. But from Lemma 5.1 we deduce that

$$L_{n+1} \notin \mathscr{I}_n(\Sigma).$$

Let $XY(\Sigma)$ be the family of sets of finite images generated by nondeterministic XY grammar where $X, Y \in \{R, C\}$.

Theorem 5.4. For $XY(\Sigma)$, the following table is true.

is closed	∪	∩		/		REL
RR	YES	YES		NO	4	YES
RC	YES	NO	1	NO	5	YES
CR	YES	NO	2	NO	6	YES
CC	YES	NO	3	NO	7	YES

9

Proof. For the "Yes cases", one can use classical constructions and for "No cases" Cases 1–7 follow from the fact that $\phi \in$ RR and $\Sigma^{**} \notin$ RR.

Reduction of Image Grammar:

Definition 5.5. Let Σ be a finite alphabet, then SIMPLE $(\Sigma) = \{u \in \Sigma^* : \text{for all } a \in X, |u|_a \le 1\}$, where $|u|_a$ is the number of occurrences of a on u. ∎

Definition 5.6. Let G be an image grammar and A be an element of $V_H \cup \Sigma_I$, then A is called H-useful iff $S \overset{*}{\underset{H}{\Rightarrow}} u_1 \, A \, u_2 : A \overset{*}{\underset{H}{\Rightarrow}} V_1 \in \Sigma_I^*$ and $u_2 \overset{*}{\underset{H}{\Rightarrow}} \omega_2 \in \Sigma_I^*$ where $u_1 \in \Sigma_I^*$.

Definition 5.7. Let G be an image grammar and A be an element of SIMPLE $(V_v) \cup$ SIMPLE (Σ). A is called V-useful iff there is $u \in H(a)$ such that

$$u \overset{*}{\underset{v}{\Rightarrow}} \begin{bmatrix} I \\ A \\ u_2 \end{bmatrix}; \ A \overset{*}{\underset{v}{\Rightarrow}} I_2 \text{ and } u_2 \overset{*}{\underset{v}{\Rightarrow}} I_3 \text{ where } I_1, I_2, I_3 \in \Sigma^{**}. \ ∎$$

Definition 5.8. An image grammar is said to be reduced iff
(i)   every element of $V_H \cup \Sigma_I$ is H-useful.
(ii) the left of every rule is V-useful and
(iii) $\text{Occ}(I^{**}(G)) = \Sigma$.

Proposition 5.9. For each image grammar G, there is an equivalent reduced grammar G^1.

Proof. Let $V_H^1 = \{v \in V_H : v \text{ is } H\text{-useful}\}$,

$$\Sigma_I^1 = \{x \in \Sigma_I : x \text{ is } H\text{-useful}\}.$$

Let $v = \{u \in$ SIMPLE $(V_v) : U \overset{+}{\Rightarrow} x \in \Sigma^{++}\}$.
   The existence of v can be illustrated by the following construction inductively.
   Let

$$V_1 = \{u \in \text{SIMPLE } (V_v) : \text{there exists } \bar{r} = (A_1 \to a_1; \ \dots ; A_n \to a_n\}$$
$$\text{such that } \text{Occ}(u) = \text{left}(\bar{r}) \text{ where } \bar{r} \in R_v\},$$

$$V_{p+1} = V_p \cup \{u \in \text{SIMPLE } (V_v) : \text{there exists}$$
$$\bar{r} = (A_1 \to a_1 \alpha_1, A_2 \to a_2 \alpha_2, \ \dots) : \text{Occ}(u) = \text{left}(\bar{r}),$$
$$(\alpha_1^T \ \dots \ \alpha_n^T) = \begin{bmatrix} \alpha_1 \\ \bar{\alpha}_k \end{bmatrix} \text{ and}$$
$$\text{SIMPLE } (\text{Occ}(\bar{\alpha}_k)) \cap V_p \ne \phi\}$$

and $V = \bigcup_{p \ge 1} V_p$.

   Let $W(s) = H(a) \cup$ SIMPLE (Σ_I^1).

$V_v^1 = \{v \in V_v :$ there exist $u \in \mathcal{R}(v \cap W(s)) : u = u_1 \, V \, u_2,$ where $\mathcal{R}(v)$ is a set of simple words on V_v reachable from some simple word belonging to V.

$$\Sigma^1 = \{a \in \Sigma : a \in \text{Occ}(u) \text{ where } u \in I^{**}(G)\}$$

$$R_v^1 = \{\bar{r} \in R_v : \bar{r} = (A_1 \rightarrow a_1\alpha_1; \ldots ; A_n \rightarrow a_n\alpha_n),$$
$$\text{left}(\bar{r}) = \text{Occ}(u) \text{ where } u \in \mathcal{R}(V \cap W(s)), \, a_i \in \Sigma^1\}.$$

$$R_H^1 = \{A \rightarrow a\alpha \in R_H : A, \, \alpha \in V_H \text{ and } a \in \Sigma_I^1\}.$$

Now it follows from the construction and Definition 5.9, that $I^{**}(G) = I^{**}(G^1)$.

Corollary 5.10. The emptiness problem for image grammars is decidable. The proof follows directly from the previous theorem.

Theorem 5.11. (Horizontal pumping lemma). Let G be a reduced image grammar, then there is an integer N, depending on G such that any image x in I^{**} such that $|x|_v > N$ can be written as $I = u \oplus v \oplus x \oplus y \oplus z$ in such a way that either V or Y is nonempty and $u \oplus v^n \oplus x \oplus y^n \oplus z \in I^{**}(G)$ for every $n \geq 1$.

The proof of the horizontal pumping lemma follows from the classical theory.

Remark. Note that each rule $\bar{r} = \{A_1 \rightarrow a_1v_1^1 \ldots v_1^n; \ldots A_p \rightarrow a_pv_p^1 \ldots v_p^n)$ can be coded with the simple rule:

$$(A_1, A_2, \ldots, A_p) \rightarrow (a_1, a_2, \ldots, a_p)(v_1^1, \ldots, v_p^1) \ldots (v_1^n, \ldots, v_p^n).$$

This type of representation of $\bar{r}$ is called *code* $(\bar{r})$.

Theorem 5.12. (Vertical pumping lemma). Let G be a reduced image grammar, then there is an integer N, depending on G such that any image x in $I^{**}(G)$, such that $|x|_H > N$, can be written as $x = u \ominus v \ominus x \ominus y \ominus z$ in such a way that either u or y is nonempty and $u \ominus v_n \ominus x \ominus y_n \oplus z \in I^{**}(G)$ for every $n \geq 0$.

The proof follows from the previous remark and the classical pumping lemma.

Corollary 5.13. Finiteness problem of image grammars is decidable.

6. CHARACTERIZATION OF IMAGE SETS

In this section we characterize XY-image sets in terms of deterministic image substitution and also in terms of Kleene closure operator.

Definition 6.1. A deterministic image substitution called DIS, for short, is a mapping from Σ to $\mathcal{P}(\Delta^{**})$. Note that in this paper we restrict ourselves to substitutions from Σ to $\mathcal{P}(\Delta_*)$, where $\mathcal{P}(X)$ is the set of all subsets of X. ∎

Each DIS-σ can be given as a sequence $\sigma = (L_a)_{a\in\Sigma}$.
We call σ regular iff each L_a^T is regular, and context-free iff each L_a^T is context-free.
Let $x \in \Sigma^*$ and $\sigma(L_a)_{a\in\Sigma}$, then

$$\sigma(x) = \{y = (y_1y_2, \ldots, y_n) \in \Delta^{**} : y_i \in \sigma(x_i)$$

and if $x_i = x_j$ then $y_i = y_j\}$.

We note that $\sigma(L) = \bigcup_{x \in L} \sigma(x)$.

Theorem 6.2. For each set of images L, the following conditions are equivalent
(i) L is CC, and
(ii) there is a sequence of context-free DIS $(\sigma_i)_{1 \leqslant i \leqslant n}$ and a sequence of context-free languages K_i such that $L = \bigcup_{i-1}^{n} \sigma_i(K_i)$.

Proof. Let L be a set of images generated by the CC grammar $G = (V_H, V_v, \Sigma, \Sigma_I, S, R_H, R_v)$.

We now exhibit a sequence of context-free languages $(K_i)_{i=1,n}$ and a sequence $(\sigma_i)_{i=1,\ldots,n}$ of context-free DIS such that $\bigcup_{i=1}^{n} \sigma_i(K_i) = L$.

Let $X_i \subset \Sigma_I$ where $X_i = \{A_1^i, \ldots, A_{n_i}^i\}$ and let $K_i = H(G) \cap X_i^*$. We note that each K_i is context-free.

We define a substitution σ_i of each X_i in the following way. Let $G_i = (V_H^{n} \cap \{S_i\}, \Sigma^{n_i}, S_i, \bar{R}_i)$ where $n_i = |X_i|$.

$\bar{R}_i$ can be defined inductively.

Let

$$R_0 = \{S_i \rightarrow (A_1^i, \ldots, A_{n_i}^i)\}$$

$$R_{j+1} = R_j \cup \{A \rightarrow \mathbf{bB} : A \in N_j \text{ where}$$
$$A \rightarrow \mathbf{bB} = code(\bar{r}) \text{ for some } \bar{r} \in R_v\}$$

$$N_{j+1} = N_j \cup \{A : A \rightarrow \mathbf{bA_1 \ A_2} \ldots \mathbf{A_n} \in R_j\}.$$

Then there exists $M > 0$ such that

$$R_M = R_{M+1}.$$

Let $\bar{R}_i = R_M$.

We define $\sigma_i(A_j^i) = \{P_j(L(G_i))\}^T$ where $P_j(a_1 a_2, \ldots, a_n) = a_j$.

Then we have $L = \bigcup_{i=1}^{n} \sigma_i(K_i)$.

(ii) $\rightarrow$ (i)

Since CC is closed under union, it suffices to prove that $\sigma(K)$ is CC where σ is CF-DIS and K is also context-free.

Let $G = (V, \bar{\Sigma}, S, R)$ be a context-free grammar generating K and $G_A = (V_A, \Sigma_A, A, R_A)$ be a context-free grammar generating $\sigma(A)$. We shall now exhibit a CC grammar to generate $\sigma(K)$.

Let $V_H = V; V_v = \bar{\Sigma} \cup (\cup V_A); \Sigma_I = \bar{\Sigma}$

$$\Sigma = \bigcup_{A \in \bar{\Sigma}} \Sigma_A; R_H = R$$

12

$$R_v = \bigcup_{\{A_1,\dots,A_{i_n}\} \subseteq \bar{\Sigma}} (R_{A_{i_1}} \times \dots \times R_{A_{i_n}}).$$

Then $G = (V_H, V_v, \Sigma, \Sigma_I, S, R_H, R_v)$ is a CC grammar generating $\sigma(K)$.

Remark. From the construction used in the proof of Theorem 6.2, the following results hold.

Theorem 6.3. For each finite image set L, the following conditions are equivalent.
(i) L is CR (respectively RR) and
(ii) there is a sequence of regular DIS $(\sigma_i)_{1 \leq i \leq n}$ and a sequence of context-free (respectively regular) languages such that:

$$L = \bigcup_{i=1}^{n} \sigma_i(K_i).$$

Theorem 6.4. For each finite image set L, the following conditions are equivalent
(i) L is RC
(ii) there is a sequence of context-free DIS$(\sigma_i)_{1 \leq i \leq n}$ and a sequence of regular languages such that $L = \bigcup_{i=1}^{n} \sigma_i(K_i)$.

Now we give an example to illustrate the first construction used in the proof of Theorem 6.2.

Example 5

Let $G = (V_H, V_v, \Sigma_I, \Sigma, S, R_H, R_v)$
where

$$R_H = \{S \rightarrow ASS_1;\ S \rightarrow A\ S_1;\ S_2 \rightarrow B\},$$

$$R_v = \{(A \rightarrow aAA_1;\ B \rightarrow cBB_1);\ (A \rightarrow a;\ B \rightarrow c);\ (A_1 \rightarrow b;\ B_1 \rightarrow d)\}.$$

$$L = \left\{ \begin{bmatrix} (a_{p+1})^n & (c_{p+1})^n \\ (b_p)^n & (d_p)^n \end{bmatrix} \begin{array}{l} n \geq 1 \\ : \\ p \leq 0 \end{array} \right\}$$

and we have

$$K_1 = \{A\}^* \cap H(G) = \phi$$

$$K_2 = \{B\}^* \cap H(G) = \phi$$

$$K_3 = \{A, B\}^* \cap H(G) = H(G)$$

$$G_1 = (V_H, S_1, \bar{R}_1, \Sigma) \text{ where } \bar{R}_1 = \phi$$

13

$G_2 = (V_H, S_2, \bar{R}_2, \Sigma)$ where $\bar{R}_2 = \phi$

$G_3 = (V_H^2, S_2, \bar{R}_2, \Sigma)$ where $\bar{R}_3$ can be constructed inductively

$\bar{R}_0 = (S_3 \rightarrow (A, B))$

$N_0 = \{(A, B)\}$

$R_1 : \{(A, B) \rightarrow (a, c)(A, B)(A_1 B_1); (A, B) \rightarrow (a, c)\}$

$N_1 = \{(A, B), (A_1, B_1)\}$

$\bar{R}_2 = R_1 \cup (A_1, B_1) \rightarrow (b, d)\}$

$N_2 = N_1$

$R_3 = R_2 = \bar{R}_3.$

Let

$$L_0 = \{(a, c)^{p+1} (b, d)^{p+1} : p \geqslant 0\}$$

$$K_s = \{A^n B^n : n \geqslant 1\}$$

$$\sigma_3(A) = P_1(L(G_3)) = \{(a^{p+1} b^P)^T : P \geqslant 0\}$$

$$\sigma_3(B) = P_2(L(G_3)) = \{(E^{p+1} d^P)^T : P \geqslant 0\}$$

$$\sigma_3(A^2 B^2) = \begin{bmatrix} (a_{p+1})^2 & (c_{p+1})^2 \\ (b_p)^2 & (d_p)^2 \end{bmatrix}.$$

Hence $L = \bigcup\limits_{i=1}^{3} \sigma_i(K_i).$

We now define the Kleene closure operator in terms of regular and context-free languages for characterizing XY-image sets. Let $\Sigma_I = \{A_1, \ldots, A_n\}$ and σ be DIS from Σ_I to $\mathcal{P}(\Sigma_*)$. Then σ is given by the tuple $\langle L_1, L_2, \ldots, L_n \rangle$ where $L_i = \sigma(A_i)$. Let $L_0 \subset \Sigma_I^*$, then $\sigma(L_0) = L_0 \odot \langle L_1, \ldots, L_n \rangle$ where $L_0 \odot \langle L_1, \ldots, L_n \rangle = \{x = y_0 \odot \langle y_1, \ldots, y_n \rangle : y_0 \in L_0$ and if $y_0(i) = y_0(j) = a_k$ then $x(i)_H = s(j)_H = y_k$ and $(y_i)_v = (y_j)_v.$

Kleene closure $(\mathcal{L}_1, \mathcal{L}_2) = \{L \bigcup\limits_{i=1}^{N} L_0^i \odot \langle L_1^i, \ldots, L_n^i \rangle : L_0^i \in \mathcal{L}_1$ and $(L_j^i)^T \in \mathcal{L}_2\}.$

Let R (respectively C) be the family of regular (respectively context-free) languages.

Theorem 6.5. For each x, $y \in \{R, C\}$ and each set L of images, the following conditions are equivalent

(i) L is generated by an XY grammar

(ii) L belongs to the Kleene closure of X and Y.

The proof follows immediately from the last three theorems.

ACKNOWLEDGEMENT

We gratefully acknowledge Prof. R. Siromoney for her comments. The third author acknowledges the financial support of C.I.E.S. and L.I.T.P.

REFERENCES

1. N. Chomsky and M. P. Shützenberger, "The algebraic theory of context-free languages", in *Computer Programming and Formal Systems*, Eds. P. Braford and D. Hirschberg, North-Holland, Amsterdam, 1963, pp. 118–161.
2. A. Rosenfeld, *Picture Languages—Formal Models for Picture Recognition*, Academic Press, 1979.
3. G. Siromoney, R. Siromoney and K. Krithivasan, "Abstract families of matrices and picture languages", *Computer Graphics and Image Processing* **1** (1972) 234–307.
4. G. Siromoney, R. Siromoney and K. Krithivasan, "Picture languages with array rewriting rules". *Info. and Control* **22** (1973) 447–470.
5. R. Siromoney and K. Krithivasan, "Parallel context-free languages", *Info. and Control* **24** (1974) 155–162.
6. P. S. Wang, "Sequential/Parallel matrix array languages", *J. Cybernetics* **5** (1975) 19–36.
7. P. S. Wang, "Hierarchical structures and complexities of isometric patterns", *IEEE Trans. PAMI* **5**, 1 (1983) 92–99.
8. C. Cook and P. S. Wang, "A Chomsky hierarchy of isotonic array grammars and languages", *Computer Graphics and Image Processing* **8** (1978) 144–152.
9. P. S. Wang, "Finite turn repetitive checking automaton and sequential/parallel matrix languages", *IEEE Trans. Computers* **30** (1981) 366–390.
10. P. S. Wang, "Parallel context-free array grammars normal forms", *Computer Graphics and Image Processing* **15** (1981) 296–300.
11. R. Siromoney, K. G. Subramanian and K. Rangarajan, "Parallel/Sequential rectangular arrays with tables", *Int. J. Computer Math.*, Section A, **6** (1977) 143–158.
12. M. Harrison, *Introduction to Formal Languages Theory*, Addison-Wesley, 1978.
13. M. Nivat, "Transduction de languages de Chomsky", Doctorat d'Etat, Université Paris VII, 1967.
14. R. Siromoney, "On equal matrix languages", *Info. and Control* **14** (1969) 135–151.
15. K. G. Subramanian, "Studies in array languages", Ph. D. thesis, Madras University, 1979.

Maurice Nivat has been a Professor in Computer Science since 1969 at the University of Paris VII. He received the Master degree and Agregation in mathematics in 1961 and the doctorat d'Etat in computer science in 1967.

He is a corresponding member of the French Academy of Sciences and is editor-in-chief of the journal *Theoretical Computer Science*. He was director of LITP (Laboratory of Theoretical Computer Science and Programming) from 1975–85. He is an advisor to the President of INRIA (National Institute for Computer Science and Automation).

Prof. Nivat is head of a research team on languages concurrency and parallelism. His areas of research are automata theory, algebraic semantics of programming languages, combinatorics, compiling, code theory, and modeling parallel and distributed systems.

He is the author of more than 100 papers and books, and several reports to the French government on training and research in computer science.

Ahmed Saoudi has been an Associate Professor since 1985 at the University of Paris XIII. He received the Master degree in computer science from the University of Louis Pasteur (Strasbourg) in 1979, the doctorat of 3rd cycle from the University of Paris VII in 1972, and the doctorat d'Etat in computer science from the University of Paris VII in 1987. In 1984 he was an Assistant Professor in Computer Science at the University of Orsay.

Prof. Saoudi is a member of LITP (Laboratory of Theoretical Computer Science and Programming) since 1980 and a member of EATCS (European Association of Theoretical Computer Science). His areas of research are automata and grammars on trees, logic and programming, parallel algorithms, syntactic pattern recognition and image processing.

V. R. Dare received his M.Sc. and M.Phil. in mathematics from Madurai University in 1976 and 1977 respectively. His Ph.D. degree is from Madras University (1986). He is at present on the faculty of the Department of Mathematics, Madras Christian College, Tambaram, Madras. He was a post-doctoral fellow at LITP (Laboratory of Theoretical Computer Science and Programming), University of Paris VII, during the year 1987–88. His research interests include topological studies of formal languages and studies on infinite words and infinite arrays.

CONTEXT-SENSITIVITY OF TWO-DIMENSIONAL REGULAR ARRAY GRAMMARS

YASUNORI YAMAMOTO

National Museum of Ethnology, Senri Expo Park, Suita-shi 565, Japan

KENICHI MORITA

Faculty of Engineering, Yamagata University, Yonezawa-shi 992, Japan

and

KAZUHIRO SUGATA

Faculty of Engineering, Tottori University, Tottori-shi 680, Japan

Received 30 April 1989

Regular array grammars (RAGs) are the lowest subclass in the Chomsky-like hierarchy of isometric array grammars. The left-hand side of each rewriting rule of RAGs has one nonterminal symbol and at most one "#" (a blank symbol). Therefore, the rewriting rules cannot sense contexts of non-# symbols. However, they can sense # as a kind of context. In this paper, we investigate this #-sensing ability, and study the language generating power of RAGs. Making good use of this ability, we show a method for RAGs to sense the contexts of local shapes of a host array in a derivation. Using this method, we give RAGs which generate the sets of all solid upright rectangles and all solid squares. On the other hand, it is proved that there is no context-free array grammar (and thus no RAG) which generates the set of all hollow upright rectangles.

Keywords: Isometric array grammars; Pattern generation.

1. INTRODUCTION

Regular array grammars (RAGs),[1] context-free array grammars (CFAGs)[1] and monotonic array grammars (MAGs)[2] are three subclasses of isometric array grammars (IAGs)[2,3] forming the Chomsky-like hierarchy.[1] They are kinds of generating mechanisms of two-dimensional patterns of symbols with a set of rewriting rules. In these grammars, both sides of each rewriting rule are required to be isometric (i.e. to have the same shape) to avoid the shearing in a generated array.

RAGs are the lowest subclass of this hierarchy, and have rewriting rules of a very simple form. The left-hand side of each rule has one nonterminal symbol and at most one #, which is a blank (or background) symbol. By such a rule, the nonterminal symbol is rewritten into a terminal symbol, and # is rewritten into a nonterminal symbol.

Because of its extreme simplicity of form, RAGs might be considered to have very weak generating power. Indeed, rewriting rules of RAGs (as well as CFAGs) cannot sense contexts of non-# symbols in a sentential form. However, they have the ability of sensing # as a kind of context. In this paper, we investigate this #-sensing ability, and show that

17

International Journal of Pattern Recognition and Artificial Intelligence Vol. 3 No. 3 & 4 (1989) 295–319

RAGs have rather high language generating power. In particular, we show that there are RAGs which can generate the set of all solid upright rectangles and all solid squares.

In order to generate rectangles or squares, RAGs must know a kind of context. That is, RAGs must check whether four edges are constructed in a straight line, or two neighboring edges have the same length. In Ref. 4, Yamamoto *et al.* showed that there is a CFAG which generates the set of solid rectangles of all sizes using the #-context. Based on this idea and developing some other techniques peculiar to RAGs, we give a method for RAGs to sense local shapes of a host array in a derivation. By this method, we give a concrete description of RAGs which generate the sets of all rectangles and all squares.

However, since RAGs (and CFAGs) can sense only #-contexts and cannot sense non-#-contexts positively, RAGs cannot generate geometrical figures which require non-#-contexts. The set of hollow upright rectangles of all sizes is an example of such figures. We prove that there is no CFAG (and thus no RAG) which generates the set of all hollow rectangles.

2.   DEFINITIONS AND NOTATIONS

Let Σ be a nonempty finite set of symbols. A (two-dimensional) *word* over Σ is a two-dimensional finite connected array of symbols in Σ. The set of all words over Σ is denoted by Σ^{2+} (the empty word is not contained in Σ^{2+}).

An *isometric array grammar* (IAG) is a system defined by a quintuple

$$G = (N, T, P, S, \#)$$

where N is a finite nonempty set of nonterminals (nonterminal symbols); T is a finite nonempty set of terminals (terminal symbols); $N \cap T = \varnothing$; P is a finite set of rewriting rules of the form $\alpha \rightarrow \beta$, where α and β are words over $N \cup T \cup \{\#\}$, and satisfy the following conditions:
(1) The shapes of α and β are geometrically identical.
(2) α contains at least one nonterminal.
(3) Terminals in α are not rewritten by the rule $\alpha \rightarrow \beta$.
(4) The application of the rule $\alpha \rightarrow \beta$ preserves the connectivity of the host array (i.e. the application of the rule to a connected array results in a connected array).
   (To be more precise, see Ref. 5.)
$S \in N$ is a start symbol; $\# \notin N \cup T$ is a special blank symbol. The #-embedded array of a word $\sigma \in (N \cup T)^{2+}$ is an infinite array over $N \cup T \cup \{\#\}$ obtained by embedding σ in two-dimensional infinite array of #s, and is denoted by $\sigma_\#$. The rewriting rule $\alpha \rightarrow \beta$ is *applicable* to the host array $\sigma \in (N \cup T)^{2+}$ if α is a subarray of $\sigma_\#$. We say that a word τ is *directly derived* from a word σ in G if $\tau_\#$ can be obtained by replacing one of the occurrences of α in $\sigma_\#$ with β for some rewriting rule $\alpha \rightarrow \beta$ in G. This is denoted by $\sigma \underset{G}{\Rightarrow} \tau$. We say that τ is *derived* from σ in G iff there is a sequence of words over $N \cup T \, \sigma = \sigma_0, \sigma_1, \ldots, \sigma_m = \tau \, (m \geq 0)$ such that $\sigma_{i-1} \underset{G}{\Rightarrow} \sigma_i \, (i = 1, \ldots, m)$. This is denoted by $\sigma \overset{*}{\underset{G}{\Rightarrow}} \tau$. The relation $\overset{*}{\underset{G}{\Rightarrow}}$ is the reflexive and transitive closure of $\underset{G}{\Rightarrow}$. We use $\Rightarrow$ for $\underset{G}{\Rightarrow}$ and $\overset{*}{\Rightarrow}$ for $\overset{*}{\underset{G}{\Rightarrow}}$ if it is clear which grammar G is used.

A *sentential form* in G is a word $\alpha \in (N \cup T)^{2+}$ such that $S \overset{*}{\Rightarrow} \alpha$. The (two-dimensional) *language generated* by G (denoted by $L(G)$) is defined by

$$L(G) = \{\alpha \mid S \overset{*}{\Rightarrow} \alpha \text{ and } \alpha \in T^{2+}\}.$$

Three subclasses of the IAGs are defined by imposing the following conditions on the form of each rewriting rule $\alpha \rightarrow \beta$:

Monotonic array grammar (MAG):

Non-# symbols in α are not rewritten into #s by the application of the rule $\alpha \rightarrow \beta$.

Context-free array grammar (CFAG):

α consists of exactly one nonterminal and possibly one more #s.

Regular array grammar (RAG):

The rewriting rule $\alpha \rightarrow \beta$ is one of the following forms:

$$\#A \rightarrow Ba, \qquad A\# \rightarrow aB,$$

$$\begin{matrix} \# & B \\ A & a \end{matrix} \rightarrow \begin{matrix} & \\ & \end{matrix}, \qquad \begin{matrix} A & a \\ \# & B \end{matrix} \rightarrow \begin{matrix} & \\ & \end{matrix},$$

$$A \rightarrow a,$$

where A and B are nonterminals and a is a terminal.

Let $\mathscr{L}[\mathscr{C}]$ be the class of languages generated by a grammar class $\mathscr{C}$. Cook and Wang[1] showed the Chomsky-like hierarchy of these grammar classes as follows:

Proposition 2.1.

$$\mathscr{L}[RAG] \subsetneqq \mathscr{L}[CFAG] \subsetneqq \mathscr{L}[MAG] \subsetneqq \mathscr{L}[IAG].$$

It is similar to Chomsky hierarchy in one-dimensional string grammars.

3. CONTEXT-SENSITIVITY OF REGULAR ARRAY GRAMMARS

In this section, we show that RAGs have some context-sensing ability. We present concrete RAGs which generate geometrical figures such as rectangles and squares. By sensing local shapes of a sentential form, these grammars make each of four edges of a sentential form aligned and the neighboring two edges to be the same length. On the other hand, there is a set of figures that is similar to solid rectangles but cannot be generated by any RAG. We prove that the set of all hollow rectangles cannot be generated by any CFAG (and thus by any RAG). At the end of this section, we give concrete rewriting rules of CFAGs that generate rectangles and squares, and compare them with those of the RAGs.

First of all, we introduce *strongly linear array grammars* (SLAGs), a subclass of the linear array grammars,[5] as an equivalent alternative to RAGs. The notion of SLAG enables us to give a simpler description of a regular array language. A large number of rewriting rules are needed if we write a concrete example of an RAG, since the rewriting rules of an RAG are restricted to very simple ones. An SLAG is defined as follows.

Let I be the set of all integers. A set $C \subset I \times I$ is said to be *connected* if for all (i, j), $(i', j') \in C$ there is a sequence $(i, j) = (i_1, j_1), \ldots, (i_n, j_n) = (i', j')$ of points of C such that

$$|i_{k+1} - i_k| + |j_{k+1} - j_k| = 1 \ (k = 1, \ldots, n - 1).$$

Each rewriting rule $\alpha \rightarrow \beta$ of an IAG $G = (N, T, P, S, \#)$ can be represented by a pair of mappings

$$\alpha_D: D \rightarrow (N \cup T \cup \{\#\}),$$
$$\beta_D: D \rightarrow (N \cup T \cup \{\#\}),$$

where D is a finite connected subset of $I \times I$, that is, D is a set of points where symbols occur in α or β.

Definition 3.1. A rewriting rule $\alpha \rightarrow \beta$ (or a pair (α_D, β_D)) of an IAG $G = (N, T, P, S, \#)$ is said to be *strongly linear* if there exists a sequence of points on D

$$(i_1, j_1), \ldots, (i_n, j_n) \qquad (n = |D|)$$

which satisfies
(i)   For each k and l $(1 \leq k, l \leq n)$, if $k \neq l$ then $(i_k, j_k) \neq (i_l, j_l)$;
(ii) $|i_{k+1} - i_k| + |j_{k+1} - j_k| = 1 \ (k = 1, 2, \ldots, n - 1)$;
(iii) $\alpha_D(i_1, j_1) \in N$, $\alpha_D(i_k, j_k) = \# \ (k = 2, \ldots, n)$;
(iv) $\beta_D(i_k, j_k) \in T(k = 1, \ldots, n - 1)$, $\beta_D(i_n, j_n) \in (N \cup T)$.

Intuitively speaking, these conditions require that
(1) the rewriting rule $\alpha \rightarrow \beta$ is of the CFAG form where β contains at most one nonterminal, and
(2) that there is a single-stroke path covering the whole of D from the position of the nonterminal in α to the position of the nonterminal in β (or to some appropriate position if β contains no nonterminal).

Definition 3.2. An IAG G is called a *strongly linear array grammar* if all its rewriting rules are strongly linear.

In Ref. 6 it is shown that an SLAG and an RAG are equivalent with respect to their language-generating power. That is,

Proposition 3.3. $\mathscr{L}(\text{SLAG}) = \mathscr{L}(\text{RAG})$.

In the following, we use an abbreviated notation to describe each rewriting rule if an SLAG has only one terminal a. In this notation, each rewriting rule is described in one array, where the left-hand side α is superimposed on the right-hand side β. Only the nonterminal in α, and the nonterminal in β (or the terminal a if β has no nonterminal),

and the single-stroke path connecting between these two symbols are described (Fig. 1).
Now we show that rectangles of all sizes can be generated by an RAG.

Definition 3.4.   Let **R** be the set of all solid upright rectangles over one letter alphabet $\{a\}$. We denote the height and the width of a rectangle $x \in \mathbf{R}$ as $h(x)$ and $w(x)$ respectively (Fig. 2).

Before we show an RAG that generates **R**, we give an SLAG G_R' that generates a subset of **R**. G_R' will make the intrinsic idea clearer.

Lemma 3.5.   Let **R**′ be the subset of **R** such that

$$\mathbf{R}' = \{x \mid x \in \mathbf{R} \text{ and } h(x) = 3k + 4,$$
$$w(x) = 4l + 8 \ (k, \ l = 0, \ 1, \ 2, \ \ldots)\}.$$

Then there exists an RAG which generates **R**′.

Proof.   From Proposition 3.3, it is sufficient to present an SLAG that generates **R**′. Let $G_R' = (N, \{a\}, P, S, \#\}$ be an SLAG such that

$$N = \{S, \ T, \ R, \ I, \ L, \ B\}.$$

(a)   (b)

Fig. 1.   An abbreviated notation of a rewriting rule of SLAG,   (a) original form, and   (b) abbreviated form.

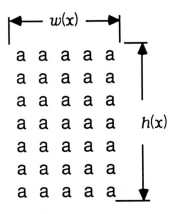

Fig. 2.   A word x in **R**.

21

P is the set of rewriting rules shown in Fig. 3.

In the following, we show $L(G'_R) = \mathbf{R}'$.

I. Suppose that the rule (S1) is applied at the first step of a derivation. By repeated
    applications of the rule (T1), the sentential form grows right and the top edge of a
    rectangle is formed (Fig. 4 (a)–(c)). When the rule (T2) is applied instead of (T1), the
    growth to the right stops. The rule (R1), which is the only available rule just after
    (T2), changes the growing direction of the sentential form to the left (Fig. 4 (d), (e)).
    By applying the rule (I1) repeatedly, the sentential form grows to the left, and the
    inside of the rectangle is formed (Fig. 4 (f)). The rules (I2) and (L) turn the growing
    direction to the right (Fig. 4 (g), (h)). Repeated applications of the rule (I3) form the
    inside of the rectangle to the right, and the rule (I4) turn the growing direction to the

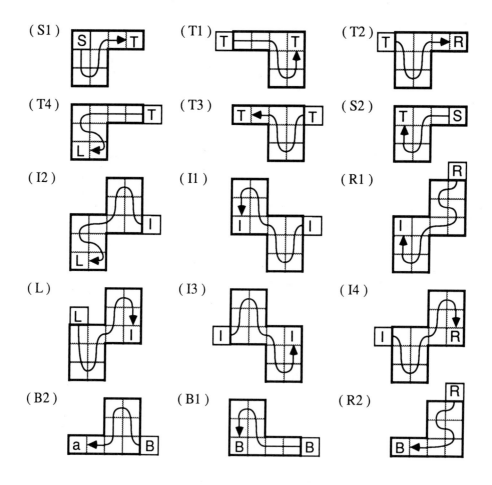

Fig. 3. Rewriting rules of G'_R.

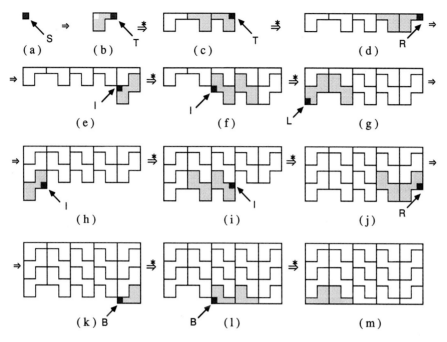

Fig. 4. A derivation by G'_R.

left again (Fig. 4 (i), (j)). At this time, if the rule (R2) happens to be applied instead of (R1), the formation of the bottom edge of the rectangle begins (Fig. 4 (k)). It proceeds by the rule (B1) and stops by the rule (B2) (Fig. 4 (l), (m)).

II. Suppose that the rule (S2) is applied at the first step of a derivation. The formation of the top edge of a rectangle proceeds to the left by rule (T3). After the growth of the top edge stops by the rule (T4) and the growing direction of the sentential form turns to the right, the derivation continues as in case I, and terminates at the left bottom of the rectangle.

G'_R derives a sentential form in a snake-like way. That is, the first pass is from left to right (in the case of I), second from right and left, and then from left to right and so on. And the last pass from right to left completes a rectangle. It is important that the direction of the growth of the sentential form changes at the same horizontal position in each pass. As a result the left and right sides of the sentential form get aligned vertically. The reason is as follows: The rewriting rules that change the developing direction are always applied only at the left or right end.

Observe the sentential form in Fig. 4 (d). We call each four columns of the sentential form in Fig. 4 (d) as a unit. The shapes of the left and right end units are

$$
\begin{array}{ll}
& \text{aaaa} \\
(1) & \text{aa} \\
& \text{aa} \quad ,
\end{array}
$$

23

while those of the inside units are

$$
(2) \quad
\begin{matrix}
\text{aaaa} \\
\text{aa} \\
\text{aa.}
\end{matrix}
$$

Then we notice the shapes of the upper part of the rewriting rules. The rewriting rules (I2), (I4) and (B2) have the shape

$$
(3) \quad
\begin{matrix}
\text{aa} \\
\text{aa} \\
\text{aaaa.}
\end{matrix}
$$

These rewriting rules change the growing direction or terminate the derivation and must be applied at the left or right end on each pass. We call them type A rules. On the other hand, the rewriting rules (I1), (I3) and (B2) have the same shape as

$$
(4) \quad
\begin{matrix}
\text{aa} \\
\text{aa} \\
\text{aaaa.}
\end{matrix}
$$

These rewriting rules continue to develop in the same direction and must be applied in the middle of the pass. We call them type B rules. Note that shape (1) is a complement of (3) and (2) is a complement of (4).

Suppose that the growth has proceeded up to the middle of the second pass (Fig. 4 (f)). The symbol I is the only nonterminal in (f). Of all rewriting rules with the nonterminal I in their left-hand side, only (I1) is applicable. This is because there is not enough blank (#) field around I to apply other rules, while the rule (I1) fits the local shape of the sentential form immediately above I. A similar argument holds for the rewriting at the left end of the second pass. Only the rule (I2) is applicable under the left end unit of the first pass.

The bottom shape of the sentential form at the end of the first pass (Fig. 4 (d)) represents the information as to whether each position is at the left or right end of a rectangle or not. Thus the applications of rewriting rules are controlled by the local shape of a sentential form which is considered to be a kind of context. At the end of the second pass, the bottom of the sentential form becomes again the same shape as in (d). This information is used in the third pass to control the rewriting.

This is why type A rules are applied only at the left or right end of a rectangle, and type B rules are applied only in the middle of it. Thus G'_R generates only solid upright rectangles.

Now we consider the sizes of rectangles derived by G'_R. In case I, derived rectangles are

$$
\{x \mid x \in R, \ h(x) = 3k + 4, \ w(x) = 4l + 8,
$$
$$
(k = 0, 2, 4, \ldots, \ l = 0, 1, 2, \ldots)\}.
$$

In case II, derived rectangles are

$$\{x \mid x \in \mathbf{R}, \; h(x) = 3k + 4, \; w(x) = 4l + 8,$$
$$(k = 1, 3, 5, \ldots, l = 0, 1, 2, \ldots)\}.$$

Thus $L(G'_R) = \mathbf{R}'$. ∎

We now show that an RAG can generate rectangles of all sizes.

Theorem 3.6. There exists an RAG which generates $\mathbf{R}$.

Proof outline. We construct an SLAG G_R which generates $\mathbf{R}$, by modifying G'_R. G'_R generates the set of solid rectangles of height 1 (mod 3) and of width 0 (mod 4). In order to generate the rectangles of height 0 or 2 (mod 3), and of width 1, 2 or 3 (mod 4), we introduce new rewriting rules to G'_R as follows.

(1) For each rule (R2), (B1) and (B2) which forms the bottom edge of rectangles, add the rewriting rule whose bottom edge is extended downward by 2 or 4 symbols. (They derive the rectangles of height 0 or 2 (mod 3) respectively.)
(2) For each rule (T2), (S2), (R1), (I4) and (R2) which forms the right edge of rectangles, add the rewriting rules whose right edge is extended by 1, 2 or 3 symbol(s) to the right. (They derive the rectangles of width 1, 2 or 3 (mod 4) respectively.)
(3) Add the rewriting rules which generate the rectangles lower in height or narrower in width than those that are generated by the above modification (1) and (2) or by G'_R.

Note that we must also introduce new nonterminals to hold the information of the height (mod 3) and the width (mod 4) of the rectangle under generation. These nonterminals are necessary to avoid the mixed applications of rewriting rules which may make the right and the bottom edges of the derived rectangle not aligned.

The entire set of rewriting rules is precisely shown in Appendix 1. ∎

Next, we consider the generation of the set of squares by RAGs. In the generation of squares, not only every edge of the derived array is aligned but also the neighboring two edges must have the same length.

Definition 3.7. Let $\mathbf{S}$ be the set of all solid upright squares over one-letter alphabet $\{a\}$. That is

$$\mathbf{S} = \{x \mid x \in \mathbf{R}, \; \text{and} \; h(x) = w(x)\}.$$

We take a similar approach to the case of rectangles. First, an RAG that generates a subset of $\mathbf{S}$ is given, and then it is modified to generate the entire set of $\mathbf{S}$.

Lemma 3.8. Let $\mathbf{S}'$ be the subset of $\mathbf{S}$ such that

$$\mathbf{S}' = \{x \mid x \in \mathbf{S}, \; \text{and} \; h(x) = 5k + 16$$
$$(k = 0, 1, 2, \ldots)\}.$$

Then there exists an RAG which generates $\mathbf{S}'$.

25

Proof. From Proposition 3.3, it is enough to prove that there exists an SLAG that generates $\mathbf{S}'$. Let $G_S' = (N, \{a\}, P, S, \#)$ be an SLAG such that

$$N = \{S, S_1, S_2, E, C, B_0, B_1, B_2, B_3\}.$$

P is the set of rewriting rules shown in Fig. 5.
We prove that $L(G_S') = \mathbf{S}'$ in the following.

I. Suppose that the rewriting rule (S1) is applied in the first step of a derivation. Then the rules (S2) and (S3) are necessarily applied in the next two steps. After that, the generation of a word proceeds in a spiral manner (Fig. 6). The rules (E1), (E3), (E5) or (E7) make an edge of the host array grow rightward, downward, leftward, or upward respectively, by repeated applications. The application of rules (E2) followed by (C1), (E4) followed by (C2), (E6) followed by (C3), or (E8) followed by (C4) rotate the growing direction 90 degrees clockwise. If the rule (C5) is used at the upper left corner of the host array, the derivation enters the last phase. The rules (B1) to (B7) make the edge of the host array aligned and the rule (B8) terminates the derivation. A square is derived as a result.

II. Suppose that the rule (S4) is applied in the first step of a derivation. The rules (S5) and (S6) can be applied just after (S4). The following derivation process is almost the same as the one obtained by rotating each sentential form in the case I derivation 180 degrees. That is, derivation processes in case I and case II are symmetric with respect to the center of the host array. The only exception is that the last phase of the derivation starts at the upper left corner.

Note that the rewriting rules (E1), (E3), (E5) and (E7) are used only in the middle of the edges of the host array and that the rewriting rules which rotate the growing directions are applied only at the corners of the host array. The reason is similar to the case of SLAG G_R' in Lemma 3.5. The local shapes of the host array such as

```
        aa                aaa
        aa        and     aaa
        aaaaa             aaaaa
```

represent "the middle of edge" and "the corner" respectively, and the shapes of rewriting rules complement them. Thus the applications of rewriting rules are controlled by the local shapes of the host array so that suitable rules are applied at suitable positions.

Now we consider the sizes of derived squares by G_S'. In case I, G_S' derives

$$\{x \mid x \in \mathbf{S}, h(x) = 5k + 16, (k = 0, 2, 4, \dots)\}.$$

In case II, G_S' derives

$$\{x \mid x \in \mathbf{S}, h(x) = 5k + 16, (k = 1, 3, 5, \dots)\}.$$

Therefore **S′** is generated by G'_S. ∎

We now show that an RAG can generate squares of all sizes.

Theorem 3.9.   There exists an RAG which generates **S**.

Proof outline.   We modify G'_S in order to construct an SLAG G_S which generates **S**. G'_S derives the set of solid squares whose four edges are of length 1 (mod 5). In order to generate the squares of length 0, 2, 3 and 4 (mod 5), we introduce new rewriting rules to G'_S as follows.

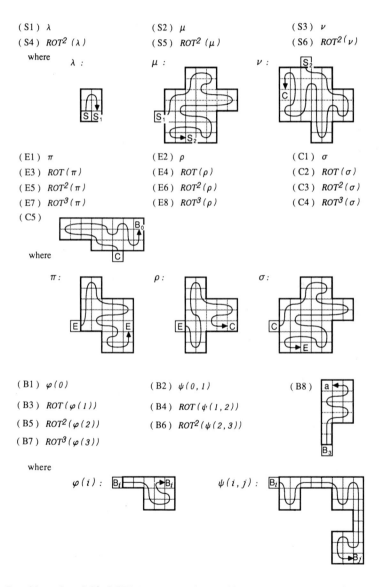

Fig. 5.   Rewriting rules of G'_S. ROT(α) represents the rewriting rule obtained by rotating both sides of the rule α 90 degrees clockwise.

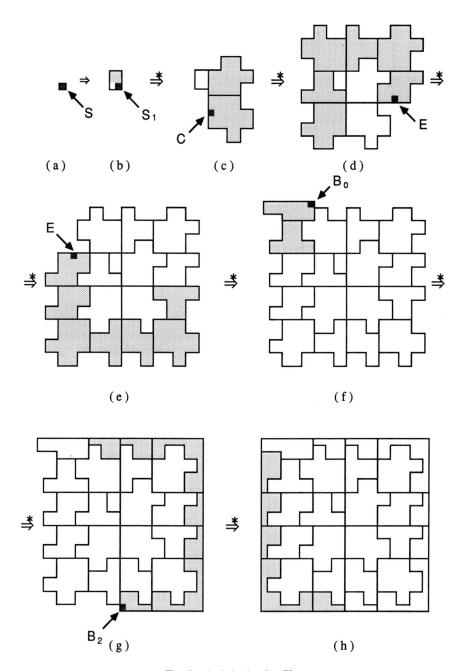

Fig. 6.   A derivation by G'_S.

(1) For each of the rules (C5) and (B1)–(B8), which form the four edges of the squares, add the rewriting rule whose outer border is extended outward by 2, 4, 6 or 8 symbol(s). (Such rewriting rules generate the squares each of whose edges is longer by 4, 8, 12 and 16 respectively. Therefore the derived squares are of length 0, 4, 3 or 2 (mod 5) respectively.)

(2) For each smaller square which is to be generated neither by the above modification nor by G'_S, add the exclusive rewriting rule which derives only such a square directly (by one step rewriting). (We can provide all such rewriting rules because the number of such squares is finite.)

We also introduce new nonterminals which hold the length (mod 5) of the square under generation to avoid the mixed applications of rewriting rules.

The entire set of rewriting rules is precisely shown in Appendix 2. ∎

In the generation of **R** and **S**, RAGs make good use of local shapes of the host array as a kind of context. This shape-sensing (or #-sensing) ability comes from the restriction "isometric". We now give a nontrivial example of a set of figures which cannot be generated by the #-sensing ability of RAGs. We show that it cannot be generated even by CFAGs.

Before proving the theorem, we mention the fact that CFAGs have a Chomsky-like normal form.[1]

Proposition 3.10. (Chomsky-like normal form).   For any language L generated by a CFAG, there exists a CFAG G such that $L = L(G)$, and each rewriting rule in G is of the form

$$\#A \to BC, \; A\# \to BC, \; \begin{matrix} \# \\ A \end{matrix} \to \begin{matrix} B \\ C \end{matrix}, \; \begin{matrix} A \\ \# \end{matrix} \to \begin{matrix} B \\ C \end{matrix}, \; \text{or } A \to a,$$

where A, B, C are nonterminals and a is a terminal.

Definition 3.11.   Let $\mathbf{R_H}$ be the set of all hollow rectangles of thickness 1 over one-letter alphabet $\{a\}$ (Fig. 7).

Theorem 3.12.   There exists no context-free array grammar which generates $\mathbf{R_H}$.

Proof.   We assume that there exists a CFAG $G = (N, \{a\}, P, S, \#)$ which generates $\mathbf{R_H}$. From Proposition 3.10, all rewriting rules in G are assumed to be of Chomsky-like normal form.

G must grow a sentential form linearly in one way or two ways from the start symbol S, because each edge of a hollow rectangle is one symbol thick. Thus the sentential form extends one arm or two arms from S, and stops its growth when a growing head (i.e. an end point) of an arm meets another end point.

For any derivation of $x \in \mathbf{R_H}$, we can find a derivation of x that satisfies the following.

(1) One arm starts growing after the other has been completed, if the derivation proceeds in two ways.

(2) In each step of the derivation, nonterminals may appear only at the two squares of each growing head.

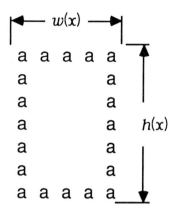

Fig. 7. A word x in $\mathbf{R_H}$.

We can obtain such a derivation by changing the order of applications of rewriting rules in the given derivation. The reason is as follows.

(1) Any rewriting in one arm does not affect those in the other arm because two arms occupy disjoint portions of the sentential form.

(2) Since G is a CFAG of Chomsky-like normal form, the rewriting rules applicable in the middle of an arm are only of the form $A \rightarrow a$. Thus, they can be applied independently and earlier than the rewritings at the growing head.

Now we consider the derivation of $x \in \mathbf{R_H}$ whose height and width are greater than n, where n is the number of nonterminals in G. Consider the formation of an edge where no start point and no meeting point exists. (If the meeting point is at a corner, we can take an edge that is not adjacent to the corner and does not contain the start point in the middle of it.) This edge is formed by growing the sentential form in one way. Our argument on the formation of this edge is similar to that of the pumping lemma in the string grammar.[7] Since the edge grows by at most one symbol of length at a time and the final length is more than n, there exists at least one nonterminal Y that appears twice at the growing head position. That is, the following derivation exists:

$$u_1 Y \overset{*}{\Rightarrow} u_1 u_2 Y \overset{*}{\Rightarrow} u_1 u_2 u_3 Z \tag{1}$$

where u_1, u_2, u_3 form a linear array over $\{a\}$ and the length of u_2 is more than or equal to one and Y, Z are nonterminals. Then the following derivation is possible by G.

$$u_1 Y \overset{*}{\Rightarrow} u_1 u_2 Y \overset{*}{\Rightarrow} u_1 u_2 u_2 Y \overset{*}{\Rightarrow} u_1 u_2 u_2 u_3 Z. \tag{2}$$

In the derivation process of x from S, if we replace the partial derivation (1) with (2), we can derive another word x' by G. Clearly x' is not in $\mathbf{R_H}$. This contradicts the assumption that $L(G) = \mathbf{R_H}$. Therefore the theorem follows. ∎

From the Chomsky-like hierarchy (Proposition 2.1), we have the following corollary.

Corollary 3.13. There exists no RAG that generates R_H.

Before ending this paper, we make a short remark about the generation of **R** and **S** by CFAGs, the grammar class higher than RAGs in the Chomsky-like hierarchy. As RAGs, CFAGs also have #-sensing ability, though they cannot sense non-# contexts in rewriting nonterminals in a host array. In Ref. 4, Yamamoto *et al.* showed the following CFAG G_1 which generates

$$\{x \mid x \in \mathbf{R} \text{ and } h(x) = 2k + 4, \ w(x) = 2l + 3$$
$$(k, \ l = 0, \ 1, \ 2, \ \ldots \ )\}$$

using #-sensing ability.

$$G_1 = (\{S, \ U, \ L, \ I, \ R\}, \ \{a\}, \ P_1, \ S, \ \#),$$

where P_1 is the set of rewriting rules shown in Fig. 8. A derivation process by G_1 is shown in Fig. 9. It is easy to modify G_1 to generate rectangles of all sizes, as we have done in the proof of Theorem 3.6.

Here, we present a CFAG which generates **S**. Consider first the following CFAG G_2.

$$G_2 = (\{S, \ D, \ D_0, \ D_1, \ L, \ I, \ R\}, \ \{a\}, \ P_2, \ S, \ \#),$$

(S1)
$$\begin{matrix} S\,\# \\ \# \end{matrix} \ \rightarrow \ \begin{matrix} a\,U \\ L \end{matrix}$$

(U1)
$$\begin{matrix} U\,\#\,\# \\ \#\,\# \end{matrix} \ \rightarrow \ \begin{matrix} a\,a\,U \\ a\,I \end{matrix}$$

(U2)
$$\begin{matrix} U\,\# \\ \#\,\# \end{matrix} \ \rightarrow \ \begin{matrix} a\,a \\ a\,R \end{matrix}$$

(L1)
$$\begin{matrix} L \\ \#\,\# \\ \# \end{matrix} \ \rightarrow \ \begin{matrix} a \\ a\,a \\ L \end{matrix}$$

(L2)
$$\begin{matrix} L \\ \# \\ \#\,\# \end{matrix} \ \rightarrow \ \begin{matrix} a \\ a \\ a\,a \end{matrix}$$

(I1)
$$\begin{matrix} I \\ \#\,\# \\ \#\,\# \end{matrix} \ \rightarrow \ \begin{matrix} a \\ a\,a \\ a\,I \end{matrix}$$

(I2)
$$\begin{matrix} I \\ \#\,\# \\ \#\,\# \end{matrix} \ \rightarrow \ \begin{matrix} a \\ a\,a \\ a\,a \end{matrix}$$

(R1)
$$\begin{matrix} R \\ \# \\ \#\,\# \end{matrix} \ \rightarrow \ \begin{matrix} a \\ a \\ a\,R \end{matrix}$$

(R2)
$$\begin{matrix} R \\ \#\,\# \\ \# \end{matrix} \ \rightarrow \ \begin{matrix} a \\ a\,a \\ a \end{matrix}$$

Fig. 8.   Rewriting rules of G_1.

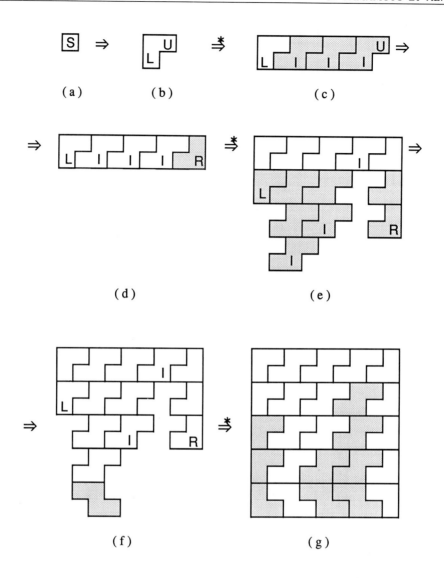

Fig. 9.   A derivation by G_1.

where P_2 is the set of rewriting rules shown in Fig. 10. A derivation process by G_2 is shown in Fig. 11. We can see that G_2 generates the following subset of **S**.

$$\{x \mid x \in \mathbf{S} \text{ and } h(x) = 2k + 6 \ (k = 0, 1, 2, \ldots)\}.$$

It is also easy to modify G_2 to generate squares of all sizes. We leave it to the reader.

We now compare G_1 and G_2 with the SLAGs G_R and G_S. These CFAGs take a different approach from G_R and G_S to generate such figures. That is, sentential forms can grow nonlinearly (i.e. the growth can branch in many ways). As a result, the numbers of nonterminals and rewriting rules are considerably reduced.

By modifying G_2, we can show that the set of all isosceles right triangles can be generated by a CFAG, although Kirsch[8] presented a grammar which generates such triangles using the method of sensing non-# context. The set of all isosceles right triangles is a nontrivial example of the two-dimensional language which cannot be generated by any RAG, because such triangles have, in general, no one-stroke-path.

4. CONCLUDING REMARKS

In this paper, we investigated the #-sensing ability of RAGs. In spite of the simplicity of the form, RAGs can sense a kind of context, and can generate some sets of context-needing figures by using this ability. We gave a concrete description of RAGs which generate all rectangles and all squares. However, it was proved that the set of all hollow rectangles cannot be generated using only #-context.

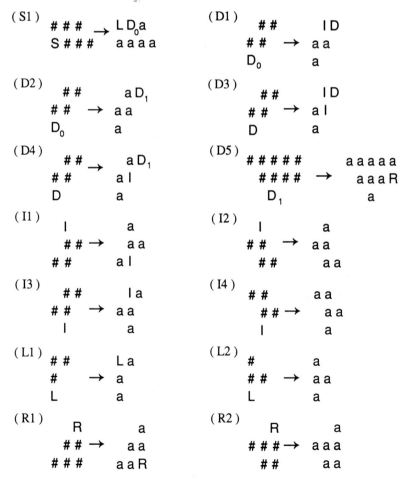

Fig. 10. Rewriting rules of G_2.

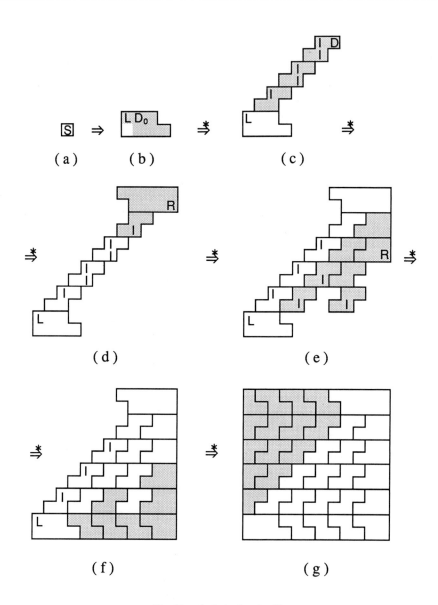

Fig. 11.   A derivation by G_2.

From the above results, it turned out that the generating power of RAGs is relatively higher than imagined from their apparent features. While RAGs have such useful abilities for describing figures, many decision problems for RAGs (and for CFAGs) have been known to be very hard. In Ref. 6, it was shown that the membership problems for RAGs and CFAGs are both NP-complete, and the emptiness and the equivalence problems for RAGs (and thus for CFAGs) are undecidable. Therefore, it will be worth studying other classes of array grammars which have enough generating power (or some context-sensing ability) and whose decision problems are easy to solve.

APPENDIX 1.   SLAG G_R.

Figure 12 shows the nonterminals and the rewriting rules to be added to G'_R (in Lemma 3.5).

The subscripts of nonterminals T, R, I and L represent the width of the rectangle under generation in mod 4, and the subscript of B represents the height in mod 3.

The added rules $\tau 1(1)$, $\tau 2(1)$, $\lambda(1)$, $\mu 1(1)$, $\mu 2(1)$, $\mu 3(1)$, (T5), (S3), (R3), (I5), (R7), (R10) and (R13) generate $x \in \mathbf{R}$ such that

$$w(x) = 4k + 9 \text{ for } k = 0, 1, 2, \ldots \text{ (i.e. 1 mod 4).}$$

The rules $\tau 1(2)$, $\tau 2(2)$, $\lambda(2)$, $\mu 1(2)$, $\mu 2(2)$, $\mu 3(2)$, (T6), (S4), (R4), (I6), (R8), (R11) and (R14) generate $x \in \mathbf{R}$ such that

$$w(x) = 4k + 10 \text{ for } k = 0, 1, 2, \ldots \text{ (i.e. 2 mod 4).}$$

The rules $\tau 1(3)$, $\tau 2(3)$, $\lambda(3)$, $\mu 1(3)$, $\mu 2(3)$, $\mu 3(3)$, (T7), (S5), (R5), (I5), (R7), (R12) and (R15) generate $x \in \mathbf{R}$ such that

$$w(x) = 4k + 11 \text{ for } k = 0, 1, 2, \ldots \text{ (i.e. 3 mod 4).}$$

The rules (B4), (B3), (R16) and (R10)–(R12) generate $x \in \mathbf{R}$ such that

$$h(x) = 3k + 8 \text{ for } k = 0, 2, 4, \ldots \text{ (i.e. 2 mod 3),}$$

if the rule (S1) (in Fig. 3) is applied at the first step of the derivation, or

$$h(x) = 3k + 8 \text{ for } k = 1, 3, 5, \ldots \text{ (i.e. 2 mod 3),}$$

if the rule (S2), (S3), (S4) or (S5) is applied at the first step of the derivation. The rules (B6), (B5), (R17) and (R13)–(R15) generate $x \in \mathbf{R}$ such that

$$h(x) = 3k + 6 \text{ for } k = 0, 2, 4, \ldots \text{ (i.e. 0 mod 3),}$$

if the rule (S1) is applied at the first step of generation, or

$$h(x) = 3k + 6 \text{ for } k = 1, 3, 5, \ldots \text{ (i.e. 0 mod 3),}$$

if the rule (S2), (S3), (S4) or (S5) is applied at the first step of generation.

There are an infinite number of rectangles which are not generated even by adding the above rules. They are

$$\{x \in \mathbf{R} \mid h(x) = 1, 2, 3, 5 \text{ or } 1 \leqslant w(x) \leqslant 7\}.$$

($\Re$1) $\tau k(i)$ $(i=1,2,3 , k=1,2)$

($\Re$2) $\lambda(i)$ $(i=1,2,3)$

($\Re$3) $\mu k(i)$ $(i=1,2,3 , k=1,2,3)$

where

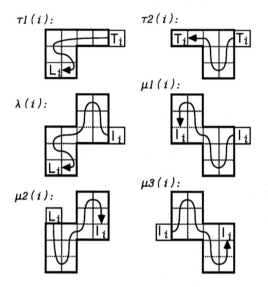

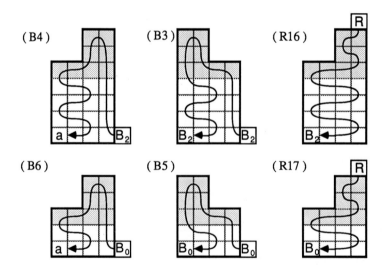

Fig. 12.   Additional rewriting rules for G_R.

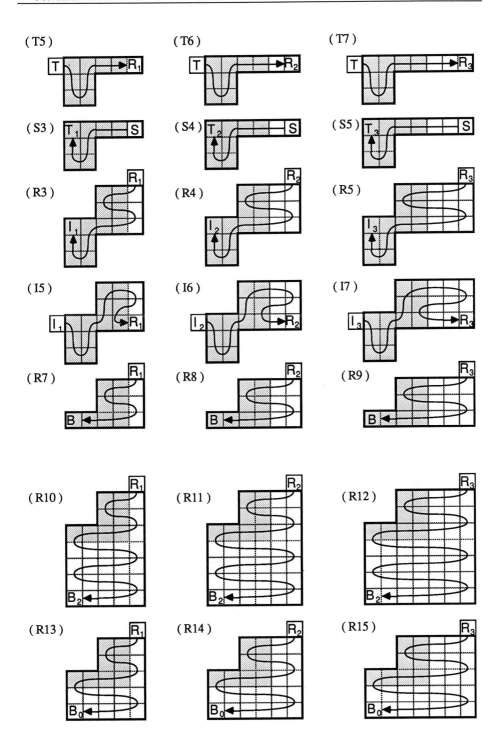

Fig. 12.   Cont'd.

They can be generated by a finite number of other rewriting rules. For example, the following rewriting rules generate the rectangles of width 3 and of any height.

$$S \# \# \to a \ a \ R_{w3}, \qquad R_{w3} \to \qquad a, \qquad R_{w3} \to a,$$
$$\# \# \# \qquad L_{w3} \ a \ a$$

$$L_{w3} \qquad \to a \qquad , \qquad L_{w3} \to a.$$
$$\# \# \# \qquad \# \# R_{w3}$$

The construction of the rest of such rules is left to the reader.

APPENDIX 2.   SLAG G_S.

Figure 13 shows the nonterminals and the rewriting rules to be added to G_S' (in Lemma 3.8).

The first digit i of the subscript of the nonterminal B_{ij} means the growing direction of edges of a square. The second digit j represents the size of the squares under generation in mod 5. The rules (C6), $\varphi 0(0)$, $\psi 0(0, 1)$, $\text{ROT}(\varphi 0(1))$, $\text{ROT}(\psi 0(1, 2))$, $\text{ROT}^2(\varphi 0(2))$, $\text{ROT}^2(\psi 0(2, 3))$, $\text{ROT}^3(\varphi 0(3))$ and (B9) generate the squares of size 0 mod 5. The rules (C7), $\varphi 2(0)$, $\psi 2(0, 1)$, $\text{ROT}(\varphi 2(1))$, $\text{ROT}(\psi 2(1, 2))$, $\text{ROT}^2(\varphi 2(2))$, $\text{ROT}^2(\psi 2(2, 3))$, $\text{ROT}^3(\varphi 2(3))$ and (B10) generate the squares of size 2 mod 5. The rules (C8), $\varphi 3(0)$, $\psi 3(0, 1)$, $\text{ROT}(\varphi 3(1))$, $\text{ROT}(\psi 3(1, 2))$, $\text{ROT}^2(\varphi 3(2))$, $\text{ROT}^2(\psi 3(2, 3))$, $\text{ROT}^3(\varphi 3(3))$ and (B11) generate the squares of size 3 mod 5. The rules (C9), $\varphi 4(0)$, $\psi 4(0, 1)$, $\text{ROT}(\varphi 4(1))$, $\text{ROT}(\psi 4(1, 2))$, $\text{ROT}^2(\varphi 4(2))$, $\text{ROT}^2(\psi 4(2, 3))$, $\text{ROT}^3(\varphi 4(3))$ and (B12) generate the squares of size 4 mod 5. The sizes of squares generated by the above rules and the rules in G_S' are

$$10k + 4l + 16 \text{ for } k = 0, 1, 2, 3, \ldots \text{ and } l = 1, 2, 3, 4,$$

if the rule (S1) (in Lemma 3.8) is used at the first step of the generation, or

$$10k + 4l + 21 \text{ for } k = 0, 1, 2, 3, \ldots \text{ and } l = 1, 2, 3, 4,$$

if the rule (S4) is used at the first step of the generation.

All that is left to do is to add the rewriting rules to derive small squares which cannot be generated by the above rules. They are

$$\{x \mid x \in \mathbf{S} \text{ and } 1 \leqslant h(x) \leqslant 15 \quad \text{ or } h(x) = 17, 18, 19, 22, 23, 27\}.$$

It is easy to provide the exclusive rewriting rules for these 21 squares. Thus the construction is left to the reader.

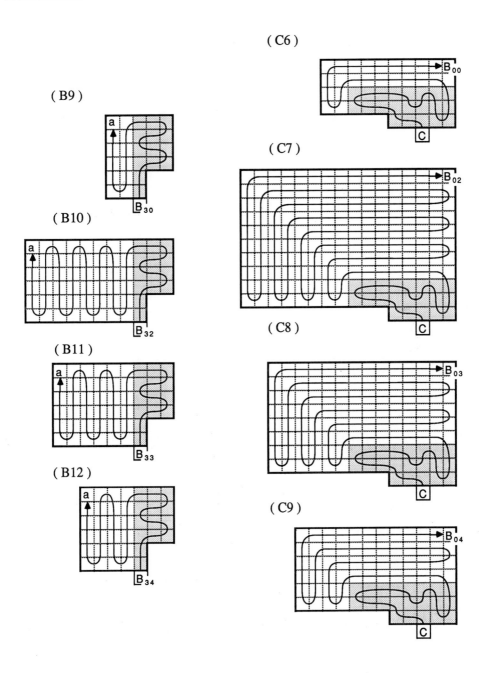

Fig. 13. Additional rewriting rules for G_S.

($\mathfrak{R}$1) $ROT^i(\varphi k(i))$ $(i = 0, 1, 2, 3,\ k = 0, 2, 3, 4)$

where

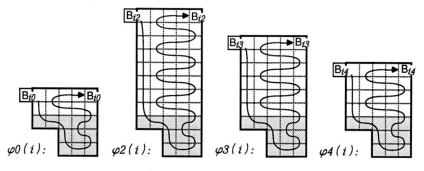

$\varphi 0(i):$ $\varphi 2(i):$ $\varphi 3(i):$ $\varphi 4(i):$

($\mathfrak{R}$2) $ROT^i(\psi k(i, i+1))$

       $(i = 0, 1, 2,\ k = 0, 2, 3, 4)$

where

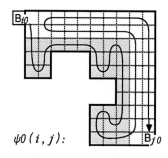

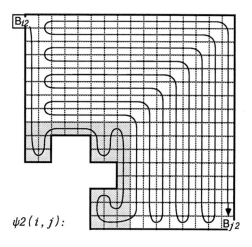

$\psi 0(i,j):$ $\psi 2(i,j):$

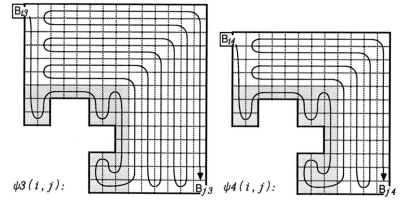

$\psi 3(i,j):$ $\psi 4(i,j):$

Fig. 13.   Cont'd.

40

REFERENCES

1. C. R. Cook and P. S. P. Wang, "A Chomsky hierarchy of isotonic array grammars and languages", *Computer Graphics and Image Processing* **8** (1978) 144–152.
2. D. L. Milgram and A. Rosenfeld, "Array automata and array grammars", *Information Processing* **71** (1972) 69–74.
3. A. Rosenfeld, "Isotonic grammars, parallel grammars, and picture grammars", in *Machine Intelligence VI*, Eds. D. Michie and B. Meltzer, University of Edinburgh Press, Scotland, 1971, pp. 281–294.
4. Y. Yamamoto, K. Morita and K. Sugata, "An isometric context-free array grammar that generates rectangles", *Trans. IECE Japan* **E65** (1982) 754–755.
5. A. Rosenfeld, *Picture Languages*, Academic Press, New York, 1979.
6. K. Morita, Y. Yamamoto and K. Sugata, "The complexity of some decision problems about two-dimensional array grammars", *Information Sciences* **30** (1983) 241–262.
7. J. E. Hopcroft and J. D. Ullman, *Introduction to Automata Theory, Languages, and Computation*, Addison-Wesley, Reading, MA, 1979.
8. R. A. Kirsch, "Computer interpretation of English text and picture patterns", *IEEE Trans. EC* **13** (1964) 363–376.
9. P. S. P. Wang, "Hierarchical structures and complexities of parallel isometric languages", *IEEE Trans. PAMI* **5** (1983) 92–99.

Yasunori Yamamoto received the B.S. and M.S. degrees in engineering from Osaka University, in 1978 and 1980 respectively. Since October 1983, he has been an Assistant Professor in the Division of Computer Ethnology of the National Museum of Ethnology. His research interests include automata and language theory, computational complexity and computer ethnology.

Kenichi Morita received the B.E., M.E. and Dr.E. degrees from Osaka University, in 1971, 1973 and 1978 respectively. From 1974 to 1987, he was a Research Associate of the Faculty of Engineering Science, Osaka University. Since 1987 he has been an Associate Professor of the Faculty of Engineering, Yamagata University, Yonezawa, Japan. His research interests include automata theory, computational complexity, formal language theory, and logic systems for knowledge and natural language processing. His other interests include listening to classical music, watching operas and running long distances very slowly (his best record of a full marathon is 4 h 5 min).

Kazuhiro Sugata received the B.S. degree in electrical engineering from Kyoto University, in 1961, and the M.S. and Ph.D. degrees in electrical engineering (1963) and computer engineering (1968) from Kyoto University respectively. From 1966 to 1971 he served in Osaka University as a research assistant and was an Assistant Professor there between 1971 to 1986. Since 1986 he has been working at the Information Processing Division of the Social Systems Engineering Department in Tottori University, Japan as a Chief Professor.

He was a member of the editorial committee of the Institute of Electronics, Information and Communication Engineers of Japan. He is also a member of the Information Processing Society of Japan. His research interests lie in automata theory, language, computational complexity, two-dimensional array grammars, array processing, speech signal compression, computer applications to speech signal processing and image processing.

GENERATING RECTANGLES USING TWO-DIMENSIONAL GRAMMARS WITH TIME AND SPACE COMPLEXITY ANALYSES

EDWARD T. LEE

Department of Electrical and Computer Engineering
University of Miami, P. O. Box 248294
Coral Gables, FL 33124, USA

SHANG-YONG ZHU and PENG-CHING CHU

Department of Computer Science
Louisiana State University, Baton Rouge, LA 70803, USA

Received 26 April 1987
Revised 20 January 1988

A two-dimensional grammar for generating all possible rectangles is presented and illustrated by examples. The time and space complexity analyses of this grammar together with a parallel context-free array grammar and a tree grammar are also presented. Generating pictures using two-dimensional grammars appears to be a fertile field for further study. The study of two-dimensional grammars has useful applications in region filling, pattern recognition, robotics, pictorial information system design and related areas.

Keywords: Grammar; Two-dimensional grammar; Derivation chain; Rectangles; Picture generation; Time and space complexity; Parallel context-free array grammars; Tree grammars.

1. INTRODUCTION

Kirsch[1] presented a two-dimensional grammar for generating all possible 45 degree right-angled triangles in a plane consisting of unit squares. Additional information regarding two-dimensional grammars may be found in Refs. 1–20. In this paper, an algorithm for generating all possible rectangles using two-dimensional grammars is presented. In addition, the time and space complexity of this grammar compared with other similar works in the literature are also investigated. There are three reasons that we select rectangles.

1. The classification of quadrangles may be found in Refs. 21 and 22 and is shown in Fig. 1. Furthermore, two-dimensional grammars for generating squares and rhombuses may be found in Ref. 6. Thus, naturally, rectangles become the next type of quadrangles to study.

2. Rectangles are an important type of quadrangle. For example, the shapes of walls usually are rectangles.

43

3. Our tacit assumption is that the two-dimensional grammar developed here will be used as part of a two-level picture generation system. A high level description of this two-level picture generation system is presented in the next section.

2. HIGH LEVEL DESCRIPTION OF A TWO-LEVEL PICTURE GENERATION SYSTEM

The block diagram of a high level description of a two-level picture generation system is shown in Fig. 2.

2.1. A First Level Picture Primitive Generation

(i) Depending on prospective applications, a set of primitive picture entities are specified.

(ii) For each primitive picture entity, specify a two-dimensional picture grammar which will be able to generate this primitive picture entity with pixels as primitive elements.

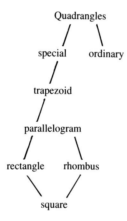

Fig. 1. Classification of quadrangles.

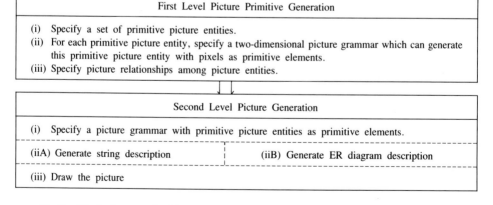

Fig. 2. Block diagram of a high level description of a two-level picture generation system.

If squares and rhombuses are primitive picture entities, then the corresponding two-dimensional picture grammar which will be able to generate all possible squares and all possible rhombuses may be found (see Ref. 6). If rectangles are primitive picture entities, then we need the corresponding two-dimensional picture grammar which is presented in Sect. 4.

2.2. Second Level Picture Generation

(i) Depending on prospective applications, a picture grammar with primitive picture entities as primitive elements is specified.

(iiA) For each element in the language, generate the corresponding string description.

(iiB) For each element in the language, generate the corresponding entity-relationship (ER) diagram description.

(iii) For each element in the language, draw the corresponding picture.

3. TWO-DIMENSIONAL GRAMMARS

A simple two-dimensional generalization of string grammars,[23,24] is to extend from one-dimensional strings to two-dimensional arrays.[1-20] The primitives are the array elements and the relation between primitives is the two-dimensional concatenation. Each production rewrites one subarray by another rather than one substring by another. Relationships between array grammars and array automata (automata with two-dimensional tapes) have been studied in Ref. 9. A detailed study on array grammars and array automata may be found in Ref. 11. As shown in Ref. 16, some properties of two-dimensional array patterns do not coincide with their one-dimensional counterparts.

Informally, a two-dimensional grammar may be viewed as a set of rules for generating the two-dimensional elements of a set. More concretely, a two-dimensional grammar is a quadruple $G = (V_N, V_T, P, S)$ in which V_T is a set of terminals, V_N is a set of nonterminals $(V_T \cap V_N = \phi)$, P is a set of two-dimensional productions, and $S \in V_N$. Essentially, the elements of V_N are labels for certain subsets of V_T^* called two-dimensional syntactic categories with S being the label for the syntactic category "two-dimensional sentences". In addition, each production rewrites one subarray by another. A two-dimensional grammar for generating all possible rectangles is presented in the following section.

4. GRAMMARS FOR GENERATING RECTANGLES

A two-dimensional grammar for generating all possible rectangles in a plane consisting of unit squares is presented as follows:

$$G = (V_N, V_T, P, S)$$

where $V_N = \{A, B, C, S\}$,
$\qquad V_T = \{t, b, l, w, a, z, r, i\}$,
$\qquad S = \{S\}$.

Furthermore,

A denotes any member of $\{S, z\}$;

B denotes any member of $\{b, r, l\}$;

C denotes anything, including blanks.

Two-dimensional productions P are shown in Fig. 3. The derivation chain for generating a 3 by 4 rectangle is shown in Fig. 4. The number above the derivation chain indicates the production rule that is used during the derivation.

5.   TIME AND SPACE COMPLEXITY ANALYSES

It is of interest to study the time and space complexity of the grammar G compared with other similar works in the literature.

For simplicity, we use the length of a derivation chain as a time complexity measure. More accurate time complexity measure should include the time for locating the production. Assume that there are n productions, and that linear search is used. Then, on the average, for locating a production, we need to search $n/2$ productions. Furthermore, we can use associative memory (content-addressable memory)[25] in order to improve retrieval time. These aspects of time complexity analysis will be presented in subsequent papers.

The length of the derivation chain for generating a 3 by 4 rectangle using G is equal to 8 as shown in Fig. 4.

In generation, a derivation chain for generating an m by n rectangle using G is shown in Fig. 5. Furthermore, a double arrow in Fig. 5 represents a derivation chain. $(n - 2) \times (2)$ above a double arrow means that production (2) is applied repeatedly $(n - 2)$ times. Similarly, $(m - 4) \times (n - 3) \times (10)$ above a double arrow means that production (10) is applied repeatedly $(m - 4) \times (n - 3)$ times.

Thus, in general, the length of the derivation chain for generating an m by n rectangle using G is equal to $[m + n + (m - 2) \times (n - 3)]$.

The regions generated by production rules in G are shown in Fig. 6. In addition, Fig. 6 may also be viewed as an abbreviation of a derivation chain.

We use the number of productions and memory requirement as space complexity measures. There are 9 productions in G. The memory requirement for G is equal to 72 memory words.

Note that, with VLSI technology, the price of memory per word becomes less expensive. Thus, for time and space complexity analyses, relatively speaking, saving time may be more important than saving memory space.

6.   PARALLEL CONTEXT-FREE ARRAY GRAMMARS

The definition of a parallel context-free array grammar may be found in Ref. 17; and the discussion of parallel context-free array grammars normal forms may be found in Ref. 15.

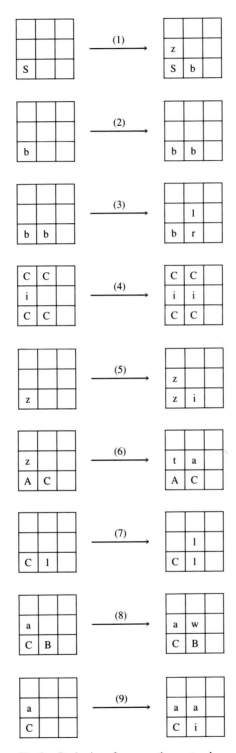

Fig. 3. Productions for generating rectangles.

47

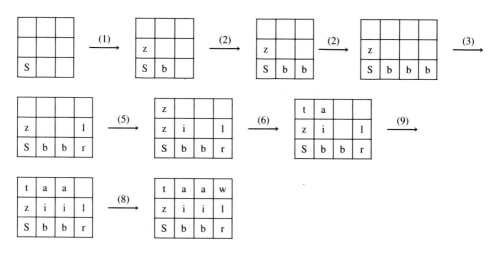

Fig. 4.   A derivation chain for generating a 3 by 4 rectangle.

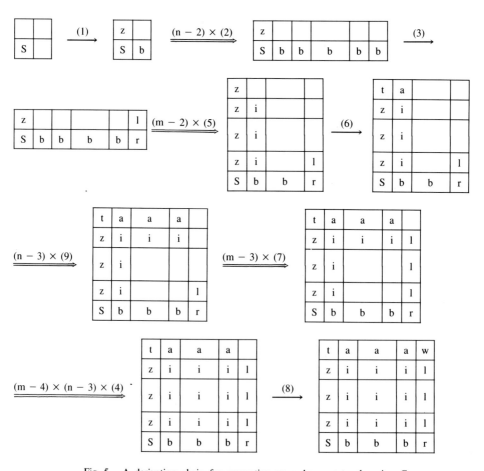

Fig. 5.   A derivation chain for generating an *m* by *n* rectangle using *G*.

6	6	9	9	8
5	5	9	9	7
5	5	4	4	7
1	5	4	4	3
0	1	2	2	3

Fig. 6.   The regions generated by production rules in G.

Example 1.   A parallel context-free array grammar $G1$ can generate all rectangles as follows:

$$G1 = [V_N, \ V_T, \ P1, \ S, \ \#]$$

where $\# \notin V_N \cup V_T$ is the blank symbol,
$V_N = \{S, A\}$,
$V_T = \{a\}$

and $P1 = \Big\{ \ S \# \overset{1}{\rightarrow} AA$

$\qquad A \# \overset{2}{\rightarrow} AA,$

$\qquad \begin{matrix} \# & \underset{3}{\rightarrow} & A \\ A & & A \end{matrix}$

$\qquad A \overset{4}{\rightarrow} a \ \Big\}$

This $G1$ can generate all rectangles with a's as shown in Fig. 7.

$$
\begin{matrix}
a & a & \ldots & a \\
a & & \ldots & a \\
a & & \ldots & a
\end{matrix}
$$

Fig. 7.   A typical rectangle generated by $G1$.

The minimum size of rectangles generated by $G1$ is 1 by 2.
   If we want to include a 2 by 1 rectangle, then we can include the following production

$$\begin{matrix} \# & \underset{5}{\rightarrow} & A \\ S & & A \end{matrix} \ .$$

49

If we want to include a, then we can include either

$$S \xrightarrow{6A} A,$$

or

$$S \xrightarrow{6B} a.$$

Note that $G1$ also generates non-rectangles. An example is shown in Fig. 8.

$$
\begin{array}{ccc}
 & a & \\
a & a & a
\end{array}
$$

Fig. 8.   A non-rectangle generated by $G1$.

The length of the derivation chain for generating a 3 by 4 rectangle using $G1$ is equal to 23.

In general, the length of the derivation chain for generating an m by n rectangle using $G1$ is equal to $(2\ mn - 1)$. It takes $(mn - 1)$ steps to generate an m by n rectangle of A. Then, it takes mn steps to transform an m by n rectangle of A to an m by n rectangle of a.

The number of productions in $G1$ is equal to 4. The memory requirement of $G1$ is equal to 14 memory words.

7.   TREE GRAMMARS

The definition of a tree grammar may be found in Ref. 5; and the discussion of fuzzy tree automata and syntactic pattern recognition may be found in Ref. 26.

Example 2.   The tree grammar

$$G2 = (V, r, P2, S)$$

where $V = \{S, a, b, \$, A, B\}$,
$\quad\quad\quad V_T = \{a, b, \$\}$,
$\quad\quad\quad r(a) = r(b) = \{2, 0\}$,
$\quad\quad\quad r(\$) = 2$,

and $P2$, is shown in Fig. 9.

A 3 by 4 rectangle and its tree representation are shown in Fig. 10. Note that $G2$ also generates non-rectangle patterns. An example is shown in Fig. 11.

The length of the derivation chain of generating a 3 by 4 rectangle is equal to 32.

In general, the length of the derivation chain of generating an m by n rectangle is equal to $(2mn + m + n + 1)$.

There are 7 productions in $G2$. The memory requirement for $G2$ is equal to 20 memory words.

The time complexity analysis with respect to G, $G1$ and $G2$, and in terms of the length of a derivation chain is shown in Table 1. Thus, for generating a rectangle, G has the shortest derivation chain.

The space complexity analysis with respect to G, $G1$ and $G2$, and in terms of the number of productions and memory requirement is shown in Table 2. $G1$ has the least number of productions and requires the least number of memory words.

Other similar works in the literature can be compared in the same manner.

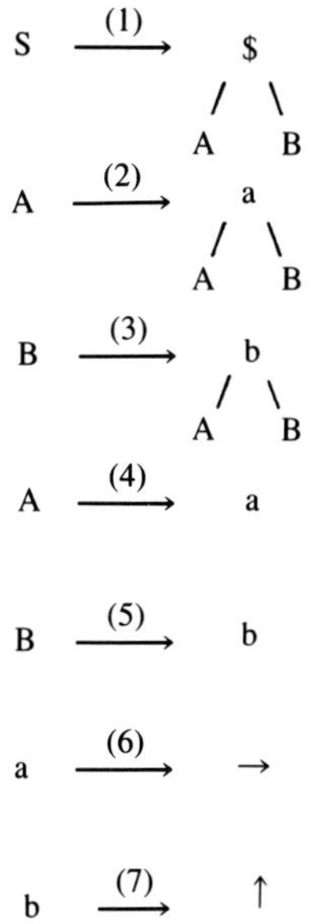

S $\xrightarrow{(1)}$ $\begin{array}{c} \$ \\ / \quad \backslash \\ A \quad B \end{array}$

A $\xrightarrow{(2)}$ $\begin{array}{c} a \\ / \quad \backslash \\ A \quad B \end{array}$

B $\xrightarrow{(3)}$ $\begin{array}{c} b \\ / \quad \backslash \\ A \quad B \end{array}$

A $\xrightarrow{(4)}$ a

B $\xrightarrow{(5)}$ b

a $\xrightarrow{(6)}$ $\rightarrow$

b $\xrightarrow{(7)}$ $\uparrow$

Fig. 9. Productions $P2$ for tree grammar $G2$.

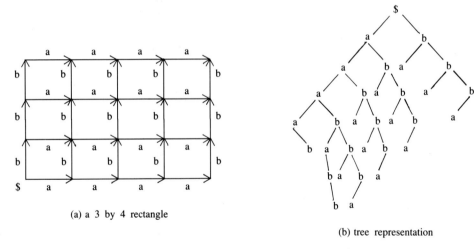

(a) a 3 by 4 rectangle

(b) tree representation

Fig. 10. A 3 by 4 rectangle generated by G2 and its tree representation.

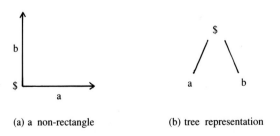

(a) a non-rectangle   (b) tree representation

Fig. 11. A non-rectangle generated by $G2$ and its tree representation.

51

Table 1.   Time complexity analysis with respect to G, $G1$ and $G2$.

	Length of a derivation chain for generating a 3 by 4 rectangle	Length of a derivation chain for generating an m by n rectangle
G	8	$m + n + (m - 2)(n - 3)$
$G1$	23	$2mn - 1$
$G2$	32	$2mn + m + n + 1$

Table 2.   Space complexity analysis with respect to G, $G1$ and $G2$.

	Number of productions	Memory requirement in terms of memory words
G	9	72
$G1$	4	14
$G2$	7	20

8.   CONCLUSION

A two-dimensional grammar for generating all possible rectangles is presented. The time and space complexity analyses of this grammar together with a parallel context-free array grammar and a tree grammar are also presented. Picture generation and picture description[7] using two-dimensional grammars offer what appear to be a fertile field for further study. Further work remains to be done. Nevertheless, even at this early stage of the development of this subject, it appears that the study of two-dimensional grammars may have useful applications in region filling,[8] pattern recognition,[10,27,28] robotics, pictorial information system design,[29,30] and related areas.

ACKNOWLEDGEMENT

This research was supported by DARPA Contract N00014-87-K-0066 and by SUSS FHTIC Grant No. 578.

REFERENCES

1. R. A. Kirsch, "Computer interpretation of English text and patterns," *IEEE Trans. Electron. Comput.* **13** (1964) 363–376.
2. K. Aizawa and A. Nakamura, "Direction-independent application of productions on 2-d arrays", *Information Processing Letters* **22** (1986) 295–301.
3. C. R. Cook and P. S. P. Wang, "A Chomsky hierarchy of isotonic array grammars and languages", *Computer Graphics and Image Processing* **8** (1978) 144–152.
4. M. F. Dacey, "The syntax of a triangle and some other figures," *Pattern Recognition* **2** (1970) 11–31.
5. K. S. Fu, *Syntactic Pattern Recognition and Applications*, Prentice Hall, 1982.
6. E. T. Lee and P. Chu, "Two-dimensional grammars for generating squares and rhombuses", *Kybernetes* **16** (1987) 121–123.
7. E. T. Lee, P. Chu and C. Peng Wu, "Applications of entity-relationship model to picture description", *Robotica* **5** (1987) 231–234.

8. E. T. Lee, Y. J. Pan and P. Chu, "An algorithm for region filling using two-dimensional grammars", *Int. J. Intelligent Systems*, **2** (1987) 255–263.
9. D. M. Milgram and A. Rosenfeld, "Array automata and array grammars", *International Federation of Information Processing Congress 71*, Booklet TA-2, North-Holland, Amsterdam, 1971, pp. 166–173.
10. T. Pavlidis, *Structural Pattern Recognition*, Springer-Verlag, Berlin, 1977.
11. A. Rosenfeld, *Picture Languages*, Academic Press, New York, 1979.
12. R. Siromoney, K. G. Subramanian and K. Rangarajan, "Parallel/sequential rectangle arrays with tables", *Int. J. Comp. Math.* **6A** (1976) 143–157.
13. R. Siromoney, "Array languages and Lindenmayer systems—A survey", in *The Book of L*, Eds. G. Rozenberg and A. Salomaa, Springer-Verlag, 1986.
14. P. S. P. Wang, "Finite-turn repetitive checking automata and sequential/parallel matrix languages", *IEEE Trans. Computers*, **30** (1981) 366–370.
15. P. S. P. Wang, "Parallel context-free array grammars normal forms", *Computer Graphics and Image Processing* **15** (1981) 296–300.
16. P. S. P. Wang, "A new hierarchy for 2-D isometric arrays", *Information Processing Letters* **15** (1982) 223–226.
17. P. S. P. Wang, "Hierarchical structures and complexities of parallel isometric languages", *IEEE Trans. Patt. Anal. Mach. Intell.* **5** (1983) 92–99.
18. P. S. P. Wang, "An application of array grammars to clustering analysis for syntactic patterns", *Pattern Recognition* **17** (1984) 441–451.
19. P. S. P. Wang and X. W. Dai, "A grammatical inference algorithm for digitized array patterns", *Proc. ICPR '86*, Paris, 1986, pp. 129–131.
20. E. Yodogawa, "A note on array grammars", *Information Processing Letters* **18** (1984) 51–54.
21. E. T. Lee, "Proximity measures for the classification of geometric figures", *Journal of Cybernetics* **2** (1972) 43–59.
22. E. T. Lee, "The shape-oriented dissimilarity of polygons and its applications to the classification of chromosome images", *Pattern Recognition* **6** (1974) 47–60.
23. J. E. Hopcroft and J. D. Ullman, *Introduction to Automata Theory, Languages, and Computation*, Addison-Wesley, 1979.
24. E. T. Lee and L. A. Zadeh, "Note on fuzzy languages", *Information Sciences* **1** (1969) 421–434.
25. F. J. Hill and G. R. Peterson, *Digital Systems: Hardware Organization and Design*, Third ed., John Wiley and Sons, 1987.
26. E. T. Lee, "Fuzzy tree automata and syntactic pattern recognition", *IEEE Trans. Patt. Anal. Mach. Intell.* **4** (1982) 445–449.
27. T. Y. Young and T. W. Calvert, *Classification Estimation and Pattern Recognition*, Elsevier Science Publishers, New York, 1974.
28. T. Y. Young and K. S. Fu, Eds., *Handbook of Pattern Recognition and Image Processing*, Academic Press, 1986.
29. E. T. Lee, "Similarity retrieval techniques", in *Pictorial Information Systems*, Eds. S. K. Chang and K. S. Fu, Springer-Verlag, 1980, pp. 128–176.
30. E. T. Lee, "Similarity retrieval for pictorial databases" in *Management and Office Information Systems*, Ed. S. K. Chang, Plenum, 1984, pp. 253–288.

 **Edward T. Lee** received his Master and Ph.D. degrees from the University of California at Berkeley. His industrial experience includes working for IBM Corporation and Systems Control, Inc. Currently, Dr. Lee is a Professor in the Department of Electrical and Computer Engineering, University of Miami.

He was awarded the Outstanding Scholarly Contribution Award at the 4th International Conference on Systems Research Informatics and Cybernetics, Baden-Baden, West Germany, August 15–21, 1988. He was also selected as a 1989 NAVY/ASEE Distinguished Summer Faculty Research Fellow.

His research interests include medical expert systems, pictorial knowledge, computer architecture and knowledge-based systems.

Photographs and biographical information of Shang-Yong Zhu and Peng-Ching Chu were not available.

SIROMONEY ARRAY GRAMMARS
AND APPLICATIONS

K. G. SUBRAMANIAN, L. REVATHI
and R. SIROMONEY

Department of Mathematics
Madras Christian College
Tambaram, Madras 600 059, India

Received 29 May 1989
Revised 10 June 1989

The Siromoney matrix model is a simple and elegant model for describing two-dimensional digital picture languages. The notion of attaching indices to nonterminals in a generative grammar, introduced and investigated by Aho, is considered in the vertical phase of a Siromoney matrix grammar (SMG). The advantage of this study is that the new model retains the simplicity and elegance of SMG but increases the generative power and enables us to describe pictures not generable by SMG. Besides certain closure properties and hierarchy results, applications of these two-dimensional grammars to describe tilings, polyominoes, distorted patterns and parquet deformations are studied.

Keywords: Matrix grammar; Indexed grammar; Tiling; Stochastic model.

1. INTRODUCTION

Syntactic methods play an important role in picture generation and description. Fu[1] has made a comprehensive review of syntactic approaches in pictorial pattern recognition. There has been considerable interest in studying array grammars that generate sets of two-dimensional picture languages, considered as digitized arrays. Rosenfeld[2] has made a compact presentation of various array grammars.

A simple and elegant model for two-dimensional picture languages was introduced in Ref. 3. Studies of different aspects of this model have been made (see for example Refs. 4–9). We refer to this model[3] of array grammars as Siromoney matrix grammars (SMG). The derivation consists of two phases: the horizontal phase uses a Chomskian string grammar to generate strings of intermediate symbols and the vertical phase uses a finite number of right-linear grammars to generate arrays of symbols from the strings of intermediates, the rewriting taking place in parallel. Other generative grammars can be used in the horizontal phase to reflect the string grammar study in the case of arrays, but incorporating other generative schemes in the vertical phase of SMG is of more interest and is advantageous for the study of the particular aspect of the picture we are concerned with. Wang[10,11] has made a detailed study of matrix grammars and recognizers by allowing for CF, CS and PS rules in the vertical generation and has noted that all the advantages of the matrix grammars carry over to this model as well. Recently, parallel generation of finite images has been examined[12] using extensions and modifications of SMG.

55

Aho[13] has introduced indexed grammars, motivated by the need to have a reasonable grammar less powerful than context-sensitive grammars but possessing properties similar to context-free grammars, thereby overcoming the inadequacy of context-free grammars in specifying syntactic structures.

In this paper, we incorporate and examine the notion of indices attached to nonterminals introduced and investigated in Refs. 13 and 14 to the vertical derivation of SMG. The advantage is that we can generate pictures that cannot be described by the earlier model,[3] such as pictures having a given proportion about a horizontal line.

Besides hierarchy results and some closure properties, we study various aspects of application of these Siromoney matrix grammars with/without indices. First, we indicate the use of SMG with/without indices in describing periodic/non-periodic tilings. Next we examine certain classes of polyominoes with the help of SMG. Thirdly, the stochastic version of SMG with indices is utilised to classify noisy versions of two-dimensional pictures of digitized rectangular arrays. Finally the application of SMG with indices in describing parquet deformation is brought out.

2. PRELIMINARIES

In this section, we first review some of the definitions of indexed grammars. For details we refer to Refs. 13 and 14.

Definition 2.1.   A right-linear indexed right-linear (RIR) grammar G is a five-tuple (N, T, F, P, S) where N, T, F are finite, pair-wise disjoint sets of nonterminals, terminals and indices respectively; P consists of two types of productions, namely
(i)   right-linear productions of the form

$$A \to xBf, \ A \in N, \ x \in T \cup \{\varepsilon\}, f \in F \cup \{\varepsilon\}, \ B \in N \cup \{\varepsilon\}, \text{ not all } \varepsilon, \text{ and}$$

(ii) indexed productions of the form

$$Af \to xB, \ A \in N, \ B \in N \cup \{\varepsilon\}, \ x \in T \cup \{\varepsilon\}, f \in F,$$

and $S \in N$ is the start symbol.

Derivations are as in a Chomskian right-linear grammar except that a nonterminal A is expanded by a production of the form (i) or an index f is consumed by a production of the form (ii).

A left-linear indexed right-linear (LIR) grammar is defined in a similar way with P consisting of
(i)   productions of the form $A \to xBf$, and
(ii) indexed productions of the form $Af \to Ba$.
LIL and RIL grammars can be defined analogously.

Matrix grammars for generation of two-dimensional digitized rectangular arrays have been introduced in Ref. 3. We call these grammars Siromoney matrix grammars (SMG). We define here an extension of these grammars with the notion of indexed nonterminals and indexed productions introduced in the vertical phase of the derivations in these grammars.

Definition 2.2. A $(CF : RIR)SMG$ $G = (G_1, G_2)$ is defined as follows:

$G_1 = (N, I, P, S)$ is a context-free (CF) grammar where N is a finite set of nonterminals, I is a finite set of k intermediate symbols $S_1, S_2, \ldots, S_k$ with $N \cap I = \phi$, and $S \in N$ is the start symbol of G_1. G_1 is called the horizontal grammar.

$G_2 = \langle G_{21}, \ldots, G_{2k} \rangle$, where each G_{2i}, $i = 1, \ldots, k$, is called a vertical grammar and $G_{2i} = (N_i, T, F_i, P_i, S_i)$ is an RIR grammar with N_i, F_i being distinct from N_j, F_j for $i \neq j$ $(1 \leq i, j \leq k)$. The intermediate symbol S_i of G_1 is in N_i and is the start symbol of G_{2i}.

The derivations are as follows: G_1 generates finite strings of intermediates as in a Chomskian CF grammar, i.e. $S \underset{G_1}{\overset{*}{\Rightarrow}} \alpha \in I^+$. The vertical derivation starts with a string of intermediates generated by G_1 and proceeds in parallel as in a matrix grammar.[3] Rules of the same type—either CF productions $A \rightarrow \alpha$ or indexed productions $Af \rightarrow \alpha$ with the length of α being the same (3, 2, 1 or 0), are applied in the vertical derivation. At every step of the vertical derivation, a row $A_1 \ldots A_m$ of nonterminals is expanded or a string of indexed nonterminals $\begin{array}{c} A_1 \ldots A_m \\ f_1 \ldots f_m \end{array}$ is rewritten, consuming the indices. A derivation ends successfully on generating an array M over T by rewriting a row of nonterminals with(without) indices by rules of the form $Af \rightarrow a$ $(A \rightarrow a)$.

The array language generated by the grammar G is given by

$$L(G) = \{M \in T^{++} / S \underset{G_1}{\overset{*}{\Rightarrow}} \alpha \text{ and } \alpha \underset{G_2}{\overset{*}{\Rightarrow}} M, \ \alpha \in I^+\}.$$

The other classes of indexed SMG, either with a regular grammar in the horizontal direction or other indexed grammars (LIR, LIL or RIL) in the vertical direction, are defined in a similar manner.

We note that the class of languages generated by $(R : RIR)SMG$ $((CF : RIR)SMG)$ properly includes the class of languages generated by RSMG (CFSMG) introduced in Ref. 3.

Example 1. The $(R : RIR)SMG$ which generates the token H of xs with the horizontal row of xs exactly in the middle is as follows:

$$G = (G_1, G_2)$$

where

$$G_1 = (\{S, A\}, \{S_1, S_2\}, \{S \rightarrow S_1A, A \rightarrow S_2A, A \rightarrow S_2, S_1\}, S)$$

generating strings of intermediates $S_1 S_2^n S_1$ for $n \geq 1$ and

$$G_2 = \langle G_{21}, G_{22} \rangle$$

where

$$G_{21} = (\{S_1, A_1, A_2, A_3\}, \{x\}, \{g_1, g_2\}, P_{21}, S_1)$$

with $P_{21} = \{S_1 \to xA_1g_2,\ A_1 \to A_2g_1,\ A_1 \to xA_1g_1,$
$\qquad\qquad A_2g_1 \to xA_3,\ A_3g_1 \to xA_3,\ A_3g_2 \to x\},$

$$G_{22} = (\{S_2,\ B_1,\ B_2,\ B_3,\ B_4\},\ \{\cdot,\ x\},\ \{f_1,\ f_2\},\ P_{22},\ S_2)$$

with $P_{22} = \{S_2 \to \cdot B_1 f_2,\ B_1 \to \cdot B_1 f_1,\ S_2 \to \cdot B_2 f_2,$
$\qquad\qquad B_1 \to \cdot B_2 f_1,\ B_2 \to B_3 f_1,\ B_3 f_1 \to xB_4,$
$\qquad\qquad B_4 f_1 \to \cdot B_4,\ B_4 f_2 \to \cdot\}.$

A sample vertical derivation is as follows:

$$
S_1 S_2 S_1 \underset{G_2}{\Rightarrow}
\begin{matrix} x & \cdot & x \\ A_1 & B_2 & A_1 \\ g_2 & f_2 & g_2 \end{matrix}
\underset{G_2}{\Rightarrow}
\begin{matrix} x & \cdot & x \\ A_2 & B_3 & A_2 \\ g_1 & f_1 & g_1 \\ g_2 & f_2 & g_2 \end{matrix}
\underset{G_2}{\Rightarrow}
\begin{matrix} x & \cdot & x \\ x & x & x \\ A_3 & B_4 & A_3 \\ g_2 & f_2 & g_2 \end{matrix}
$$

$$
\underset{G_2}{\Rightarrow}
\begin{matrix} x & \cdot & x \\ x & x & x \\ x & \cdot & x \end{matrix}
$$

We first state certain closure properties of the indexed SMG which can be easily proved as in the case of Siromoney matrix grammars.[3]

Proposition 2.3.

(i) The class of languages generated by $(X : Y)$SMG where $X \in \{R, CF\}$ and $Y \in \{RIR, RIL, LIR, LIL\}$ is closed under the operations of translation, reflection about vertical and base, half-turn, column catenation and column Kleene plus.

(ii) The row catenation and row Kleene plus of the family of finite matrices can be generated by an $(R : RIR)$SMG.

We denote the family of array languages generated by an $(X : Y)$SMG by $(X : Y)$ itself, $X \in \{R, CF\}$, $Y \in \{RIR, RIL, LIR, LIL\}$.

We now compare various families of indexed Siromoney matrix languages (SML).

Theorem 2.4.

(i) $(R : Y) \subsetneqq (CF : Y)$ for $Y \in \{RIR, LIL, RIL, LIR\}$

(ii) $(X : RIR) = (X : LIL) \subsetneqq (X : RIL) = (X : LIR)$ for $X \in \{R, CF\}$.

Proof.   (i) follows from the fact that the family of regular languages is properly contained in the family of CF languages.

In (ii) the result that $(X : RIR) = (X : LIL)$ $((X : RIL) = (X : LIR))$ follows by observing that the family of languages of $(X : RIR)$SMG $((X : RIL)$SMG) is closed under reflection about the base and that the reversal of the right sides of the vertical RIR (RIL) rules are simply LIL (LIR) rules.

That $(X : RIR) \subseteq (X : RIL)$ follows by noting that a matrix language generated by an $(X : RIR)$SMG is also generable by an $(X : RIL)$SMG, for, the family of languages generated by the RIR grammars is equivalent to that of context-free grammars and those generated by the RIL grammars properly contains the family of context-free languages.

To prove proper inclusion, we consider the matrix language L, obtained from strings of intermediates $S_1^n S_2 S_1^n$ $(n \geqslant 1)$ and the vertical languages

$$
L_1 = \left\{ \begin{pmatrix} \begin{pmatrix} a \\ a \\ a \end{pmatrix}_n \\ \begin{pmatrix} b \\ b \\ b \end{pmatrix}_n \end{pmatrix}, \ n > 0 \right\} \text{ and } L_2 = \left\{ \begin{pmatrix} \begin{pmatrix} a \\ a \end{pmatrix}_n \\ \begin{pmatrix} c \\ c \end{pmatrix}_n \\ \begin{pmatrix} b \\ b \end{pmatrix}_n \end{pmatrix}, \ n > 0 \right\}
$$

corresponding to intermediates S_1 and S_2 respectively. A member of L is got from a word $S_1^n S_2 S_1^n$ by replacing each S_1 by an element of L_1 and S_2 by an element of L_2, subject to the condition of column catenation (namely, the elements have the same number of rows). L can be generated by a (CF : RIL)SMG while it cannot be generated by a (CF : RIR)SMG. ∎

We now give the necessary definitions of image grammars introduced in Ref. 12 for generation of finite images that are rectangular arrays of digitized symbols and compare the families of languages generated by them with the families of indexed SML.

Definition 2.5.

(i) A CR image grammar has two phases of generation as in a Siromoney matrix grammar.[3] The horizontal rules are of the form

$$H \to A \text{ or } H \to AH_1 H_2 \ldots H_n \ (n \geqslant 1),$$

where A is an intermediate and H, H_i are nonterminals, and the vertical rules are of the form

$$(V_1 \to a_1 V_1', \ \ldots, \ V_p \to a_p V_p') \text{ or } (V_1 \to a_1, \ \ldots, \ V_p \to a_p),$$

V_i, V_i' are nonterminals and a_i are terminals.

(ii) An RR image grammar has horizontal rules of the form

$$H \to A \text{ or } H \to AH_1$$

where A is an intermediate and H, H_1 are nonterminals, and the vertical rules are of the form mentioned in (i).

A vertical rule is used to rewrite a row of nonterminals vertically in parallel.

Definition 2.6. A deterministic image grammar is one in which there is exactly one rule for every nonterminal in the vertical grammar.[12]

Theorem 2.7. For every deterministic CR (RR) image grammar, there exists an equivalent (CF : RIR)SMG ((R : RIR)SMG).

Proof.   Consider a deterministic CR image grammar

$$G = (V_H, \ V_V, \ \Sigma_I, \ \Sigma, \ S, \ R_H, \ R_V).$$

We construct an equivalent (CF : RIR)SMG as follows.

The horizontal components of G are retained, i.e. if $G' = (G_1, \ G_2)$ is a (CF : RIR)SMG, then $G_1 = (V_H, \ \Sigma_I, \ R_H, \ S)$.

The vertical grammar is $G = \langle G_{2i} \rangle$, $1 \leqslant i \leqslant n$, where G_{2i} has the ith intermediate S_i as the start symbol.

P_i is defined as follows.

$P_i = \{S_i \to a_i V_i' \ f / S_i \to a_i V_i'$ is the ith rule in some table in $R_V\} \cup \{V_i f \to a_i V_i''$, $V_i'' \to V_i' g / f \neq g$ and $V_i \to a_i V_i'$ is the ith rule in some table in R_V and $(V_{i1} \to b_i V_i f / 1 \leqslant i \leqslant n)$ is a set of rules already in $P_i\} \cup \{V_i f \to a_i / V_i \to a_i$ is the ith rule in a table in R_V and $(V_{i1} \to b_i V_i f / 1 \leqslant i \leqslant n)$ is already in $P_i\}$. F_i, $1 \leqslant i \leqslant n$, is the collection of all the indices introduced in the set P_i. It is clear that $S \overset{*}{\underset{G'}{\Rightarrow}} \alpha \in \Sigma^{**}$ iff $S \overset{*}{\underset{G}{\Rightarrow}} \alpha \in \Sigma^{**}$.   ∎

Remark.   In fact, it can be shown that there exists an equivalent (CF : RIR)SMG for a CR image grammar in which every nonterminal has at most one nonterminal and at most one terminal rule.

3.   SMG AND TILING

It is well-known that the Siromoney matrix model (SMM)[3] has wide applications.[6,7,9,15,16] Another area where it is found useful is in tiling. Informally, by a tiling of a plane we mean a set of tiles that cover the plane with no gaps or no overlaps. Here, we indicate the use of SMG and indexed SMG in describing tilings. We first generate a finite array by a regular Siromoney matrix grammar (RSMG) and using the properties of RSMG, obtain a tiling for a set of tiles satisfying a given property. As a specific case, we describe the method of obtaining a tiling with the prototiles of heptiamonds which are formed by seven equilateral triangles.

For the basic definition of tilings, we refer to Ref. 17.

Definition 3.1.   If the symmetry group[17] of a tiling contains at least two translations in non-parallel directions, then the tiling is said to be periodic.

We now restrict our attention to the study of periodic tilings.

Theorem 3.2.   Any periodic tiling can be described by an RSMG.

Proof.   We give an informal proof. With any periodic tiling, we can associate a lattice, and the points of the lattice can be regarded as the vertices of a parallelogram tiling, since such a tiling is possible for any parallelogram. Hence, if the configuration of the tiles in one of the parallelograms is known, then the rest of the tiling can be constructed by repeating this configuration in every parallelogram. That is, the tiling could be constructed progressively by translating a parallelogram in two non-parallel directions.[17]

A finite parallelogram-shaped array which is a finite matrix language (FML) can be generated by an RSMG. Since the row and column Kleene plus of FML can be considered to be linear translations[3] in two non-parallel directions, an RSMG can be constructed to generate the above matrix language. Thus, the tiling of a parallelogram tile can be described by an RSMG. ∎

We now discuss the method of describing the tiling whose prototile is any heptiamond (except one particular heptiamond) using SMG.

Example 2.   A heptiamond is a tile formed by seven equilateral triangles, each of side one unit. The twenty-four possible heptiamonds are shown in Fig. 1.

Out of these twenty-four heptiamonds, all except the last one are prototiles of a tiling and so from now on, we deal only with these twenty-three heptiamonds.

In order to get a tiling by the heptiamonds, we generate the finite array

$$
\begin{array}{cccc}
a(1,\ 1) & a(1,\ 2) & \cdots & a(1,\ q) \\
a(2,\ 1) & a(2,\ 2) & \cdots & a(2,\ q) \\
\cdot & & & \cdot \\
\cdot & & & \cdot \\
\cdot & & & \cdot \\
a(p,\ 1) & a(p,\ 2) & \cdots & a(p,\ q)
\end{array}
$$

by an RSMG, where $p,\ q > 0$.
   Let $R = \{a(m,\ n)/1 \leqslant m \leqslant p,\ 1 \leqslant n \leqslant q\}$.

Fig. 1.   Heptiamonds.

Fig. 2. Primitives of heptiamonds.

We define a coding h from R to the elements of the set S, where $S = \{a_1, a_2, a_3, a_4,$ $b_1, b_2, b_3, b_4, b_5, b_6, a, b\}$. Here, $a_1, a_2, a_3, a_4, b_1, b_2, b_3, b_4, b_5, b_6, a$ and b respectively stand for the primitives shown in Fig. 2.

The figure represented by an element of S is an equilateral triangle of side one unit, where the sides denoted in dotted lines represent virtual sides.

Choosing the coding differently, we obtain tilings of various heptiamonds, since the finite array generated then, varies.

The coding h chosen to obtain the tilings is such that

(i) $h(a(i, j))$ is defined for $1 \leqslant j \leqslant q$ and

(ii) the coding of the remaining elements of the array is defined by the relation $h(a(i + 1, 1 + ((j + r) \bmod q))) = h(a(i, j))$, $1 \leqslant i < p$, $1 \leqslant j \leqslant q$, where r is the repetition number.

Thus, a coding is defined for the entire array of size $p \times q$ if it is defined for the first row of the array and the repetition number r is known.

We write $h(a(i, j)) = x$ as $a(i, j) \to x$.

As an illustration, consider the following coding

$$
\begin{array}{ll}
a(1, 1) \to a_1 & a(1, 8) \to a \\
a(1, 2) \to b_4 & a(1, 9) \to a_4 \\
a(1, 3) \to a_4 & a(1, 10) \to b_4 \\
a(1, 4) \to b_4 & a(1, 11) \to a_4 \\
a(1, 5) \to b & a(1, 12) \to b_2 \\
a(1, 6) \to b_2 & a(1, 13) \to a_3 \\
a(1, 7) \to a_1 & a(1, 14) \to b_3
\end{array}
$$

with $r = 8$, $p = 14$ and $q = 14$.

With this coding applied to the finite matrix, we obtain the basic pattern given in Fig. 3, which when translated linearly in two perpendicular directions yields a tiling whose prototile is shown in Fig. 4.

Non-periodic tilings can be described by SMG with indices.

Example 3. The non-periodic tiling shown in Fig. 5 can be generated by the (R : RIR)SMG $G = (G_1, G_2)$ where

$$G_1 = (\{S\}, \{S_1, S_2\}, S, \{S \to S_1 S_2 S, S \to S_1 S_2\})\text{ and}$$

$$G_2 = \langle G_{21}, G_{22} \rangle.$$

G_{21} and G_{22} are given by

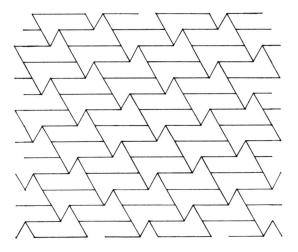

Fig. 3.   Tiling by a heptiamond.

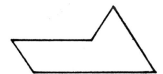

Fig. 4.   Prototile of Fig. 3.

$$G_{21} = (\{S_1, A_1, B_1\}, \{a_1, b_1\}, \{f_1, g_1\}, S_1, \{S_1 \rightarrow a_1A_1f_1,$$
$$A_1 \rightarrow a_1A_1g_1, A_1 \rightarrow b_1B_1, B_1g_1 \rightarrow a_1B_1, B_1f_1 \rightarrow a_1\}).$$

$$G_{22} = (\{S_2, A_2, B_2\}, \{a_2, b_2\}, \{f_2, g_2\}, S_2, \{S_2 \rightarrow a_2A_2f_2,$$
$$A_2 \rightarrow a_2A_2g_2, A_2 \rightarrow b_2B_2, B_2g_2 \rightarrow a_2B_2, B_2f_2 \rightarrow a_2\}).$$

An array generated by this grammar is

$$
\begin{array}{cccccccc}
a_1 & a_2 & a_1 & a_2 & a_1 & a_2 & a_1 & a_2 \\
a_1 & a_2 & a_1 & a_2 & a_1 & a_2 & a_1 & a_2 \\
b_1 & b_2 & b_1 & b_2 & b_1 & b_2 & b_1 & b_2 \\
a_1 & a_2 & a_1 & a_2 & a_1 & a_2 & a_1 & a_2 \\
a_1 & a_2 & a_1 & a_2 & a_1 & a_2 & a_1 & a_2 \\
\end{array}
$$

We denote by a_1, a_2, b_1 and b_2 the primitives shown in Fig. 6.

In a_1 and b_1, the horizontal side is 3/4 of the vertical and in a_2 and b_2, the horizontal
side is 1/4 of the vertical. The sides in dotted lines denote virtual sides.

With this representation, we get the tiling pattern shown in Fig. 5.

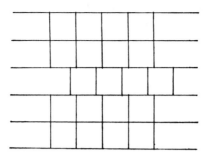

Fig. 5.   A non-periodic tiling.

Fig. 6.   Primitives of the tiling in Fig. 5.

4.   SMG AND POLYOMINOES

The polyominoes are a simple basic pattern of a tile whose study is of current interest[18,19] and the SMG is quite useful in examining certain classes of polyominoes. We give below some of the definitions required for our discussion.

Definition 4.1.

(i)   A polyomino is a point in the plane $Z \times Z$, each point being represented by a square tile of side one unit.

(ii) A polyomino is said to be connected if there exists a path, consisting of horizontal and vertical lines alone, between any two tiles. For example, the polyomino in Fig. 7(a) is connected while that in Fig. 7(b) is not.

(iii) A polyomino is said to be H-convex (V-convex) if its intersection with any horizontal (vertical) strip is connected and is contained in it.

(iv) A polyomino is convex iff it is H-convex and V-convex.

(v)   A V-convex polyomino is said to row-span a vertical strip of width n iff it has at least one row of size n.

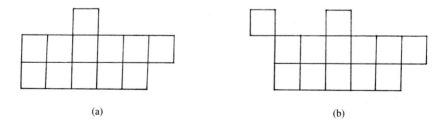

(a)   (b)

Fig. 7.   (a) A connected polyomino and (b) a polyomino which is not connected.

Let us consider vertical strips of finite length and consider the class of all polyominoes restricted to these strips. In order to study such polyominoes in the context of SMG, we also make provision to consider arrays of varying row-size and column-size within it, by modifying the SMG in the following manner.

(i) We remove the restriction of applying the same type of rules at any step of the vertical derivation from the SMG.

(ii) Two rows of intermediates are derived in the horizontal derivation so that vertical derivations can proceed upward from the first row and downward from the second row.

This class of extended SMG has been studied in Ref. 5.

The following theorem gives a necessary and sufficient condition for a class of connected polyominoes to be V-convex.

Theorem 4.2. A connected polyomino which row-spans a vertical strip of finite length is V-convex iff it is generated by an extended SMG.

Proof. Consider an extended SMG G over the single terminal alphabet $\{a\}$. The terminal a stands for a unit square tile. Then obviously any connected polyomino generated by G is V-convex.

Conversely, consider any connected V-convex polyomino which row-spans a vertical strip of length n. Then, we first generate an intermediate string of length n, duplicated twice. This can be done by the grammar

$$G = \left(\{S\}, \ \{S_1\}, \ \left\{ S \to \begin{matrix} S_1 \\ S_1 \end{matrix} S, \ S \to \begin{matrix} S_1 \\ S_1 \end{matrix} \right\}, \ S \right).$$

Hence we have,

$$S \overset{*}{\Rightarrow} \begin{matrix} S_1 & S_1 & \ldots & S_1 \\ S_1 & S_1 & \ldots & S_1 \end{matrix} \quad (n \text{ times}).$$

Since the polyomino is V-convex and row-spans a vertical strip of length n, we observe that if it has two rows of length n, then they should be consecutive.

We now split the polyomino into two parts, i.e. we make a cut just above the first row of length n. Then using the production set $\{S_1 \to \varepsilon, \ S_1 \to aS_1\}$, we can generate the polyomino in the following manner.

Consider the upper part of the polyomino. Let P be the set of positions in the last row of the upper part which is filled up by the tiles. Use the rule $S_1 \to \varepsilon$ to the top row of intermediates to get the last row of the upper part. In all other positions apply the production $S_1 \to aS_1$ upward as if it were $\begin{matrix} S_1 \\ a \\ \uparrow \\ S_1 \end{matrix}$.

Since the polyomino is V-convex, the positions in P will not contain any tile in the upper part. In all other positions, use the second rule as many times as necessary followed by $S_1 \rightarrow \varepsilon$.

Now consider the lower part. First, the rule $S_1 \rightarrow aS_1$ is applied to all intermediates and from then on, the generation is similar to that of the upper part. Thus G generates the given polyomino. ■

We now consider the H-convex nature of a V-convex connected polyomino that row-spans a vertical strip of finite length.

Let $f_t(i)$, $1 \leq i \leq n, t = 1, 2$ denote the length of the ith column of a given polyomino up and down the rows of length n. Obviously, $f_t(i) > 1$.

For a given j, let $P_t(j)$, $t = 1$, 2 be the set $\{f_t(i)/1 \leq i \leq j\}$ and $S_t(j) = \{f_t(i)/j < i \leq n\}$.

Theorem 4.3. A connected polyomino which row-spans a vertical strip of finite length and is generated by an extended SMG is convex if all columns of maximum height occur together; $P_t(m)$ is a non-decreasing sequence and $S_t(m)$ is a non-increasing sequence where m corresponds to the maximum element of $\{f_t(i)/1 \leq i \leq n\}$.

Proof. That the polyomino considered is V-convex follows from the previous theorem. Hence it is enough to prove that it is H-convex. Let $f_t(m_t)$ be the maximum element of the set $\{f_t(i)/1 \leq i \leq n\}$. If $P_1(m_1)$ and $S_1(m_1)$ are non-decreasing and non-increasing sequences respectively, then since the polyomino is V-convex, it has to be H-convex too, for it is not possible to have a segment as shown in Fig. 8, with gaps in the middle of any horizontal segment. Thus all rows in the upper part of the polyomino are connected. By a similar argument, it can be noticed that the lower part is also connected and thus the polyomino is H-convex, thereby showing that it is convex. ■

5.   SMG AND NOISY PATTERNS

In order to recognize and classify pictures in their noisy and distorted versions, SMGs have been effectively used in Ref. 9. We illustrate the use of indices in the stochastic matrix model described in Ref. 9.

We assume that the reader is familiar with the basics of stochastic grammars and languages.[9]

Definition 5.1. A stochastic (R : RIR)SMG is a stochastic matrix grammar[9] wherein an RIR grammar is used for vertical derivations.

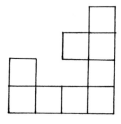

Fig. 8.   Impossible polyomino in Theorem 4.3.

We now construct a stochastic (R : RIR)SMG to describe distorted and noisy patterns of two alphabetic letters E and F and classify them. In the following figure, sixteen arrays are given, of which A_1 to A_{11} belong to the pattern class P_1 consisting of the alphabet letter E and its noisy versions. A_6 to A_{16} belong to the pattern class P_2 representing the alphabet letter F and its noisy versions. The common elements of P_1 and P_2 are A_6 to A_{11}, out of which the patterns in A_6, A_7 and A_8 resemble E more than F, i.e. they have greater probability of belonging to P_1. In the same way, A_9, A_{10} and A_{11} have a greater probability of belonging to P_2. Taking these into consideration, we construct a suitable model to achieve this probability assignment.

```
X X X X      X X X X      X X X X      X X X X
X . . .      X . . .      X . . .      X . . .
X X X X      X X X X      X X X X      X X X X
X . . .      X . . .      X . . .      X . . .
X X X X      X X X .      X X . X      X . X X
   A₁           A₂           A₃           A₄


X X X X      X X X X      X X X X      X X X X
X . . .      X . . .      X . . .      X . . .
X X X X      X X X X      X X X X      X X X X
X . . .      X . . .      X . . .      X . . .
. X X X      . . X X      . X . X      . X X .
   A₅           A₆           A₇           A₈


X X X X      X X X X      X X X X      X X X X
X . . .      X . . .      X . . .      X . . .
X X X X      X X X X      X X X X      X X X X
X . . .      X . . .      X . . .      X . . .
X . . X      X . X .      X X . .      . . . X
   A₉           A₁₀          A₁₁          A₁₂


X X X X      X X X X      X X X X      X X X X
X . . .      X . . .      X . . .      X . . .
X X X X      X X X X      X X X X      X X X X
X . . .      X . . .      X . . .      X . . .
. X . .      . . X .      . . . .      X . . .
  A₁₃          A₁₄          A₁₅          A₁₆
```

Let $G = (G_1, G_2)$ with $L(G_1) = (S_1 S_2 S_3 S_4, 1)$. For convenience, in the grammar for the vertical derivation, a table like $\{A_1 \to xB_1,\ A_2 \to \cdot B_2,\ A_3 \to \cdot B_3,\ A_4 \to \cdot B_4\}$ is written as $\langle A \rangle \to (x,\ \cdot,\ \cdot,\ \cdot)\langle B \rangle$. G_2 is given by the tables,

$P_V = \{(T_1,\ 1),\ (T_2,\ 1),\ (T_3,\ 1/2),\ (T_4,\ 1/2),\ (T_5,\ 1/4),\ (T_6,\ 1/4),\ (T_7,\ 1/12),$
$(T_8,\ 1/12),\ (T_9,\ 1/12),\ (T_{10},\ 1/12),\ (T_{11},\ 1/27),\ (T_{12},\ 1/27),\ (T_{13},\ 1/27),$
$(T_{14},\ 1/54),\ (T_{15},\ 1/54),\ (T_{16},\ 1/54)\}$

where

$$
\begin{aligned}
T_1 &= \langle S \rangle \rightarrow (x, \ x, \ x, \ x)\langle A \rangle \\
T_2 &= \langle A \rangle \rightarrow (x, \ \cdot, \ \cdot, \ \cdot)\langle B \rangle f \\
T_3 &= \langle B \rangle \rightarrow (x, \ \cdot, \ \cdot, \ \cdot)\langle B \rangle g \\
T_4 &= \langle B \rangle \rightarrow (x, \ x, \ x, \ x)\langle C \rangle g \\
T_5 &= \langle C \rangle g \rightarrow (x, \ \cdot, \ \cdot, \ \cdot)\langle C \rangle \\
T_6 &= \langle C \rangle f \rightarrow (x, \ x, \ x, \ x) \\
T_7 &= \langle C \rangle f \rightarrow (x, \ x, \ x, \ \cdot) \\
T_8 &= \langle C \rangle f \rightarrow (x, \ x, \ \cdot, \ x) \\
T_9 &= \langle C \rangle f \rightarrow (x, \ \cdot, \ x, \ x) \\
T_{10} &= \langle C \rangle f \rightarrow (\cdot, \ x, \ x, \ x) \\
T_{11} &= \langle C \rangle f \rightarrow (\cdot, \ \cdot, \ x, \ x) \\
T_{12} &= \langle C \rangle f \rightarrow (\cdot, \ x, \ \cdot, \ x) \\
T_{13} &= \langle C \rangle f \rightarrow (\cdot, \ x, \ x, \ \cdot) \\
T_{14} &= \langle C \rangle f \rightarrow (x, \ \cdot, \ \cdot, \ x) \\
T_{15} &= \langle C \rangle f \rightarrow (x, \ \cdot, \ x, \ \cdot) \\
T_{16} &= \langle C \rangle f \rightarrow (x, \ x, \ \cdot, \ \cdot).
\end{aligned}
$$

The grammar G describes the elements of the pattern class P_1.

The pattern class P_2 consisting of A_6 to A_{16} representing the alphabet F and its noisy versions is described by the grammar $G' = (G_1', G_2')$ where $L(G_1') = (S_1 S_2 S_3 S_4, 1)$ and the production tables for G_2' are given by

$$
\begin{aligned}
P_V = \{ &(T_1, \ 1), \ (T_2, \ 1), \ (T_3, \ 1/2), \ (T_4, \ 1/2), \ (T_5, \ 1/4), \ (T_6, \ 1/4), \ (T_7, \ 1/12), \\
&(T_8, \ 1/12), \ (T_9, \ 1/12), \ (T_{10}, \ 1/12), \ (T_{11}, \ 1/27), \ (T_{12}, \ 1/27), \ (T_{13}, \ 1/27), \\
&(T_{14}, \ 1/54), \ (T_{15}, \ 1/54), \ (T_{16}, \ 1/54) \}
\end{aligned}
$$

where

$$
\begin{aligned}
T_1 &= \langle S \rangle \rightarrow (x, \ x, \ x, \ x)\langle A \rangle \\
T_2 &= \langle A \rangle \rightarrow (x, \ \cdot, \ \cdot, \ \cdot)\langle B \rangle f \\
T_3 &= \langle B \rangle \rightarrow (x, \ \cdot, \ \cdot, \ \cdot)\langle B \rangle g \\
T_4 &= \langle B \rangle \rightarrow (x, \ x, \ x, \ x)\langle C \rangle g \\
T_5 &= \langle C \rangle g \rightarrow (x, \ \cdot, \ \cdot, \ \cdot)\langle C \rangle \\
T_6 &= \langle C \rangle f \rightarrow (x, \ \cdot, \ \cdot, \ \cdot) \\
T_7 &= \langle C \rangle f \rightarrow (\cdot, \ x, \ \cdot, \ \cdot) \\
T_8 &= \langle C \rangle f \rightarrow (\cdot, \ \cdot, \ x, \ \cdot) \\
T_9 &= \langle C \rangle f \rightarrow (\cdot, \ \cdot, \ \cdot, \ x) \\
T_{10} &= \langle C \rangle f \rightarrow (\cdot, \ \cdot, \ \cdot, \ \cdot) \\
T_{11} &= \langle C \rangle f \rightarrow (x, \ \cdot, \ \cdot, \ x) \\
T_{12} &= \langle C \rangle f \rightarrow (x, \ \cdot, \ x, \ \cdot) \\
T_{13} &= \langle C \rangle f \rightarrow (x, \ x, \ \cdot, \ \cdot) \\
T_{14} &= \langle C \rangle f \rightarrow (\cdot, \ \cdot, \ x, \ x) \\
T_{15} &= \langle C \rangle f \rightarrow (\cdot, \ x, \ \cdot, \ x) \\
T_{16} &= \langle C \rangle f \rightarrow (\cdot, \ x, \ x, \ \cdot).
\end{aligned}
$$

From the grammar G we note that the probabilities are $p(A_1) = 1/32$, $p(A_2) = 1/96$, $p(A_3) = 1/96$, $p(A_4) = 1/96$, $p(A_5) = 1/96$, $p(A_6) = 1/216$, $p(A_7) = 1/216$, $p(A_8) = 1/216$, $p(A_9) = 1/432$, $p(A_{10}) = 1/432$, $p(A_{11}) = 1/432$.

From the grammar G', the probabilities are $p(A_6) = 1/432$, $p(A_7) = 1/432$, $p(A_8) = 1/432$, $p(A_9) = 1/216$, $p(A_{10}) = 1/216$, $p(A_{11}) = 1/216$, $p(A_{12}) = 1/96$, $p(A_{13}) = 1/96$, $p(A_{14}) = 1/96$, $p(A_{15}) = 1/96$, $p(A_{16}) = 1/32$.

The undistorted versions of E and F have the highest probability $1/32$ by G and G' respectively. Also, the probability assigned by G to A_6, A_7 and A_8 ($= 1/216$) is greater than that assigned by G' ($= 1/432$) and hence they are classified as distorted versions of E. Similarly the probability assigned by G and G' to A_9, A_{10}, A_{11} are $1/432$ and $1/216$ respectively and thus they are classified as belonging to the class of noisy versions of F, during the process of recognition.

It is interesting to note here that by a slight modification of the grammars G and G', we can classify E and F of any size.

6. SMG AND PARQUET DEFORMATION

Yet another interesting application of the indexed SMG is in the description of parquet deformation. A parquet deformation is one in which a regular tessellation of the plane gets deformed progressively in one dimension and at each stage there is a unit cell that combines with itself so that it covers an infinite plane exactly.[20] In Ref. 6, some parquet deformations have been described using the concept of attaching a weight function to the terminals of an array. Here we illustrate how indices in the vertical grammar help us to describe interesting parquet deformations in which the pattern shifts at varying speeds in the upper half and lower half of the picture. This is a feature that cannot be described by the earlier technique.

Consider the (R : RIR)SMG $G = (G_1, G_{2i})$ $i = 1, 2$, where G_1 is a regular grammar generating the language $(S_1 S_2)^* S_1$ of intermediates.

G_{21} consists of the productions $\{S_1 \to aA_1, A_1 \to bS_1 f_1, A_1 \to bB_1 f_1, B_1 \to cC_1, C_1 f_1 \to bB_1, C_1 f_1 \to b\}$ with the set of flags $\{f_1\}$ and the set of terminals $\{a, b, c\}$. G_{22} has the production set consisting of $\{S_2 \to bA_2, A_2 \to aS_2 f_2, A_2 \to aB_2 f_2, B_2 \to bC_2, C_2 f_2 \to cB_2, C_2 f_2 \to c\}$ with the set of flags $\{f_2\}$ and the set of terminals as in G_{21}.

A typical array generated by this grammar G is of the form

```
a  b  a  b  a
b  a  b  a  b
a  b  a  b  a
b  a  b  a  b
c  b  c  b  c
b  c  b  c  b
c  b  c  b  c
b  c  b  c  b
```

69

The functions f_a, f_b for the terminals a and b are as in Ref. 6. That is, $f_b(i, j) = \phi$ (blank). $f_a(i, j)$ and $f_c(i, j)$ are primitives defined with reference to a hexagonal frame as in Fig. 9.

As in Ref. 6, O is the center of the hexagon and p_1, p_2, p_3 the centers of the three parallelograms. The sides of the three parallelograms are fixed with respect to the center O. Three line segments $x_1 p_1 y_1$, $x_2 p_2 y_2$, $x_3 p_3 y_3$ passing through the points p_1, p_2, p_3 and with end points on ABOF, BCDO and FODE respectively, rotate clockwise around axes perpendicular to the plane of the hexagon.

Each of a and c is replaced by a regular hexagon of side d, and bs are replaced by blanks. Two hexagons corresponding to two successive horizontal as are placed such that their centers are $3d$ apart. Two hexagons corresponding to two successive vertical as or two successive vertical cs or an a succeeded vertically by a c are placed such that their centers are at a distance of $3d$ from each other.

The function $f_{p_1}(i, j)$, $f_{p_2}(i, j)$, $f_{p_3}(i, j)$ denote the angles ϕ_1, ϕ_2, ϕ_3 described by $x_1 p_1$, $x_2 p_2$, $x_3 p_3$ from lines parallel to AB through p_1, p_2, p_3 respectively.

For the terminal a, ϕ_1, ϕ_2 and ϕ_3 are as defined below:

$$\phi_1 = f_{p_1}(i, j) = \frac{2\pi}{3} - \frac{\pi(t - 1)}{20}$$

$$\phi_2 = f_{p_2}(i, j) = \pi - \frac{\pi(t - 1)}{20}$$

$$\phi_3 = f_{p_3}(i, j) = \frac{\pi}{3} - \frac{\pi(t - 1)}{20}.$$

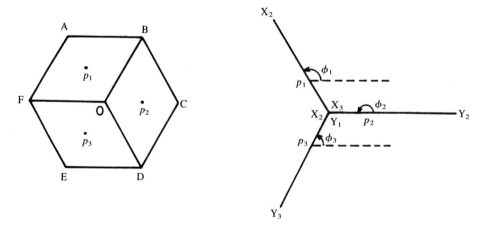

Fig. 9.   Primitives of the functions f_a and f_c.

As for the terminal c,

$$\phi_1 = f_{p_1}(i, j) = \frac{2\pi}{3} - \frac{\pi(t - 1)}{10}$$

$$\phi_2 = f_{p_2}(i, j) = \pi - \frac{\pi(t - 1)}{10}$$

$$\phi_3 = f_{p_3}(i, j) = \frac{\pi}{3} - \frac{\pi(t - 1)}{10}.$$

With these functions f_a, f_b and f_c, the parquet deformation obtained is made up of two parts—a parquet deformation known as "Consternation"[6,20] and another part of equal size in which the deformation is twice as rapid as in the upper part.

7. CONCLUSION

The simple and elegant model introduced in Ref. 3 describes several classes of two-dimensional digitized pictures. In this paper we have examined the notion of attaching indices to nonterminals (introduced in Ref. 13) in the vertical derivations of this model. The advantage is that we are able to describe pictures having a given proportion. about a horizontal line. These are not generable by earlier SMG. The SMG with/without indices are found useful in describing tiling patterns, noisy pictures, polyominoes and parquet deformations. The effects of attaching indices to nonterminals in other array grammars[7,9,21] are being investigated.

ACKNOWLEDGEMENT

We thank Mr C. R. Boyd for his help in the preparation of the paper and in drawing the figures.

REFERENCES

1. K. S. Fu, *Syntactic Methods in Pattern Recognition*, Academic Press, 1974.
2. A. Rosenfeld, *Picture Languages*, Academic Press, 1979.
3. G. Siromoney, R. Siromoney and K. Krithivasan, "Abstract families of matrices and picture languages", *Computer Graphics and Image Processing* **1** (1972) 234–307.
4. K. Krithivasan and R. Siromoney, "Characterizations of regular and context-free matrices", *Int. J. Comput. Math.* **4A** (1974) 229–245.
5. K. Krithivasan, "Variations of the matrix models", *Int. J. Comput. Math.* **6A** (1977) 171–190.
6. K. Krithivasan and A. Das, "Treating terminals as function values of time", *Lecture Notes in Computer Science 181*, Springer, 1984, pp. 188–201.
7. R. Siromoney, K. Krithivasan and G. Siromoney, "n-Dimensional array languages and description of crystal symmetry— I and II", *Proc. Indian Acad. Sci.* **78** (1973) 72–88, 130–139.
8. R. Siromoney, K. G. Subramanian and K. Rangarajan, "Parallel/sequential rectangular arrays with tables", *Int. J. Comput. Math.* **6A** (1977) 143–158.

9. G. Siromoney, R. Siromoney and K. G. Subramanian, "Note on stochastic table arrays", *Computer Graphics and Image Processing* **18** (1982) 202–211.
10. P. S. Wang, "Sequential/parallel matrix array languages", *J. Cybernetics* **5** (1975) 19–36.
11. P. S. Wang, "Finite-turn repetitive checking automata and sequential/parallel matrix languages", *IEEE Computers* **30** (1981) 366–370.
12. M. Nivat, A. Saoudi and V. R. Dare, "Parallel generation of finite images", *Int. J. of Pattern Recognition and Artificial Intelligence* **3** (1989) 279–294.
13. A. V. Aho, "Indexed grammars—An extension of context-free grammars", *J. ACM* **15** (1968) 647–671.
14. J. Duske and R. Parchmann, "Linear indexed languages", *Theoretical Computer Science* **32** (1984) 47–60.
15. R. Siromoney and G. Siromoney, "Extended controlled table L-arrays", *Information and Control* **35** (1977) 119–130.
16. K. G. Subramanian and R. Siromoney, "On array grammars and languages", *Cybernetics and Systems* **18** (1987) 77–98.
17. B. Grünbaum and G. C. Shephard, *Tilings and Patterns*, W. H. Freeman and Company, New York, 1987.
18. D. Beauquier and M. Nivat, "Codicity and simplicity in the plane", Technical Report 88–65, Laboratoire Informatique Theorique Et Programmation, Univ. Paris VII, Nov. 1988.
19. D. Beauquier and M. Nivat, "Tilings with polyominoes", Technical Report 88–66, Laboratoire Informatique Theorique Et Programmation, Univ. Paris VII, Nov. 1988.
20. D. R. Hofstadter, "Metamagical Themas: Parquet deformations: patterns of tiles that shift gradually in one dimension", *Scientific American* **249**, **1** (1983).
21. G. Siromoney, R. Siromoney and K. Krithivasan, "Picture languages with array rewriting rules", *Information and Control* **22** (1973) 447–470.

K. G. Subramanian received the M.Sc. degree in mathematics in 1969 and the Ph.D. degree in 1980 from Madras University. Since 1970, he has been on the teaching faculty of the Department of Mathematics, Madras Christian College, Tambaram, Madras. In the academic year 1984–85, he visited the Institut National de Recherche en Informatique et Automatique and the University of Paris under a French government scholarship. He is author or coauthor of about thirty research papers in his fields of interest which include formal languages, automata, array and graph languages, cryptography, infinite words, codes and Thue systems. He has presented papers at several conferences in India.

L. Revathi received the M.Sc. degree in mathematics in 1984 and the M.Phil. degree in 1985 from Madras University. She is at present on the teaching faculty of the Department of Mathematics at Madras Christian College, Tambaram, Madras. She is doing research in the areas of rewriting systems and array languages.

Rani Siromoney received the B.A. (Hons.) in mathematics from Madras University in 1950, the A.M. degree in 1960 from Columbia University, New York, where she was a Fulbright Smith-Mundt scholar and the Ph.D. degree from Madras University in 1970. From 1951 to 1979, she was on the teaching faculty of the Department of Mathematics, Madras Christian College, Tambaram, Madras. She was chairman of the department from 1979 to 1988. She is at present Professor Emeritus appointed by the University Grants Commission, Government of India and directs the research program at the Department of Mathematics, Madras Christian College, where she has built a strong and active research group in the areas of formal grammars and languages, automata, picture and graph languages, pattern recognition, cryptography, infinite words, codes, Thue systems and other related areas of theoretical computer science.

She is author or coauthor of more than fifty research papers and four books. She is on the editorial board of the journals *Theoretical Computer Science* and *International Journal of Foundations of Computer Science*. She was a member of the program committee for the conferences on Foundations of Software Technology and Theoretical Computer Science organized by the Tata Institute of Fundamental Research, Bombay, from 1980–88. She was a consultant at the University of Maryland in 1974 and has delivered special lectures and presented papers at various conferences at national and international levels. She is the recipient of awards such as "Distinguished Author", "Best Teacher" and "Outstanding Woman Professional", from different organizations in India.

TWO-DIMENSIONAL THREE-WAY ARRAY GRAMMARS AND THEIR ACCEPTORS

KENICHI MORITA

Faculty of Engineering, Yamagata University, Yonezawa-shi 992, Japan

YASUNORI YAMAMOTO

National Museum of Ethnology, Senri Expo Park, Suita-shi 565, Japan

KAZUHIRO SUGATA

Faculty of Engineering, Tottori University, Tottori-shi 680, Japan

Received 22 April 1989
Revised 10 May 1989

Two kinds of three-way isometric array grammars are proposed as subclasses of an isometric monotonic array grammar. They are a three-way horizontally context-sensitive array grammar (3HCSAG) and a three-way immediately terminating array grammar (3ITAG). In these three-way grammars, patterns of symbols can grow only in the leftward, rightward and downward directions. We show that their generating abilities of rectangular languages are precisely characterized by some kinds of three-way two-dimensional Turing machines or related acceptors. In this paper, the following results are proved. First, 3HCSAG is characterized by a nondeterministic two-dimensional three-way Turing machine with space-bound n (n is the width of a rectangular input) and a nondeterministic one-way parallel/sequential array acceptor. Second, 3ITAG is characterized by a nondeterministic two-dimensional three-way real-time (or linear-time) restricted Turing machine, a nondeterministic one-dimensional bounded cellular acceptor and a nondeterministic two-dimensional one-line tessellation acceptor.

Keywords: Isometric array grammar; Three-way array grammar; Array acceptor; Two-dimensional tape automaton.

1. INTRODUCTION

An isometric array grammar (IAG)[1,2] is a system that generates a set of two-dimensional patterns of symbols by isometric rewriting rules. In IAG, blank symbols (#) may be padded to keep the left-hand and right-hand sides of a rewriting rule isometric (i.e. having the same shape). Many subclasses of IAG have been proposed until now. For example, a monotonic array grammar (MAG),[1] a context-free array grammar (CFAG),[3,4] and a regular array grammar (RAG)[3,4] form a Chomsky-like hierarchy in IAG. For IAGs and MAGs, it is known that there are classes of acceptors which exactly characterize their generating abilities.[1] More precisely, the classes of languages generated by IAGs and MAGs agree with the classes of languages accepted by two-dimensional Turing machines and nondeterministic two-dimensional linear bounded automata respectively. However, very little is known as to whether there are "natural" classes of acceptors which characterize other grammars.

International Journal of Pattern Recognition and Artificial Intelligence Vol. 3 No. 3 & 4 (1989) 353–376
© World Scientific Publishing Company

In this paper, we propose two classes of isometric three-way array grammars which are subclasses of MAG. They are a three-way horizontally context-sensitive array grammar (3HCSAG) and a three-way immediately terminating array grammar (3ITAG). In these three-way grammars, patterns of symbols can grow only in three directions (i.e. leftward, rightward and downward) in the derivation. We show that if we consider only rectangular languages, their generating abilities are precisely characterized by some natural classes of acceptors having rectangular input tapes.

3HCSAG is a subclass of MAG, in which the left-hand side of each rewriting rule can contain non-# symbols only in the uppermost row. Therefore, its context-sensing ability (of non-# symbols) is only horizontal, and thus it has a context-free-like nature in the vertical direction. 3ITAG is a subclass of 3HCSAG. In 3ITAG, the left-hand side of each rewriting rule contains no terminal symbols, and every nonterminal symbol in the left-hand side must be "immediately" rewritten into a terminal one.

In this paper, we investigate the generating abilities of these grammar classes, and show that they are characterized by some three-way (or similar) acceptors, which read rectangular input tapes from top to bottom. The main results of this paper are as follows.

(1) The class of rectangular languages generated by 3HCSAGs agrees with the classes of languages accepted by nondeterministic two-dimensonal three-way Turing machines with space-bound n (n is the width of a rectangular input) and nondeterministic one-way parallel/sequential array acceptors.

(2) The class of rectangular languages generated by 3ITAGs agrees with the classes of languages accepted by nondeterministic two-dimensional three-way real-time (or linear-time) restricted Turing machines, nondeterministic one-dimensional bounded cellular acceptors and nondeterministic two-dimensional one-line tessellation acceptors.

2. DEFINITIONS AND NOTATIONS

2.1. Isometric Array Grammars

Let X be a nonempty finite set of symbols. A two-dimensional connected array of symbols in X is called a (two-dimensional) *word* over X. The set of all words over X is denoted by X^{2+} (empty word is not contained in X^{2+}).

An *isometric array grammar* (IAG) is defined as a quintuple

$$G = (N, T, P, S, \#),$$

where N and T are nonempty finite sets of *nonterminals* (nonterminal symbols) and *terminals* (terminal symbols) respectively. We assume N and T contain no common element. S ($\in N$) is a *start symbol* and # ($\notin N \cup T$) is a *blank symbol*. P is a finite set of *rewriting rules* of the form $\mathbf{u} \to \mathbf{v}$, where $\mathbf{u}$ and $\mathbf{v}$ are elements of $(N \cup T \cup \{\#\})^{2+}$ and satisfies the following conditions.

(1) (a) The shapes of $\mathbf{u}$ and $\mathbf{v}$ are geometrically identical.

(b) $\mathbf{u}$ contains one or more nonterminals.

(c) Terminals in $\mathbf{u}$ are not rewritten by the rule $\mathbf{u} \to \mathbf{v}$.

(d) The application of $\mathbf{u} \to \mathbf{v}$ preserves the connectivity of the host array (i.e. the array to be rewritten). (To be more precise, see Ref. 2.)

The *#-embedded array* of a word $\mathbf{x} \in (N \cup T)^{2+}$ is an infinite array over $(N \cup T \cup \{\#\})$ obtained by embedding $\mathbf{x}$ in the two-dimensional infinite array of #s, and is denoted by $\mathbf{x}_\#$. We say that the rewriting rule $\mathbf{u} \to \mathbf{v}$ ($\in P$) is *applicable* to $\mathbf{x}$, iff $\mathbf{u}$ occurs in $\mathbf{x}_\#$ as a subarray. We say that a word $\mathbf{y}$ is *directly derived* from a word $\mathbf{x}$ in G, iff $\mathbf{y}_\#$ can be obtained by replacing one of the occurrences of $\mathbf{u}$ in $\mathbf{x}_\#$ with $\mathbf{v}$ for some applicable rule $\mathbf{u} \to \mathbf{v}$. This is denoted by $\mathbf{x} \underset{G}{\Rightarrow} \mathbf{y}$. The reflexive and transitive closure of the relation $\underset{G}{\Rightarrow}$ is denoted by $\underset{G}{\overset{*}{\Rightarrow}}$. That is, $\mathbf{x} \underset{G}{\overset{*}{\Rightarrow}} \mathbf{y}$ iff there exist some n ($= 0, 1, 2, \ldots$) and $\mathbf{z}_0, \mathbf{z}_1, \ldots, \mathbf{z}_n \in (N \cup T)^{2+}$ that satisfy the following.

$$\mathbf{x} = \mathbf{z}_0 \underset{G}{\Rightarrow} \mathbf{z}_1 \underset{G}{\Rightarrow} \cdots \underset{G}{\Rightarrow} \mathbf{z}_n = \mathbf{y}.$$

The above is called a *derivation* of $\mathbf{y}$ from $\mathbf{x}$ in G. If there is a derivation of $\mathbf{y}$ from $\mathbf{x}$ with length n, we write it as $\mathbf{x} \underset{G}{\overset{n}{\Rightarrow}} \mathbf{y}$. In what follows, if G is understood, the notations $\Rightarrow$, $\overset{*}{\Rightarrow}$ and $\overset{n}{\Rightarrow}$ are used instead of $\underset{G}{\Rightarrow}$, $\underset{G}{\overset{*}{\Rightarrow}}$ and $\underset{G}{\overset{n}{\Rightarrow}}$.

A *sentential form* of G is a word $\mathbf{x} \in (N \cup T)^{2+}$ such that $S \underset{G}{\overset{*}{\Rightarrow}} \mathbf{x}$. The *language* generated by G is the set of all sentential forms of G consisting only of terminals, and is denoted by $L(G)$. That is,

$$L(G) = \{\mathbf{w} \mid S \underset{G}{\overset{*}{\Rightarrow}} \mathbf{w} \text{ and } \mathbf{w} \in T^{2+}\}.$$

If every word in $L(G)$ is a rectangular-shaped array, $L(G)$ is said to be a *rectangular language*.

A *monotonic array grammar* (MAG) is a subclass of IAG which satisfies the following condition.

(2) In each rule $\mathbf{u} \to \mathbf{v}$, non-# symbols in $\mathbf{u}$ are not rewritten into #s by the application of $\mathbf{u} \to \mathbf{v}$.

2.2. Three-Way Array Grammars

We now define two kinds of three-way array grammars, which are subclasses of IAG. If each rewriting rule $\mathbf{u} \to \mathbf{v}$ of an IAG G satisfies the conditions (3) or (4) shown below, G is said to be a *three-way horizontally context-sensitive array grammar* (3HCSAG) or a *three-way immediately terminating array grammar* (3ITAG) respectively. (Of course G satisfies (1)(a)–(d) above.)

3HCSAG:

(3) (a) $\mathbf{u}$ contains one or more non-# symbols *only* in the uppermost row.

    (b) $\mathbf{v}$ does not contain #s.

3ITAG:

(4) (a) $\mathbf{u}$ does not contain terminals.

    (b) $\mathbf{u}$ contains one or more nonterminals *only* in the uppermost row.

    (c) $\mathbf{v}$ does not contain #s.

(d) By the application of the rule **u** → **v**, nonterminals in **u** must be rewritten into terminals.

From the above definitions, it is clear that 3HCSAG is a subclass of MAG and 3ITAG is a subclass of 3HCSAG.

In these three-way grammars, sentential forms grow only in the leftward, rightward and downward directions (by (3)(a) and (4)(b)). And, as in MAG, non-# symbols are never erased (by (3)(b) and (4)(c)).

Each rewriting rule can sense context with the uppermost row of the left-hand side of it, but cannot sense context ranging over two or more rows (by (3)(a) and (4)(b)). In other words, their context-sensitivity is only horizontal. (Note that, here we use the term "context-sensitivity" of a rewriting rule as the ability of sensing a partial array of *non-#symbols* in a host array.)

In 3ITAG, rewriting rules cannot sense context including terminals (by (4)(a)). In addition, every nonterminal must be immediately rewritten into a terminal if a rewriting rule is applied to this nonterminal (by (4)(d)).

2.3. Acceptors

The two-dimensional three-way Turing machine is a system consisting of a rectangular input tape, a read-only input tape head, a one-way rightward infinite storage tape, a read-write storage tape head and a finite-state control. The input tape is divided into squares (like a checkerboard), and in each square an input symbol is written. The input head can move left, right and down but not up, and cannot go beyond border symbols ($s) attached to the input tape (Fig. 1).

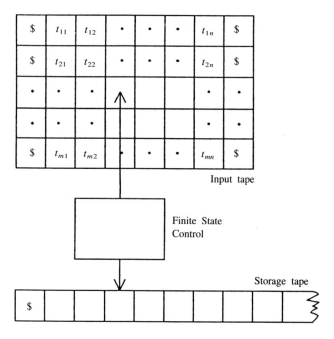

Fig. 1.   A two-dimensional three-way Turing machine.

Formally, a *nondeterministic two-dimensional three-way Turing machine* (N3TM) is defined by

$$M = (Q, T, A, f, q_0, \$, a_0, F),$$

where Q is a nonempty finite set of states, T and A are nonempty finite sets of input tape symbols and storage tape symbols respectively, q_0 is an initial state $(q_0 \in Q)$, $\$$ is a border symbol for the input and the storage tapes ($\$ \notin T \cup A$), a_0 is a blank symbol of the storage tape ($a_0 \in A$) and F is a set of final (halting) states ($F \subseteq Q$). f is a move function

$$f: Q \times (T \cup \{\$\}) \times (A \cup \{\$\}) \rightarrow 2^{Q \times (A \cup \{\$\}) \times \{L,R,D,N\} \times \{L,R,N\}},$$

where L, R, D and N represent the move directions (left, right, down and no-move respectively) of the heads.

Let $\mathbf{w}$ be an $m \times n$ array (i.e. rectangular word) over T. We assume $\mathbf{w}$ (with border symbols) is given to M as an input. Further, we assume M starts from the initial state with the input head at the leftmost square of the topmost row of $\mathbf{w}$ and the storage head at the leftmost square. If there is a move sequence in which M halts in a final state at some column of the mth row, $\mathbf{w}$ is said to be *accepted* by M. The set of all rectangular words accepted by M is called the language accepted by M and denoted by $L(M)$.

If, for any input $\mathbf{w}$ of size $m \times n$, M uses at most $L(m, n)$ squares of the storage tape when accepting $\mathbf{w}$, M is said to be an $L(m, n)$ *space-bounded nondeterministic two-dimensional three-way Turing machine* (N3TM($L(m, n)$)), where $L(m, n)$ is an integer function of m and n.

If M satisfies the following condition (5), M is called a *nondeterministic two-dimensional three-way linear-time restricted Turing machine* (N3LTM).

(5) (a) Horizontal movements of the input head coincide with those of the storage head. That is, if the input head moves to the direction L, R, D, then the storage head moves to L, R, N, respectively.

(b) There exists a constant k (≥ 0) that satisfies the following: For any rectangular input $\mathbf{w} \in T^{2+}$, M reads each square of $\mathbf{w}$ at most k times when accepting $\mathbf{w}$.

In particular, an N3LTM with $k = 1$ is called a *nondeterministic two-dimensional three-way real-time restricted Turing machine* (N3RTM).

By the above definition, it is clear that an N3LTM uses at most $(n + 2)$ squares of the storage tape for any input of size $m \times n$ when accepting it.

A *nondeterministic one-dimensional bounded cellular acceptor* (NBCA) which was introduced in Ref. 5, is a system defined as follows:

$$M = (\mathbf{Z}, H, Q, T, g, q_0, R).$$

$\mathbf{Z}$ is the set of all integers, and an identical finite automaton (called a cell) is placed at each point of $\mathbf{Z}$. H is a finite subset of $\mathbf{Z}$ representing a neighborhood template (here, we assume $H = \{-1, 0, 1\}$). Q is a set of states of a cell, which includes a special boundary state $q_\$$. T is a set of input symbols. g is a mapping

$$g : Q^3 \times T \to 2^Q,$$

called a local function. q_0 is the initial state $(q_0 \in Q)$. R is a regular set over $Q-\{q_\$\}$, which represents accepting configurations of M. (A *configuration* is an array of states of the n cells of M.)

Intuitively, NBCA M is an acceptor acting as follows (to be more precise, see Ref. 5). Given a rectangular word $\mathbf{w} \in T^{2+}$ of size $m \times n$, the n cells with coordinates 1 through n are set to the state q_0. The cellular array reads $\mathbf{w}$ one row a step moving downward. Each cell transits its state according to the local function g (states of the cells with coordinate 0 and $(n + 1)$ are fixed to $q_\$$). We say M accepts $\mathbf{w}$ if the configuration of M just after reading the last row of $\mathbf{w}$ is in the set R.

2.4. Notations

Let $\mathbf{A}$ represent a class of array grammars or acceptors. The class of two-dimensional languages generated or accepted by $\mathbf{A}$ is denoted by $\mathscr{L}[\mathbf{A}]$ (e.g. $\mathscr{L}[3ITAG]$, $\mathscr{L}[N3LTM]$). The class of rectangular languages generated by a grammar class $\mathbf{A}$ is denoted by $\mathscr{L}^R[\mathbf{A}]$. That is,

$$\mathscr{L}^R[\mathbf{A}] = \{L \mid L \in \mathscr{L}[\mathbf{A}] \text{ and } L \text{ is a rectangular language}\}.$$

Note that, since the acceptors defined here take only rectangular words as inputs, the languages accepted by them are of course rectangular.

3.   EQUIVALENCE OF 3HCSAG AND N3TM(n)

In this section, we show that a language generated by a 3HCSAG is accepted by an N3TM(n) (i.e. N3TM with space bound $L(m, n) = n$) and its converse. In this sense, 3HCSAG and N3TM(n) are equivalent.

From the definition of 3HCSAG, the left-hand side of each rewriting rule contains non-# symbols only in the uppermost row. Therefore, 3HCSAG has context-free-like nature in the vertical direction. Here, we define the notion of "uppermost derivation", which is an analog of "leftmost derivation" in the usual context-free grammar for strings, and show that for any derivation in 3HCSAG there is an equivalent uppermost derivation.

Let G be a 3HCSAG, and let

$$\mathbf{x}_0 \Rightarrow \mathbf{x}_1 \Rightarrow \ldots \Rightarrow \mathbf{x}_n$$

be a derivation in G. We now assign a "row-number" to each row of $\mathbf{x}_i$ $(i = 0, 1, \ldots, n)$. Row-number 1 is assigned to the top row of each $\mathbf{x}_i$. Note that, since G is a three-way grammar, this numbering matches between any two $\mathbf{x}_i$s. Let

$$\text{row}[\mathbf{x}_i \Rightarrow \mathbf{x}_{i+1}] \quad (i = 0, 1, \ldots, n - 1)$$

denote the row-number of the uppermost row of the rewritten part in the derivation $\mathbf{x}_i \Rightarrow \mathbf{x}_{i+1}$.

We say that $x_0 \Rightarrow x_1 \Rightarrow \ldots \Rightarrow x_n$ is an *uppermost derivation* iff

$$\text{row}[x_i \Rightarrow x_{i+1}] \leqslant \text{row}[x_{i+1} \Rightarrow x_{i+2}]$$

holds for all i (= 0, 1, . . . , $n - 2$). If there is an uppermost derivation from x to x', we write it as $x \overset{*}{\underset{um}{\Rightarrow}} x'$. In particular, if there is an uppermost derivation of length n, we write it as $x \overset{n}{\underset{um}{\Rightarrow}} x'$.

Lemma 3.1. Let G be a 3HCSAG, and let $x_1 \Rightarrow x \Rightarrow x_2$ be a derivation in G. If

$$\text{row}[x_1 \Rightarrow x] > \text{row}[x \Rightarrow x_2],$$

then there exists $x' \in (N \cup T)^{2+}$ which satisfies the following three conditions,

$$x_1 \Rightarrow x' \Rightarrow x_2,$$
$$\text{row}[x_1 \Rightarrow x'] = \text{row}[x \Rightarrow x_2],$$
$$\text{row}[x' \Rightarrow x_2] = \text{row}[x_1 \Rightarrow x].$$

Proof. Let $u_1 \rightarrow v_1$ and $u_2 \rightarrow v_2$ be the rules applied in the derivations $x_1 \Rightarrow x$ and $x \Rightarrow x_2$ respectively. Then the following assertion holds: the two portions rewritten by the rules $u_1 \rightarrow v_1$ and $u_2 \rightarrow v_2$ have (geometrically) no common area (Fig. 2). The reason is as follows. Since $\text{row}[x_1 \Rightarrow x] > \text{row}[x \Rightarrow x_2]$, the topmost rows of u_1 (or v_1) and u_2 (or v_2) do not overlap in these applications. Furthermore, since v_1 contains no #s and all the portion of u_2 except the top row consists only of #s, v_1 cannot have a common area with u_2. Therefore, these two applications of the rules do not interact with each other, and thus we can exchange the order of applications.

Let x' be the word obtained from x_1 by applying the rule $u_2 \rightarrow v_2$ at the same position as in the derivation $x \Rightarrow x_2$. Then, by applying $u_1 \rightarrow v_1$ to x' at the same position as in $x_1 \Rightarrow x$ we can obtain x_2. Clearly, this x' satisfies the above three conditions. ■

The following lemma shows that for any derivation there is an equivalent uppermost derivation.

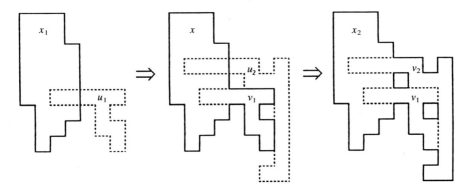

Fig. 2.   A derivation in 3HCSAG.

Lemma 3.2. Let $G = (N, T, P, S, \#)$ be a 3HCSAG. For any $\mathbf{x}$ and $\mathbf{x}'$, if $\mathbf{x} \overset{n}{\Rightarrow} \mathbf{x}'$ then $\mathbf{x} \underset{um}{\overset{n}{\Rightarrow}} \mathbf{x}'$.

Proof. We prove this by the induction on the number of steps n of a derivation. Consider the case $n > 1$, since the case $n = 1$ is obvious. Let $\mathbf{x}''$ be a word such that

$$\mathbf{x} \overset{n-1}{\Rightarrow} \mathbf{x}'' \Rightarrow \mathbf{x}'.$$

From the inductive hypothesis, $\mathbf{x} \underset{um}{\overset{n-1}{\Rightarrow}} \mathbf{x}''$. Thus there are $\mathbf{y}_0, \mathbf{y}_1, \ldots, \mathbf{y}_{n-1}$ which satisfies the following conditions.
(1) $\mathbf{x} = \mathbf{y}_0 \Rightarrow \mathbf{y}_1 \Rightarrow \ldots \Rightarrow \mathbf{y}_{n-1} = \mathbf{x}''$
(2) $\text{row}[\mathbf{y}_i \Rightarrow \mathbf{y}_{i+1}] \leqslant \text{row}[\mathbf{y}_{i+1} \Rightarrow \mathbf{y}_{i+2}]$ $(i = 0, 1, \ldots, n - 3)$
   Here, if $\text{row}[\mathbf{y}_{n-2} \Rightarrow \mathbf{y}_{n-1}] \leqslant \text{row}[\mathbf{y}_{n-1} \Rightarrow \mathbf{x}']$, then

$$\mathbf{x} = \mathbf{y}_0 \Rightarrow \mathbf{y}_1 \Rightarrow \ldots \Rightarrow \mathbf{y}_{n-1} \Rightarrow \mathbf{x}'$$

is an uppermost derivation and the lemma holds. Thus, in the following, we assume
(3) $\text{row}[\mathbf{y}_{n-2} \Rightarrow \mathbf{y}_{n-1}] > \text{row}[\mathbf{y}_{n-1} \Rightarrow \mathbf{x}']$.
Let k be as follows:
(4) $k = \min\{i \mid \text{row}[\mathbf{y}_{n-1} \Rightarrow \mathbf{x}'] < \text{row}[\mathbf{y}_i \Rightarrow \mathbf{y}_{i+1}]\}$.
We now consider the derivation
(5) $\mathbf{x} = \mathbf{y}_0 \Rightarrow \mathbf{y}_1 \Rightarrow \ldots \Rightarrow \mathbf{y}_{n-2} \Rightarrow \mathbf{y}_{n-1} \Rightarrow \mathbf{x}'$.
First, we apply Lemma 3.1 to the last two steps of (5), since (3) holds. As a result, we can obtain $\mathbf{z}_{n-1}$ which satisfies the following:

$$\mathbf{y}_{n-2} \Rightarrow \mathbf{z}_{n-1} \Rightarrow \mathbf{x}',$$
$$\text{row}[\mathbf{y}_{n-2} \Rightarrow \mathbf{z}_{n-1}] = \text{row}[\mathbf{y}_{n-1} \Rightarrow \mathbf{x}'],$$
$$\text{row}[\mathbf{z}_{n-1} \Rightarrow \mathbf{x}'] = \text{row}[\mathbf{y}_{n-2} \Rightarrow \mathbf{y}_{n-1}].$$

Replace the last two steps of (5) by $\mathbf{y}_{n-2} \Rightarrow \mathbf{z}_{n-1} \Rightarrow \mathbf{x}'$. Next, apply Lemma 3.1 to $\mathbf{y}_{n-3} \Rightarrow \mathbf{y}_{n-2} \Rightarrow \mathbf{z}_{n-1}$, and replace it by $\mathbf{y}_{n-3} \Rightarrow \mathbf{z}_{n-2} \Rightarrow \mathbf{z}_{n-1}$, where $\mathbf{z}_{n-2}$ is the word obtained by Lemma 3.1. Repeating this procedure for the partial derivation

$$\mathbf{y}_i \Rightarrow \mathbf{y}_{i+1} \Rightarrow \mathbf{z}_{i+2}$$

from $i = n - 2$ to k, we can obtain the next derivation.
(6) $\mathbf{x} = \mathbf{y}_0 \Rightarrow \mathbf{y}_1 \Rightarrow \ldots \Rightarrow \mathbf{y}_k \Rightarrow \mathbf{z}_{k+1} \Rightarrow \ldots \Rightarrow \mathbf{z}_{n-1} \Rightarrow \mathbf{x}'$
It is easily seen that the following relations hold. (Here, we assume $\mathbf{z}_n = \mathbf{x}'$).

$$\text{row}[\mathbf{z}_i \Rightarrow \mathbf{z}_{i+1}] = \text{row}[\mathbf{y}_{i-1} \Rightarrow \mathbf{y}_i] \qquad (k + 1 \leqslant i \leqslant n - 1)$$
$$\text{row}[\mathbf{y}_k \Rightarrow \mathbf{z}_{k+1}] = \text{row}[\mathbf{y}_{n-1} \Rightarrow \mathbf{x}']$$

From these and (2), (3) and (4),

$$\text{row}[\mathbf{z}_i \Rightarrow \mathbf{z}_{i+1}] \leqslant \text{row}[\mathbf{z}_{i+1} \Rightarrow \mathbf{z}_{i+2}] \quad (k + 1 \leqslant i \leqslant n - 2)$$
$$\text{row}[\mathbf{y}_{k-1} \Rightarrow \mathbf{y}_k] \leqslant \text{row}[\mathbf{y}_k \Rightarrow \mathbf{z}_{k+1}] < \text{row}[\mathbf{z}_{k+1} \Rightarrow \mathbf{z}_{k+2}]$$

are derived. Thus (6) is an uppermost derivation. ∎

Note that in the case of $\mathbf{x} = S$ and $\mathbf{x}' \in T^{2+}$, an uppermost derivation means that one of the uppermost nonterminals in a sentential form is rewritten in each step of the derivation $S \underset{um}{\Rightarrow} \mathbf{x}'$.

Lemma 3.3. $\mathscr{L}^R[\text{3HCSAG}] \subseteq \mathscr{L}[\text{N3TM}(n)]$.

Proof. From any given 3HCSAG $G = (N, T, P, S, \#)$, construct an N3TM(n) $M = (Q, T, A, f, q_0, \$, a_0, F)$ as follows.

Let the height of a rewriting rule $\mathbf{u} \to \mathbf{v}$ be the number of rows of $\mathbf{u}$ (or $\mathbf{v}$). Let h be the maximum height of the rules in P. M uses the storage tape divided into h tracks. Given a (rectangular) input $\mathbf{w} \in T^{2+}$, M executes the following algorithm.

begin
    mark n squares of the storage tape;
    comment in the following, M uses only these n squares;
    write #s in all the n squares of the tracks 1 to h;
    select nondeterministically one square from n, and rewrite the symbol # on the
        track 1 into S;
    while M is not in a halting state **do**
        if there is (are) a nonterminal(s) on the track 1 **then**
            begin
                select nondeterministically a rule $\mathbf{u} \to \mathbf{v}$ from P;
                if $\mathbf{u} \to \mathbf{v}$ is applicable at some position where the top row of $\mathbf{u}$ is on the
                    first track **then**
                    select one of the applicable positions and execute the rewriting on the tape
                else halt without accepting the input
            end
        else
            if the contents of the row of the input tape where the input head is positioned
                agrees with the contents of the track 1 of the storage tape **then**
                begin
                    transfer the contents of the track $i + 1$ into the track i ($i = 1, 2, \ldots,$
                    $h - 1$);
                    write #s in all the squares of the track h;
                    if the track 1 consists only of #s **then** halt in a final state
                    else shift the input head downward one row
                end
            else halt without accepting the input
end

If $w \in L(G)$, then there is an uppermost derivation of w from Lemma 3.2. It is easy to see that M accepts w when M correctly guesses the rewriting rule and the application position in each step of the uppermost derivation. Conversely, if M accepts the input $w \in T^{2+}$, then by applying the rewriting rules as M did, we can derive w from S in G. Thus $L(M) = L(G)$. ■

Lemma 3.4. $\mathcal{L}[\text{N3TM}(n)] \subseteq \mathcal{L}^R[\text{3HCSAG}]$.

Proof.   Let $M = (Q, T, A, f, q_0, \$, a_0, F)$ be a given N3TM(n). We can assume, without loss of generality, that the horizontal movements of the input head of M coincide with those of the storage head (i.e. if the input head is at the ith column then the storage head is at the ith square from the left). This is because, by adding new symbols to A, M can easily simulate an N3TM(n) whose horizontal movements of the two heads do not coincide. Furthermore, it is assumed that when M halts, the input head is at the first column.

We now construct a 3HCSAG $G = (N, T, P, S, \#)$ in the following manner.

$$N = \{S, X\} \cup (Q \times T \times A \times \{L, C, R\})$$
$$\cup (T \times A \times \{L, C, R\}) \cup (\{*\} \times A)$$

The set P of rewriting rules is determined as follows.
(1) For each $t \in T$, include the following rules in P.

$$S \# \to [q_0, t, a_0, L] X$$
$$X \# \to [t, a_0, C] X$$
$$X \to [t, a_0, R]$$

(2) (a) For each $q, q' \in Q,\quad t, t' \in T,\quad a, a', a'' \in A,\quad Z \in \{L, C\},$
$Z' \in \{C, R\}$ which satisfy

$$(q', a', R, R) \in f(q, t, a),$$

include the following rule in P.

$$[q, t, a, Z][t', a'', Z'] \to [t, a', Z][q', t', a'', Z']$$

(b) For each $q, q', q'' \in Q,\quad t \in T,\quad a, a' \in A$ which satisfy

$$(q', a', R, R) \in f(q, t, a), \text{ and}$$
$$(q'', a_0, L, L) \in f(q', \$, a_0),$$

include the following rule in P.

$$[q, t, a, R] \to [q'', t, a', R]$$

(c) For each $q, q' \in Q$,　$t, t' \in T$,　$a, a', a'' \in A$,　$Z \in \{L, C\}$, $Z' \in \{C, R\}$ which satisfy

$$(q', a', L, L) \in f(q, t, a),$$

include the following rule in P.

$$[t', a'', Z][q, t, a, Z'] \to [q', t', a'', Z][t, a', Z']$$

(d) For each $q, q', q'' \in Q$,　$t \in T$,　$a, a' \in A$ which satisfy

$$(q', a', L, L) \in f(q, t, a), \text{ and}$$
$$(q'', \$, R, R) \in f(q', \$, \$),$$

include the following rule in P.

$$[q, t, a, L] \to [q'', t, a', L]$$

(e) For each $q, q' \in Q$, $t \in T$, $a, a' \in A$, $Z \in \{L, C, R\}$ which satisfy

$$(q', a', N, N) \in f(q, t, a),$$

include the following rule in P.

$$[q, t, a, Z] \to [q', t, a', Z]$$

(f) For each $q, q' \in Q$,　$t, t' \in T$,　$a, a' \in A$,　$Z \in \{L, C, R\}$ which satisfy

$$(q', a', D, N) \in f(q, t, a),$$

include the following rule in P.

$$\begin{array}{ll} [q, t, a, Z] & t \\ \# & \to \ [q', t', a', Z] \end{array}$$

(3) For each $t, t' \in T$,　$a \in A$,　$Z \in \{L, C, R\}$, include the following rule in P.

$$\begin{array}{ll} [t, a, Z] & t \\ \# & \to \ [t', a, Z] \end{array}$$

(4) (a) For each $q_f \in F$,　$t \in T$,　$a \in A$, include the following rule in P.

$$[q_f, t, a, L] \to [*, t]$$

85

(b) For each $t, t' \in T$, $a \in A$, $Z \in \{C, R\}$, include the following rule in P.

$$[*, t][t', a, Z] \rightarrow t[*, t']$$

(c) For each $t \in T$, include the following rule in P.

$$[*, t] \rightarrow t$$

A nonterminal $[q, t, a, Z]$ in $(Q \times T \times A \times \{L, C, R\})$ represents that M is scanning the input tape square with symbol t and the storage tape square with symbol a in state q. $Z = L$ ($Z = C, Z = R$, respectively) means that these squares are at the leftmost (middle, rightmost) position on the tape. A nonterminal $[t, a, Z]$ in $(T \times A \times \{L, C, R\})$ represents that some input tape square with symbol t and some storage tape square with symbol a are at the same distance from the left (Z represents the same meaning as above).

The set P of rewriting rules of G guesses a rectangular word $\mathbf{w} \in T^{2+}$ row by row, and simulates the movements of M on the input $\mathbf{w}$.

The rewriting rules in (1) guess the first row of $\mathbf{w}$, and initialize the computational configuration of M. The rules in (2)(a) ((c), (e), respectively) are for simulating the movements of M, and are used when M shifts the input head to the right (left, or no-move) inside the tape. The rules in (2)(b) and (d) are used to simulate two steps of M at the right and the left borders of the input tape. (2)(f) is for the case when M shifts the input head downwards. The input symbols in the next row of $\mathbf{w}$ are guessed by (2)(f) and (3). The rules in (4) are used when M halts in a final state at the leftmost square of the bottom row of $\mathbf{w}$. If the sentential form generated so far is rectangular, the rules in (4) change all the remaining nonterminals into terminals, and terminate the derivation. (Although G cannot generate a word of width 1, it is not hard to modify G so that it can generate such words).

By the above, it is seen that $\mathbf{w}$ is generated by G iff $\mathbf{w}$ is accepted by M, and thus $L(G) = L(M)$. ■

From Lemmas 3.3 and 3.4, the next theorem follows.

Theorem 3.5. $\mathscr{L}^R[\text{3HCSAG}] = \mathscr{L}[\text{N3TM}(n)]$.

In Ref. 6, it is shown that the accepting abilities of a nondeterministic parallel/sequential array acceptor (NPSA), which was introduced in Ref. 7, and a nondeterministic two-dimensional (four-way) Turing machine with space-bound $L(m, n) = n$ are equivalent. In a similar manner, we can show that a nondeterministic one-way parallel/sequential array acceptor (N1WPSA), which is a variant of NPSA whose scanner can move only downward, and an N3TM(n) are equivalent. That is,

$$\mathscr{L}[\text{N1WPSA}] = \mathscr{L}[\text{N3TM}(n)]$$

From this and Theorem 3.5, the next corollary is derived.

Corollary 3.6. $\mathscr{L}^R[\text{3HCSAG}] = \mathscr{L}[\text{N1WPSA}]$.

4. EQUIVALENCE OF 3ITAG, NBCA, N3LTM AND N3RTM

In this section, we show that the class of rectangular languages generated by 3ITAGs agrees with the classes of languages accepted by NBCAs, N3LTMs and N3RTMs. This is proved by showing the following relations in order.

$$\mathscr{L}[\text{NBCA}] \subseteq \mathscr{L}^R[\text{3ITAG}] \quad \text{(Lemma 4.1)}$$
$$\mathscr{L}^R[\text{3ITAG}] \subseteq \mathscr{L}[\text{N3LTM}] \quad \text{(Lemma 4.2)}$$
$$\mathscr{L}[\text{N3LTM}] \subseteq \mathscr{L}[\text{N3RTM}] \quad \text{(Lemma 4.3)}$$
$$\mathscr{L}[\text{N3RTM}] \subseteq \mathscr{L}[\text{NBCA}] \quad \text{(Lemma 4.4)}$$

Lemma 4.1. $\mathscr{L}[\text{NBCA}] \subseteq \mathscr{L}^R[\text{3ITAG}]$.

Proof. Let $M = (\mathbf{Z}, H, Q, T, g, q_0, R)$ be a given NBCA. Let $A = (P_A, Q, h, p_0, F_A)$ be a finite automaton which accepts the regular set R, where P_A is a set of internal states, Q is a set of input symbols (and also the state set of M), $h : P_A \times Q \to P_A$ is a state-transition function, $p_0 \ (\in P_A)$ is an initial state, and F_A is a set of final states $(F_A \subseteq P_A)$.

We now give a 3ITAG $G = (N, T, P, S, \#)$ such that $L(G) = L(M)$. (For simplicity, we assume that M accepts neither 1-row, 2-row, nor 1-column words. For the case where M accepts such words, essentially the same method as below can be applied to construct G.)

The set N of nonterminals is as follows:

$$N = \{S, X, Y\} \cup (Q \times T \times \{0, 1\} \times Q^3)$$
$$\cup (Q \times T \times \{0, 1\} \times Q^3 \times P_A \times Q).$$

The set P of rewriting rules is determined as follows.
(1) (a) For each $q_r \in Q$, $t_j, t_e \in T$ which satisfy

$$q_r \in g(q_\$, q_0, q_0, t_j)$$

include the following rule in P.

$$
\begin{array}{ccc}
S \quad \# & & t_j \qquad\qquad Y \\
\# & \to & \\
& & [q_r, t_e, 1, q_\$, q_0, q_0]
\end{array}
$$

(b) For each $q_r \in Q$, $t_j, t_e \in T$ which satisfies

$$q_r \in g(q_0, q_0, q_0, t_j)$$

include the following rules in P.

$$
\begin{array}{ccc}
X \quad \# & & t_j \qquad\qquad Y \\
\# & \to & \\
& & [q_r, t_e, 1, q_0, q_0, q_0]
\end{array}
$$

87

$$\begin{matrix} Y & \# \\ & \# \end{matrix} \rightarrow \begin{matrix} t_j \\ [q_r, \ t_e, \ 0, \ q_0, \ q_0, \ q_0] \end{matrix} \quad X$$

(c) For each $q_r \in Q$, $t_j, \ t_e \in T$ which satisfy

$$q_r \in g(q_0, \ q_0, \ q_\$, \ t_j)$$

include the following rules in P.

$$\begin{matrix} X & & t_j \\ \# & \rightarrow & [q_r, \ t_e, \ 1, \ q_0, \ q_0, \ q_\$] \\ Y & & t_j \\ \# & \rightarrow & [q_r, \ t_e, \ 0, \ q_0, \ q_0, \ q_\$] \end{matrix}$$

(2) (a) For each $q_h, \ q_i, \ q_a, \ q_b, \ q_c, \ q_d, \ q_r, \ q_s, \ q_x, \ q_y \in Q$, $t_j, \ t_k, \ t_e, \ t_f \in T$ which satisfy

(i) $q_r \in g(q_x, \ q_h, \ q_i, \ t_j)$
(ii) $q_s \in g(q_h, \ q_i, \ q_y, \ t_k)$
(iii) $q_x = q_\$$ iff $q_a = q_\$$
(iv) $q_y = q_\$$ iff $q_d = q_\$$
include the following rule in P.

$$\begin{matrix} [q_h, \ t_j, \ 0, \ q_a, \ q_b, \ q_c] & [q_i, \ t_k, \ 1, \ q_b, \ q_c, \ q_d] \\ \# & \# \end{matrix} \rightarrow$$

$$\begin{matrix} t_j & & t_k \\ [q_r, \ t_e, \ 1, \ q_x, \ q_h, \ q_i] & [q_s, \ t_f, \ 0, \ q_h, \ q_i, \ q_y] \end{matrix}$$

(b) For each $q_h, \ q_a, \ q_b, \ q_r, \ q_x \in Q$, $t_j, \ t_e \in T$ which satisfy

$$q_r \in g(q_\$, \ q_h, \ q_x, \ t_j)$$

include the following rule in P.

$$\begin{matrix} [q_h, \ t_j, \ 1, \ q_\$, \ q_a, \ q_b] & & t_j \\ \# & \rightarrow & [q_r, \ t_e, \ 0, \ q_\$, \ q_h, \ q_x] \end{matrix}$$

(c) For each $q_h, \ q_a, \ q_b, \ q_r, \ q_x \in Q$, $t_j, \ t_e \in T$ which satisfy

$$q_r \in g(q_x, \ q_h, \ q_\$, \ t_j)$$

include the following rule in P.

$$\begin{matrix} [q_h, \ t_j, \ 0, \ q_a, \ q_b, \ q_\$] & & t_j \\ \# & \rightarrow & [q_r, \ t_e, \ 1, \ q_x, \ q_h, \ q_\$] \end{matrix}$$

(3) (a) For each $q_h, q_i, q_a, q_b, q_c, q_d, q_r, q_s, q_x, q_y, q_z \in Q,$ $t_j, t_k, t_e, t_f \in T,$
    $p_v, p_w \in P_A$ which satisfy
    (i) $q_r \in g(q_x, q_h, q_i, t_j)$
    (ii) $q_s \in g(q_h, q_i, q_y, t_k)$
    (iii) $h(p_v, q) = p_w$ for some $q \in g(q_z, q_r, q_s, t_e)$
    (iv) $p_v = p_0$ iff $q_a = q_s$
    (v) $q_x = q_z = q_s$ iff $q_a = q_s$
    (vi) $q_y = q_s$ iff $q_d = q_s$
    include the following rule in P.

$$\begin{array}{cc} [q_h, t_j, 0, q_a, q_b, q_c]\ [q_i, t_k, 1, q_b, q_c, q_d] \\ \#\qquad\qquad\qquad\qquad \# \end{array} \rightarrow$$

$$\begin{array}{cc} t_j & t_k \\ [q_r, t_e, 1, q_x, q_h, q_i, p_v, q_z]\ [q_s, t_f, 0, q_h, q_i, q_y, p_w, q_r] \end{array}$$

(b) For each $q_h, q_a, q_b, q_r, q_x \in Q,$ $t_j, t_e \in T$ which satisfy

$$q_r \in g(q_s, q_h, q_x, t_j)$$

include the following rule in P.

$$\begin{array}{c} [q_h, t_j, 1, q_s, q_a, q_b] \\ \# \end{array} \rightarrow \begin{array}{c} t_j \\ [q_r, t_e, 0, q_s, q_h, q_x, p_0, q_s] \end{array}$$

(c) For each $q_h, q_a, q_b, q_r, q_x, q_z \in Q,$ $t_j, t_e \in T,$ $p_v \in P_A$ which satisfy

$$q_r \in g(q_x, q_h, q_s, t_j)$$

include the following rule in P.

$$\begin{array}{c} [q_h, t_j, 0, q_a, q_b, q_s] \\ \# \end{array} \rightarrow \begin{array}{c} t_j \\ [q_r, t_e, 1, q_x, q_h, q_s, p_v, q_z] \end{array}$$

(4) (a) For each $q_h, q_i, q_a, q_b, q_c, q_d, q_z \in Q,$ $t_j, t_k \in T,$ $p_v, p_w \in P_A$ which
    satisfy
    (i) $h(p_v, q) = p_w$ for some $q \in g(q_z, q_h, q_i, t_j)$
    (ii) if $q_d = q_s$ then $h(p_w, q) \in F_A$ for some $q \in g(q_h, q_i, q_s, t_k)$
    include the following rule in P.

$$[q_h, t_j, 0, q_a, q_b, q_c, p_v, q_z]\ [q_i, t_k, 1, q_b, q_c, q_d, p_w, q_h] \rightarrow t_j t_k$$

(b) For each $q_h, q_a, q_b \in Q,$ $t_j \in T$ include the following rule in P.

$$[q_h, t_j, 1, q_s, q_a, q_b, p_0, q_s] \rightarrow t_j$$

(c) For each $q_h, q_a, q_b, q_z \in Q$, $t_j \in T$, $p_v \in P_A$ which satisfy

$$h(p_v, q) \in F_A \text{ for some } q \in g(q_z, q_h, q_\$, t_j)$$

include the following rule in P.

$$[q_h, t_j, 0, q_a, q_b, q_\$, p_v, q_z] \to t_j$$

The rewriting rules of G guess a rectangular word $\mathbf{w}$ over T, and simulate the movements of M on $\mathbf{w}$. G derives the terminal word $\mathbf{w}$ iff M accepts it. (It is easily seen that every terminal word derived from S is rectangular.)

We now partition the set N of nonterminals into the following two sets:

$$N_0 = \{S, X\} \cup (Q \times T \times \{0\} \times Q^3) \cup (Q \times T \times \{0\} \times Q^3 \times P_A \times Q),$$
$$N_1 = \{Y\} \cup (Q \times T \times \{1\} \times Q^3) \cup (Q \times T \times \{1\} \times Q^3 \times P_A \times Q).$$

Suppose that the position where the start symbol S first appears in a derivation is assigned to be the first column of the first row. Then, from the rewriting rules defined above, it is easily seen that a nonterminal which appears at the jth column of the ith row is in N_0 (N_1, respectively) if $i + j$ is even (odd).

A nonterminal $[q_h, t_j, z, q_a, q_b, q_c]$ in $(Q \times T \times \{0, 1\} \times Q^3)$ which appears in a derivation represents the following facts.

(i) t_j is written at the corresponding position of the input $\mathbf{w}$ of M.

(ii) The cell of M which came to this position reads t_j in state q_h.

(iii) q_a, q_b and q_c are the previous states of the left-neighboring cell, the cell at this position and the right-neighboring cell respectively.

(iv) If $z = 0$ ($z = 1$, respectively) then $q_c(q_a)$ is a guessed state. The present state q_h of the cell depends on this guess. Note that, when $q_a = q_\$$ or $q_c = q_\$$ (i.e. the cell is at the leftmost or rightmost column), the value is always correct regardless of z.

In 3ITAG, since every nonterminal in the left-hand side of a rule must be rewritten into a terminal, the information stored in a nonterminal can be (directly) used only once. Thus, when simulating an NBCA, each nonterminal, which keeps the present state of a cell, can know the state of only one of the neighboring two cells from the right- or left-neighboring nonterminal, but not both. Therefore, the state of the other neighboring cell must be guessed, and the state transition is performed according to this guess. In the next row, by reading the nonterminal on the other side, it is verified whether this guess was correct. q_a, q_b and q_c above are used for this purpose.

A nonterminal $[q_h, t_j, z, q_a, q_b, q_c, p_v, q_z]$ in $(Q \times T \times \{0, 1\} \times Q^3 \times P_A \times Q)$ can appear at the bottom of each column of a sentential form. The meanings of the first six items are the same as above. In addition, p_v and q_z have the following meanings.

(v) p_v is the state of the finite automaton A at this column when A is reading the last configuration of M. If $z = 1$, p_v is a guessed state.

(vi) q_z is the present state of the left-neighboring cell. If $z = 1$, q_z is a guessed state.

The rewriting rules in (1) guess the first and second rows of an input $\mathbf{w} \in T^{2+}$. At the same time, they simulate the one step movement of each cell of M, which was initially in the state q_0, and create such a configuration in a sentential form.

The rules in (2) guess a new row of **w**, and simulate the movements of M (except at the top row and the bottom two rows of **w**). (2)(b) and (c) are for the cases where the nonterminal is at the leftmost or rightmost column, but their functions are essentially the same as in (2)(a). The rule (2)(a) simulates the movements of two cells C_1 and C_2 which are reading the symbols t_j and t_k respectively. It is clear that this rule requires the previously guessed states q_c in $[q_h, t_j, 0, q_a, q_b, q_c]$ and q_b in $[q_i, t_k, 1, q_b, q_c, q_d]$ to be correct. It then guesses the present states of C_1's left-neighboring cell and C_2's right-neighboring cell (they are q_x and q_y). According to these guesses, it simulates the state transitions of C_1 and C_2 (their next states are q_r and q_s).

The rules in (3) are for simulating M at the bottom two rows. In addition to the function in (2), they have a function to check if the last configuration **c** of M is in the regular set R. That is, these rules simulate the automaton A on the input **c**. The nonterminal $[q_r, t_e, 1, q_x, q_h, q_i, p_v, q_z]$ in (3)(a) represents that A reads the last state of the cell at this position in the state p_v, and that the state of the left-neighboring cell is q_z. The nonterminal $[q_s, t_f, 0, q_h, q_i, q_y, p_w, q_r]$ represents that A reads the last state of the cell at this position in the state p_w. Since p_w is a state such that $h(p_v, q) = p_w$ for some $q \in g(q_z, q_r, q_s, t_e)$, if the guesses of p_v and q_z are correct, A can transit its state from p_v to p_w. Rules in (3)(b) and (c) also work as in (3)(a).

The rules in (4) have the final checking function of the unchecked (remaining) guesses. The checking mechanism is similar to that of (2) or (3). In addition to this, these rules check if A becomes a final state after reading the last configuration **c** of M. If the sentential form generated so far passes these checks and is rectangular, then a terminal word is generated.

From the above construction, it is clear that $L(G)$ agrees with the language accepted by M. ∎

Lemma 4.2. $\mathscr{L}^R[\text{3ITAG}] \subseteq \mathscr{L}[\text{N3LTM}]$.

Proof. Let $G = (N, T, P, S, \#)$ be a given 3ITAG. An N3LTM M which simulates derivations in G is constructed as follows.

Since 3ITAG is a subclass of 3HCSAG, Lemma 3.2 also holds for 3ITAG. Thus it is sufficient for M to simulate only the uppermost derivations in G.

Let r_m (c_m, respectively) be the maximum number of rows (columns) of the rewriting rules in P. When a rewriting rule $\mathbf{u} \to \mathbf{v}$ is applied to a sentential form $\mathbf{x}$, the uppermost row of the rewritten part is called the *application row* of the rewriting rule.

M uses the storage tape divided into r_m tracks. If an input $\mathbf{w} \in T^{2+}$ is given, M executes the following algorithm, assuming that there is an uppermost derivation of $\mathbf{w}$.

begin
 mark n squares of the storage tape;
 write #s in all the n squares of the tracks 1 to r_m;
 select nondeterministically one square from n, and rewrite the symbol # on the track 1
  into S;

while M is not in a halting state   **do**
  begin
        guess all the rewritings (i.e. applications of rewriting rules) applied at the row
          where the input head is now scanning, and write this information on the storage
          tape;
        if these rewritings are applicable and "consistent" (explained later) in the
          application order **then** execute all the rewritings on the storage tape
        else   halt without accepting the input;
        if the contents of the row of the input tape where the input head is now
          positioning agree with the contents of the track 1 of the storage tape   **then**
          begin
                transfer the contents of the track $i + 1$ into the track i ($i = 1, 2, \ldots,$
                  $r_m - 1$);
                write #s in all the squares of the track r_m;
                if the track 1 consists only of #s   **then** halt in a final state
                else shift the input head downward one row
          end
        else   halt without accepting the input
    end
end

  In the above algorithm, at each row of **w**, M guesses the set of all the rewritings applied
at that row in the uppermost derivation of **w**. In 3ITAG, rewriting rules can be applied at
most twice at each square. Thus, M can perform the tasks of guessing the set of rewritings
and write them at the corresponding position on the storage tape (as in Fig. 3) during one
scan of the storage head from left to right. Note that any two rewritings among them never
overlap in their applications area except at the application row, because the symbols in the
left-hand side of a rewriting rule except the first row are all #s and those of the right-hand
side are all non-# symbols.

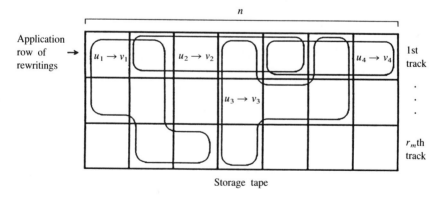

Fig. 3.   Guessing the set of rewritings and recording them on the storage tape.

If the guessed rewritings are applicable in some order to the symbol array written in the storage tape, then these rewritings should be performed on the tape. However, if M performs them in the actual order as in the derivation of $\mathbf{w}$, the storage head may scan the tape many times (the number of times being proportional to n). To avoid this, M performs them from left to right regardless of the actual order. Namely, M scans the storage tape from left to right, and each time M finds a rewriting, M checks if it is applicable or not. This is done by using the information of the present symbol array in its application area and the other rewritings which are overlapping with this rewriting. If it is applicable, M performs it on the tape.

Now, note that any two rewritings which have an overlapping area have a unique precedence (order) of applications (if they are both applicable). This is because every rewriting rule of 3ITAG rewrites each symbol in the left-hand side into a different type of symbol (i.e. it rewrites # into a non-#symbol and a nonterminal into a terminal).

The remaining task M must do is to check if these precedences between pairs of rewritings are consistent as a whole (i.e. these precedences form a partial order). For example, in Fig. 3, inconsistency arises if $\mathbf{u}_2 \to \mathbf{v}_2$ precedes $\mathbf{u}_3 \to \mathbf{v}_3$, $\mathbf{u}_3 \to \mathbf{v}_3$ precedes $\mathbf{u}_4 \to \mathbf{v}_4$ and $\mathbf{u}_4 \to \mathbf{v}_4$ precedes $\mathbf{u}_2 \to \mathbf{v}_2$.

Since the guessed rewritings may overlap at most twice at each square of the application row, and do not overlap in the other rows, the number of the rewritings at the ith column (i.e. the rewritings which have common areas with the ith column) is at most $r_m + 1$. Scanning from left to right, M keeps track of the partial order among the rewritings at each column. Assume M is recording the partial order among the rewritings at the ith column, which is computed from the precedences obtained in the first i columns. At the $(i + 1)$th column, using newly obtained precedences at this column, M can easily compute the partial order among the rewritings at the $(i + 1)$th column. Since $r_m + 1$ is a constant, M can do this in its finite state control. If an inconsistent loop arises (i.e. the precedences do not form a partial order), M halts without accepting the input.

By the above, it is seen that $L(M) = L(G)$. ∎

Lemma 4.3. $\mathscr{L}[\text{N3LTM}] \subseteq \mathscr{L}[\text{N3RTM}]$.

Proof. For any N3LTM $M_L = (Q, T, A, f, q_0, \$, a_0, F)$, construct an N3RTM M_R which simulates M_L as follows.

We can assume that, without loss of generality, when M_L moves its input head downward, it does so at the first column on the tape (this is done by increasing the number of storage tape symbols). Further, we assume that M_L reads each input square at most k times when it accepts the input.

Suppose a rectangular word $\mathbf{w} \in T^{2+}$ of size $m \times n$ is given to M_L. If we divide the entire move sequence of M_L at the downward movements of the input head, m segments of move sequences can be obtained. Although $\mathbf{w}$ is two-dimensional, input head movements are one-dimensional in each of these segments. Furthermore, since horizontal movements of the input head agree with those of the storage head, M_L can be regarded as a one-dimensional one-tape Turing machine. Thus we can use the notion of "crossing sequence"[8] for a one-tape Turing machine to analyze the movements of M_L in one segment.

The *crossing sequence* of M_L at a square on **w** is a sequence of movements on that square which is picked out from the entire sequence of movements of M_L. More precisely, it is an element of

$$\bigcup_{i=0}^{k} (Q \times \{L, R, D\} \times A \times Q \times \{L, R, D, H\})^i,$$

where $[q, d, a, q', d'] \in (Q \times \{L, R, D\} \times A \times Q \times \{L, R, D, H\})$ represents that M_L enters the square in state q, moving the input head to the direction d, then rewrites the storage tape symbol into a, and leaves in state q', moving the head to the direction d'. Note that $d' = H$ means that q' is a halting state.

Given an input **w**, M_R executes the following algorithm.

begin
  scan : = "right";
  while M_R is not in a halting state **do**
    begin
      while M_R has not yet reached the opposite border of the row where the input head
        is now positioning **do**
        begin
          guess a crossing sequence of M_L at the square where the input head of M_R is
            now scanning;
          write the symbol which is finally written at the square of M_L's storage tape by
            this guessed crossing sequence, in the M_R's storage tape;
          if scan = "right" **then** shift the heads to the right
          else shift the heads to the left
        end;
      if any two neighboring crossing sequences guessed in this row connect
        coherently, and the crossing sequence at the first column of this row also
        connects coherently to that of the above row (except in the first row where M_L
        starts from the initial state at the leftmost square) **then**
      if M_L halts in a final state in this row **then** halt in a final state
      else **begin**
          shift the input head downward;
          if scan = "right" **then** scan : = "left"
          else scan : = "right"
        end
     else halt without accepting the input
    end
end

In this algorithm, in scanning the input tape in the snake-like (zigzag) order, M_R nondeterministically guesses a crossing sequence of M_L at each square of the input (including the border square) and checks if the guesses are correct. Of course, these crossing sequences must be compatible with M_L's move function f.

Each time the outermost **while** loop is executed, a move sequence of M_L in one row is simulated. Assume that M_R has executed this **while** loop i times and completed the simulation of M_L up to the ith row, and it is in the $(i + 1)$th row. At that time, M_R is recording M_L's last state in the above row (i.e. the state when M_L goes down to this row) in its finite-state memory and the contents of the storage tape of M_L are stored in the storage tape of M_R. In the $(i + 1)$th execution of the **while** loop, where guessing a crossing sequence at each square occurs, M_R checks if it connects coherently to the crossing sequence at the neighboring square and writes the storage tape symbol which is finally written by the guessed crossing sequence. At the square of the first column M_R also checks that M_L's last state in the ith row connects to the crossing sequence of this square.

If all the guessed crossing sequences in the $(i + 1)$th row pass these checks, the simulation of M_L up to the $(i + 1)$th row is completed. M_R repeats this procedure and if M_L halts in a final state, M_R also does so.

By the above, it is clear that M_R accepts the same language as M_L.   ∎

Lemma 4.4. $\mathscr{L}[\text{N3RTM}] \subseteq \mathscr{L}[\text{NBCA}]$.

Proof.   For any N3RTM M_R, we can construct an NBCA M_C which simulates M_R as follows.

Assume a rectangular input $\mathbf{w} \in T^{2+}$ of size $m \times n$ is given to M_C. In each row of $\mathbf{w}$, the jth cell of M_C guesses a crossing sequence of M_R at that square and records the symbol written in the jth square of the storage tape. Note that since M_R is an N3RTM, the length of each crossing sequence is at most 1. Coherency checking of the neighboring crossing sequences are done by communicating with the neighboring cells in the next step. At the column where M_R's input head goes down, the cell also checks vertical coherency of the crossing sequences. If coherency breaks at some cell, it becomes a rejecting state.

In the last configuration of M_C just after it has read the mth row, if there is no rejecting cell, and there is a crossing sequence in which M_R halts in a final state, then $\mathbf{w}$ should be accepted. It is easy to construct a finite automaton that checks the above conditions by reading the last configuration of M_C. Thus the set of accepting configurations of M_C is the regular set accepted by the finite automaton.

It is clear that the above constructed M_C accepts the same language as M_R.   ∎

From Lemmas 4.1–4.4, the following theorem follows.

Theorem 4.5. $\mathscr{L}^R[\text{3ITAG}] = \mathscr{L}[\text{N3LTM}] = \mathscr{L}[\text{N3RTM}] = \mathscr{L}[\text{NBCA}]$.

In Ref. 9, it is shown that the class of languages accepted by nondeterministic two-dimensional on-line tessellation acceptors (2-ota) agrees with $\mathscr{L}[\text{NBCA}]$. Thus the following corollary is obtained.

Corollary 4.6. $\mathscr{L}^R[\text{3ITAG}] = \mathscr{L}[\text{2-ota}]$.

5. HIERARCHY OF THE GRAMMAR CLASSES

In this section, we show the hierarchy of the classes of languages generated by 3HCSAGs, 3ITAGs, MAGs and accepted by some kinds of automata.

Let NLBA denote a nondeterministic two-dimensional linear bounded automaton (which is called a tape-bounded (or, array-bounded) array acceptor in Ref. 2 (or Ref. 7)). And let NFA denote a nondeterministic two-dimensional finite automaton. Note that, here, each of these automata is assumed to have a four-way head and a rectangular input tape.

Theorem 5.1. $\mathscr{L}[\text{NFA}] \subsetneqq \mathscr{L}^R[\text{3ITAG}] \subsetneqq \mathscr{L}^R[\text{3HCSAG}] \subsetneqq \mathscr{L}^R[\text{MAG}]$.

Proof. The following relation is shown in Ref. 10.

$$\mathscr{L}[\text{NFA}] \subsetneqq \mathscr{L}[\text{2-ota}] \subsetneqq \mathscr{L}[\text{N1WPSA}]$$

From this and Corollaries 3.6 and 4.6,

$$\mathscr{L}[\text{NFA}] \subsetneqq \mathscr{L}^R[\text{3ITAG}] \subsetneqq \mathscr{L}^R[\text{3HCSAG}]$$

is derived. In Ref. 2, it is shown that $\mathscr{L}[\text{MAG}]$ agrees with the class of languages accepted by NLBAs with inputs of any shape. In a similar manner,

$$\mathscr{L}^R[\text{MAG}] = \mathscr{L}[\text{NLBA}]$$

can be proved. On the other hand, in Ref. 7

$$\mathscr{L}[\text{NPSA}] \subsetneqq \mathscr{L}[\text{NLBA}]$$

is shown. From these results, Corollary 3.6, and the fact that N1WPSA is a subclass of NPSA, $\mathscr{L}^R[\text{3HCSAG}] \subsetneqq \mathscr{L}^R[\text{MAG}]$ is derived. ∎

6. CONCLUDING REMARKS

In this paper, we introduced two kinds of three-way array grammars and showed that their generating abilities of rectangular languages are precisely characterized by some classes of two-dimensional acceptors. Hierarchy of these grammar classes is also shown. The results obtained in this paper (Theorems 3.5, 4.5, 5.1 and Corollaries 3.6, 4.6) are summarized as follows.

$$\mathscr{L}^R[\text{MAG}] = \mathscr{L}[\text{NLBA}]$$

$$\cup\dagger$$
$$\mathscr{L}^R[\text{3HCSAG}] = \mathscr{L}[\text{N3TM}(n)] = \mathscr{L}[\text{N1WPSA}]$$

$$\bigcup \dagger$$

$$\mathcal{L}^R[\text{3ITAG}] = \mathcal{L}[\text{N3LTM}] = \mathcal{L}[\text{N3RTM}] = \mathcal{L}[\text{NBCA}] = \mathcal{L}[\text{2-ota}]$$

$$\bigcup \dagger$$

$$\mathcal{L}[\text{NFA}]$$

From these results, we can derive the properties of the three-way grammars using the known results of these acceptors. For example, we can show that there is a 3ITAG which generates the following language L_C.

$$L_C = \{\mathbf{w} \mid \mathbf{w} \text{ is a rectangular word over } \{0, 1\}$$
$$\text{and 1's in } \mathbf{w} \text{ form a connected pattern}\}$$

This is because an N3LTM can accept L_C by using essentially the same algorithm shown in Ref. 7 for a deterministic 1WPSA.

It is left for future study whether there are other useful classes of three-way array grammars.

REFERENCES

1. D. L. Milgram and A. Rosenfeld, "Array automata and array grammars", in *Information Processing 71*, North-Holland, 1972, pp. 69–74.
2. A. Rosenfeld, *Picture Languages*, Academic Press, New York, 1979.
3. C. R. Cook and P. S. P. Wang, "A Chomsky hierarchy of isotonic array grammars and languages", *Computer Graphics and Image Processing* **8** (1978) 144–152.
4. P. S. P. Wang, "Hierarchical structures and complexities of parallel isometrical languages", *IEEE Trans. PAMI* **5** (1983) 92–99.
5. S. Seki, "Real-time recognition of two-dimensional tapes by cellular automata", *Information Sciences* **19** (1979) 179–198.
6. K. Morita, H. Umeo and K. Sugata, "Language recognition abilities of several two-dimensional tape automata and their relation to tape complexities", *Trans. IECE Japan* **J60-D** (1977) 1077–1084.
7. A. Rosenfeld and D. L. Milgram, "Parallel/sequential array automata", *Information Processing Letters* **2** (1973) 43–46.
8. F. C. Hennie, "One-tape, off-line Turing machine computations", *Information and Control* **8** (1965) 553–578.
9. K. Inoue and A. Nakamura, "On the relation between two-dimensional on-line tessellation acceptors and one-dimensional bounded cellular acceptors", *Trans. IECE Japan* **J59-D** (1976) 613–620.
10. K. Inoue and A. Nakamura, "Some properties of two-dimensional on-line tessellation acceptors", *Information Sciences* **13** (1977) 95–121.

Kenichi Morita received the B.E., M.E. and Dr.E. degrees from Osaka University, in 1971, 1973 and 1978 respectively. From 1974 to 1987, he was a Research Associate of the Faculty of Engineering Science, Osaka University. Since 1987 he has been an Associate Professor of the Faculty of Engineering, Yamagata University, Yonezawa, Japan. His research interests include automata theory, computational complexity, formal language theory, and logic systems for knowledge and natural language processing. His other interests include listening to classical music, watching operas and running long distances very slowly (his best record of a full marathon is 4 h 5 min).

Yasunori Yamamoto received the B.S. and M.S. degrees in engineering from Osaka University, in 1978 and 1980 respectively. Since October 1983, he has been an Assistant Professor in the Division of Computer Ethnology of the National Museum of Ethnology. His research interests include automata and language theory, computational complexity and computer ethnology.

Kazuhiro Sugata received the B.S. degree in electrical engineering from Kyoto University, in 1961, and the M.S. and Ph.D. degrees in electrical engineering (1963) and computer engineering (1968) from Kyoto University respectively. From 1966 to 1971 he served in Osaka University as a research assistant and was an Assistant Professor there between 1971 to 1986. Since 1986 he has been working at the Information Processing Division of the Social Systems Engineering Department in Tottori University, Japan as a Chief Professor.

He was a member of the editorial committee of the Institute of Electronics, Information and Communication Engineers of Japan. He is also a member of the Information Processing Society of Japan. His research interests lie in automata theory, language, computational complexity, two-dimensional array grammars, array processing, speech signal compression, computer applications to speech signal processing and image processing.

PUSHDOWN RECOGNIZERS FOR ARRAY PATTERNS

H. J. LIN

Mathematics Department, Northeastern University, Boston, MA 02115, USA

P. S. P. WANG

MIT Artificial Intelligence Laboratory, Cambridge, MA 02139, USA
on leave from College of Computer Science, Northeastern University, Boston, MA 02115, USA

Received 20 December 1988
Revised 1 March 1989

We investigate the factors that make it difficult to generalize pushdown automata for one-dimensional strings to two-dimensional arrays. Then we resolve the problems and construct two-dimensional pushdown array automata (PDAA). The relationship between isometric context-free array languages and pushdown array automata is established. Several examples of array automata are presented, and a pushdown array automaton is tested on VAX8650/VMS using PASCAL.

Keywords: Array patterns; Array grammars; Pushdown array automata; Parsing; Pattern recognition.

1. INTRODUCTION

For the past decades, automata for two-dimensional arrays or patterns have been widely studied and applied.[1-10] In this paper we investigate the difficulty in extending pushdown automata for one-dimensional strings to those for two-dimensional arrays. It is observed that the two-dimensional automata need to handle two things; one is to decide the directions in which the input head can move in order to avoid redundant parsing, and the other is to check if the input array is completely parsed. The problems can be overcome if the machine can parse the input array completely but not redundantly.

We use two kinds of memories; one stores all parsed array squares which are possible to be parsed again and another stores all unparsed neighbors of those parsed array squares. With the former, the machine can avoid redundant parsing, and with the latter, the machine can check whether the input array is completely parsed or not.

Due to the decision for the directions by the input head, some languages can be accepted by nondeterministic pushdown array automata (NPDAA) but not by any deterministic pushdown array automata (DPDAA); thus, $\mathcal{L}(\text{DPDAA}) \subsetneqq \mathcal{L}(\text{NPDAA})$ (where $\mathcal{L}(\cdot)$ denotes the set of languages recognized by $\cdot$). We will study the modification for the input arrays so that they can be accepted by deterministic array automata.

In Sect. 2, some basic notations and definitions of array grammars are introduced. PDAA are presented in Sect. 3. The relationship between PDAA and ICFAG is discussed in Sect. 4. A technique of recognizing noisy patterns is discussed in Sect. 5. Finally, some future research topics are discussed in Sect. 6. A preliminary version of this paper

99

International Journal of Pattern Recognition and Artificial Intelligence Vol. 3 No. 3 & 4 (1989) 377–392
© World Scientific Publishing Company

was presented at the 1988 International Computer Symposium, Taipei, Taiwan, R. O. C.[11]

2. DEFINITIONS AND NOTATIONS FOR ARRAY GRAMMARS

An array grammar (AG) is a quintuple $G = (V_N, V_T, P, S, \#)$, where V_N is a nonempty finite set of nonterminals, V_T is a nonempty finite set of terminals, $V_N \cap V_T = \phi$, $S \in V_N$ is the start symbol, $\# \notin V_N \cup V_T$ is the blank symbol and P is a set of production rules. Each member of P is of the form $\alpha \to \beta$ and can be explained as follows: Let J be a finite connected subset of I^2, where I is the set of integers. α and β are mappings from J to $V_N \cup V_T \cup \{\#\} = V$ such that $\alpha(i) = a \in V_T$, then $\beta(i) = a$; that is, terminals are never rewritten.

An array A is a mapping from I^2 to V. A production rule $\alpha \to \beta$ is applicable to A if a translation τ of the domain J of α such that $A|\tau J = \alpha$. We say that A directly produces A' (or A' is directly derivable from A), written as $A \Rightarrow A'$, if for $\alpha \to \beta$ applicable to A, $A|\tau J = \alpha$, $A'|\tau J = \beta$ and $A'|(I^2 - J) = A|(I^2 - J)$. Let $\overset{*}{\Rightarrow}$ be the transitive closure of $\Rightarrow$. Then for $A \overset{*}{\Rightarrow} B$, B is said to be derivable from A and is called a sentential form.

An initial array A_S is a mapping $I \to \{\#, S\}$, such that $\{i|A_S(i) = S\}$ is a singleton. A terminal array A_T is a mapping from I^2 to $V_T \cup \{\#\}$. The array language generated by an AG is $L(G) = \{B|A_S \overset{*}{\Rightarrow} B, B \text{ is a terminal}\}$. B is also called a sentence of the grammar G.

In order to avoid a shearing effect,[6] in each rule $\alpha \to \beta$, α and β must be isometric; that is, geometrically identical. An AG is called monotonic if it can never erase; that is, for each rule $\alpha \to \beta$, if $\beta(i) = \#$, then $\alpha(i) = \#$.

Each member in I^2 is of the form $[x, y]$, called a vertex in I^2, where x and y are two elements in I; that is, two integers. A vertex $p = [x, y]$ has two types of neighbors[12]:
(a) its four horizontal and vertical neighbors $[u, v]$ such that $|x - u| + |y - v| = 1$ and
(b) its four diagonal neighbors $[u, v]$ such that $|x - u| = |y - v| = 1$.
We shall refer to the neighbors of type (a) as the 4-neighbors of p, and to the neighbors of both types, collectively, as the 8-neighbors of p. The former neighbors are said to be 4-adjacent to p, and the latter, 8-adjacent.

By a path π of length n from p to q in I^2 we mean a sequence of vertices $p = p_0p_1 \ldots p_n = q$, such that p_i is adjacent to p_{i-1}, $1 \leqslant i \leqslant n$. Note that this comprises two definitions in one, namely, 4- and 8-path, depending on whether we use the definition of 4- or 8-adjacency.

We use the definition of 8-adjacency throughout this paper, but for the purpose of simple illustration we use the definition of 4-adjacency for all examples in Sects. 3 and 4.

With the definition of 8-adjacency, the array square has 8 neighbors in 8 directions which are denoted by "up", "down", "right", "left", "up-right", "up-left", "down-right" and "down-left"; or abbreviated by U, D, R, L, U_r, U_l, D_r and D_l respectively. For the purpose of simple expression, we let $I_U = [-1, 0]$, $I_D = [1, 0]$, $I_R = [0, 1]$, $I_L = [0, -1]$, $I_{U_r} = [-1, 1]$, $I_{U_l} = [-1, -1]$, $I_{D_r} = [1, 1]$, $I_{D_l} = [1, -1]$, and $I_T = [0, 0]$ where "T" denotes "stationary". Thus neighbors of

$[i, j]$, which are shown in Fig. 1, can be denoted as follows:

$[i, j]$-$U = [i, j] + I_U = [i - 1, j]$, $[i, j]$-$D = [i, j] + I_D = [i + 1, j]$,

$[i, j]$-$R = [i, j] + I_R = [i, j + 1]$, $[i, j]$-$L = [i, j] + I_L = [i, j - 1]$,

$[i, j]$-$U_r = [i, j] + I_{U_r} = [i - 1, j + 1]$, $[i, j]$-$U_l = [i, j] + I_{U_l} = [i - 1, j - 1]$,

$[i, j]$-$D_r = [i, j] + I_{D_r} = [i + 1, j + 1]$, $[i, j]$-$D_l = [i, j] + I_{D_l} = [i + 1, j - 1]$,

and $[i, j]$-$T = [i, j]$.

We let $Dir_4 = \{U, D, R, L, T\}$ and $Dir_8 = \{U, D, R, L, U_r, U_l, D_r, D_l, T\}$ be under the definitions of 4- and 8-adjacency respectively. For every $d \in Dir_8$, let $\bar{d}$ be the opposite direction of d. For example, $\bar{R} = L$, $\bar{U}_l = D_r$, and $\bar{T} = T$; thus $[i, j]$-$\bar{R} = [i, j]$-$L = [i, j - 1]$ and $[i, j]$-$\bar{U}_l = [i, j]$-$D_r = [i + 1, j + 1]$. $[i, j]$-d is called the *neighbor-d* of $[i, j]$.

Definition 2.1. An array is connected if there is a path of non-# symbols between every pair of non-# symbols.

Definition 2.2. Let $G = (V_N, V_T, P, S, \#)$ be an isometric array grammar:

(1) G is of type 0 (isometric, IAG) if there are no restrictions on P;

(2) G is of type 1 (monotonic, IMAG) if both sides of each rule are connected and the image of each left-side symbol is in $V_N \cup V_T$; that is, #s cannot be created;

(3) G is of type 2 (context-free, ICFAG) if it is monotonic and the left side of each rule contains exactly one nonterminal symbol in a field of #s;

(4) G is of type 3 (regular, IRAG) if every rewriting rule is of the form

$$A \rightarrow a, \; \#A \rightarrow Ba, \; A\# \rightarrow aB, \; \begin{matrix} \# \\ A \end{matrix} \rightarrow \begin{matrix} B \\ a \end{matrix}, \; \begin{matrix} a \\ \# \end{matrix} \rightarrow \begin{matrix} A \\ B \end{matrix}, \; \begin{matrix} a \\ \# \end{matrix} \rightarrow \begin{matrix} \# \\ B \end{matrix} \begin{matrix} B \\ A \end{matrix}, \; \begin{matrix} B \\ A \end{matrix} \rightarrow \begin{matrix} A \\ a \end{matrix}, \; \begin{matrix} a \\ \# \end{matrix} \rightarrow \begin{matrix} a \\ B \end{matrix}$$

or $\begin{matrix} \# \\ A \end{matrix} \rightarrow \begin{matrix} B \\ a \end{matrix}$, where A and B are nonterminal symbols and a is a terminal symbol.

Let IAL, IMAL, ICFAL, and IRAL denote the isometric, monotonic, context-free and regular array languages respectively.

Theorem 2.3.[13] Any ICFAG with the definition of 8-adjacency can be generated by an ICFAG whose writing rules are of the forms:

$$\#A \rightarrow BC, \; A\# \rightarrow BC, \; A \rightarrow a, \; \begin{matrix} \# \\ A \end{matrix} \rightarrow \begin{matrix} B \\ C \end{matrix} \begin{matrix} A \\ \# \end{matrix} \rightarrow \begin{matrix} B \\ C \end{matrix} \begin{matrix} \# \\ A \end{matrix} \rightarrow \begin{matrix} B \\ C \end{matrix} \begin{matrix} A \\ \# \end{matrix} \rightarrow \begin{matrix} B \\ C \end{matrix} \begin{matrix} \# \\ A \end{matrix} \rightarrow \begin{matrix} B \\ C \end{matrix}$$

$[i - 1, j - 1]$	$[i - 1, j]$	$[i - 1, j + 1]$
$[i, j - 1]$	$[i, j]$	$[i, j + 1]$
$[i + 1, j - 1]$	$[i + 1, j]$	$[i + 1, j + 1]$

Fig. 1. The array square $[i, j]$ with its neighbors.

or $\dfrac{A\quad B}{\#\quad C}$, where A, B and C are nonterminal symbols and a is a terminal symbol.

Arrays α and β are adjacent if there exist i and j adjacent in I^2, such that $\alpha(i) \neq \#$ and $\beta(i) \neq \#$.

If α and β are two nonsuperimposed adjacent arrays then we use $\alpha \oplus \beta$ to denote the junction of α and β; that is, for any i in I^2.

$$(\alpha \oplus \beta)(i) = \begin{cases} \alpha(i) & \text{if } \alpha(i) \neq \# \\ \beta(i) & \text{if } \beta(i) \neq \# \\ \# & \text{if } \alpha(i) = \beta(i) = \#. \end{cases}$$

If $\{i | \alpha(i) \neq \#\} = \{j\}$ is a singleton and $\alpha(j) = a$, then we say α is a single array containing the symbol a. For an array square of an array r with a non-# symbol, if it has at least three non-# neighbors then it is said to be crowded; otherwise, it is said to be simple.

3.   DEFINITION OF A PDAA (PUSHDOWN ARRAY AUTOMATON)

Suppose that Z is a stack of triple elements; that is, every element of Z is of the form (a, b, c). If Z is represented as a string $(a_1, b_1, c_1)(a_2, b_2, c_2) \ldots (a_n, b_n, c_n)$, then it can be treated as a triple stack. α, P and R have a one-to-one corresponding relation; thus they always have the same number of elements.

A pushdown array automaton M is a system $(Q, \Sigma, \Gamma, \delta, q_0, Dir)$, where Q is a finite set of states, Σ is an input alphabet, Γ is a stack alphabet, $(\supset \Sigma)$ q_0 in Q is the initial state, Z_0 in Γ/Σ is a particular stack symbol called the start symbol, Dir is the set of directions $= \{U, D, R, L, T\}$ or $\{U, D, R, L, U_r, U_l, D_r, D_l, T\}$, depending on whether the definition of 4- or 8-adjacency is applied, and δ is a transition from $Q \times (\Sigma \cup \{\varepsilon\}) \times \Gamma$ to $2^{Dir \times Q \times \Gamma^*}$.

The transition δ is classified into three different types as follows:

Type 1: $(q, \varepsilon, A) \rightarrow (d, q', BC)$, i.e. $(d, q', BC) \in \delta(q, \varepsilon, A)$, where A, B and $C \in \Gamma/\Sigma$, $d \in Dir/\{T\}$, and q and $q' \in Q$;

Type 2: $(q, a, A) \rightarrow (d, q', C)$, i.e. $(d, q', C) \in \delta(q, a, A)$, where $a \in \Sigma$, A and $C \in \Gamma/\Sigma$, $d \in Dir/\{T\}$, and q and $q' \in Q$;

Type 3: $(q, a, A) \rightarrow (T, q', \varepsilon)$, i.e. $(T, q', \varepsilon) \in \delta(q, a, A)$, where $a \in \Sigma, A \in \Gamma/\Sigma$, and q and $q' \in Q$;

Here, we define the instantaneous description (ID) as the configuration of a PDAA at a given instant, which records
(1) the state,
(2) unexpended (or unread) input,
(3) stack contents,
(4) coordinates of the stack symbols,
(5) directions from which the stack symbols cannot be scanned,

(6) a set of coordinates of scanned crowded array squares, and
(7) a set of coordinates of some unscanned array squares.
Thus, we define an ID to be of the form $(q, w, Z, ST0, ST1, ST2, check)$, or $(q, w, (\alpha, P, R), ST0, ST1, ST2, check)$, where

> q is a state,
> w is an array of input symbols,
> $Z = (\alpha, P, R)$ is a triple stack, where α is a string of stack symbols in Γ^*,
> $P \in J^*$ is the string of coordinates of all the corresponding stack symbols in α,
> $R \in (2^{Dir/\{T\}})^*$ is the string of sets of restricting directions for all the corresponding stack symbols,
> $ST0 \in 2^J$ is the set of coordinates of scanned simple array squares,
> $ST1 \in 2^J$ is the set of coordinates of scanned crowded array squares, and
> $ST2 \in 2^J$ is the set of coordinates of some unscanned array squares.

If STACK is a stack, then we use $Top(\text{STACK})$ to denote the top symbol in STACK. As the machine is in the configuration $(q, w, (\alpha, P, R), set0, set1, set2, check)$, the input head points at the array square of $Top(P)$, $check \in \{yes, no\}$, whose value is always given by "*yes*" for the initial ID, and is given by the flow-chart PDAA Checking Parsable in Appendix 1 for the other IDs. For the type 1 transition $(d, q', BC) \in \delta(q, \varepsilon, A)$, we say $(q, w, (A\gamma, P, R), set0, set1, set2, check) \vdash_M (q', w, (BC\gamma, P', R'), set0', set1', set2', check')$ if $check = check' = yes$, where $w \in \Sigma^{**}$, A, B and C are in Γ/Σ, γ is a string of stack symbols, and the value of $check$ is obtained from the flowchart PDAA Checking Parsable. Here, the PDAA, in state q with the top stack symbol A can enter state q' and replace symbol A with BC, independently of the input symbol, meanwhile, the top symbols of P and R are replaced with $\dfrac{p}{p'}$ and $\dfrac{r \cup \{d\}}{\{\bar{d}\}}$ respectively (that is, for each of P and R, one element is popped and two elements are pushed), where $p = Top(P)$, $p' = p + I_d$, and $r = Top(R)$. The contents of $ST1$ and $ST2$ are updated in the flowchart PDAA Checking Parsable, and then the input head is moved to the array square of $Top(P')$. No input is read for every move of a configuration according to the type 1 transition. For the type 2 transition $(d, q', C) \in \delta(q, a, A)$, we say $(q, w \oplus \bar{a}, (A\gamma, P, R), set0, set1, set2, check) \vdash_M (q', w, (C\gamma, P', R'), set0', set1', set2', check')$, if $check = check' = yes$, where A and $C \in \Gamma/\Sigma$, $w \in \Sigma^{**}$, $\bar{a}$ is some single array containing the symbol $a \in \Sigma$ and γ is a string of stack symbols. In the former ID, $(q, w \oplus \bar{a}, (Ar, P, R), set0, set1, set2, check)$, the input head points at the input symbol a of $\bar{a}$; that is $\bar{a}(Top(P)) = a$. Here the PDAA in state q with the topmost stack symbol A and the input symbol a can read a, enter state q', and then replace the topmost symbol A with C, replace the topmost symbols of P and R with $p' (= Top(P) + I_d)$ and $\{\bar{d}\}$ respectively, and then move the input head one array square in the direction of d (i.e. move it to the array square of $p' = Top(P')$). For the type 3 transition $(d, q', \varepsilon) \in \delta(q, a, A)$ (it is trivial that $d = T$, and so $p' = p$), we say $(q, w \oplus \bar{a}, (A\gamma, P, R),$

103

*set*0, *set*1, *set*2, *check*) $\vdash_M$ (q', w, (γ, P', R'), *set*0', *set*1', *set*2', *check*') if *check* = *check*' = *yes*, where $w \in \Sigma^{**}$, $\tilde{a}$ is some single array containing the symbol a, $A \in \Gamma/\Sigma$, and γ is the string of stack symbols. Here, the DPAA in state q, with the top stack symbol A and input symbol a, can read a, enter state q', remove *Top*($A\gamma$, P, R) from the stack to obtain the new stack (γ, P', R'), and move the input head to the array square of *Top*(P'). Note that in any ID (q, w, (A, P, R), *set*0, *set*1, *set*2, *check*), the input head always points at the array square of *Top*(P).

We define $L(M)$, the language accepted by M, to be $\{w \in \Sigma^{**} \mid (q_0, w, (Z_0, (0, 0),$ $\varepsilon), \phi, \phi, \phi, yes) \vdash_M^* (q, \varepsilon, (\varepsilon, \varepsilon, \varepsilon), set0, set1, \phi, yes)$ for some $q \in Q$ and *set*0, *set*1 $\in 2^J\}$.

We say that a PDAA $M = (Q, \Sigma, \Gamma, \delta, q_0, Dir)$ is deterministic if:
(1) for each q in Q and Z in Γ, whenever $\delta(q, \varepsilon, Z)$ is nonempty, then $\delta(q, a, Z)$ is empty for all a in Σ; and
(2) for no q in Q, Z in Γ, and a in $\Sigma \cup \{\varepsilon\}$ does $\delta(q, a, Z)$ contain more than one element.

A parsing example of array pattern is shown in Appendix 2 and a PDAA architecture is shown in Appendix 3.

4. EQUIVALENCE OF PDAA AND ICFAG

It is easy to show that for any ICFAG G, there exists another ICFAG $G' = (V_N, V_T, P, S, \#)$ equivalent to G, whose rewriting rules can be found among the forms $A \vec{d} BC$, $A \vec{d} aC$, and $A \rightarrow a$, where A, B and $C \in V_N$, $a \in V_T$ and $d \in Dir/\{T\}$. For the purpose of convenience, the rewriting rules of ICFAGs discussed in this section are all restricted to these three forms.

A pushdown array automaton is tested on a VAX8650/VMS using PASCAL.

Lemma 4.1. If L is an ICFAL, then there exists a PDAA M such that $L = L(M)$.

Proof. Let $G = (V_N, V_T, S, P, \#)$ be an ICFAG generating L. Let $M = (\{q\}, V_T, V_N \cup V_T, \delta, q, S, Dir)$, where
(1) $\delta(q, \varepsilon, A)$ contains (d, q, BC) as a transition of type 1 whenever $A \vec{d} BC$ is in P, for each A, B, and $C \in V_N$,
(2) $\delta(q, a, A)$ contains (d, q, C) as a transition of type 2 whenever $A \vec{d} aC$ is in P, for each A and $C \in V_N$ and each $a \in \Sigma$, and
(3) $\delta(q, a, A)$ contains (T, q, ε) as a transition of type 3 whenever $A \rightarrow a$ is in P, for each $A \in V_N$ and each $a \in \Sigma$.
It is easy to show that $L(G) = L(M)$.

Example 4.2. Consider the ICFAG $G_3 = (\{S, A, A', B, C\}, \{a\}, P, S, \#)$ with $P = \{S\# \rightarrow AB,$

$B \rightarrow a, \quad \dfrac{A}{\#} \rightarrow \dfrac{a\ A}{A}, \quad \dfrac{A}{\#} \rightarrow \dfrac{a\ A'}{A'}, \quad \dfrac{A'}{\#} \rightarrow \dfrac{B\ C}{C}, \quad \dfrac{C}{\#} \rightarrow \dfrac{a}{C}, C \rightarrow a\}$, which generates the language

$$L_3 = \begin{array}{c} l \left\{ \begin{array}{l} \overbrace{aa \ldots a}^{m} \\ a \\ \cdot \\ \cdot \\ \cdot \end{array} \right. \\ \left. \begin{array}{l} a \quad n \quad m, k, l \geq 1, n \geq 0. \\ \underline{aa \ldots a} \end{array} \right. \\ k \left\{ \begin{array}{l} a \\ \cdot \\ \cdot \\ a \end{array} \right. \end{array}$$

The corresponding PDAA, according to the technique used in constructing an automaton in the proof of Lemma 4.1, is $M_3 = (\{q\}, \{a\}, \{S, A, B, C, a\}, \delta, q, S, Dir)$ with $\delta(q, \varepsilon, S) = \{(R, q, AB)\}$, $\delta(q, a, A) = \{(D, q, A), (D, q, A')\}$, $\delta(q, \varepsilon, A') = \{(D, q, BC)\}$, $\delta(q, a, B) = \{(R, q, B), (T, q, \varepsilon)\}$, and $\delta(q, a, C) = \{(D, q, C), (T, q, \varepsilon)\}$.

An example of acceptable configurations of the PDAA M_3 with an input array from L_3 is shown in Appendix 2.

Lemma 4.3. If $L = L(M)$ for some PDAA $M = (Q, \Sigma, \Gamma, \delta, q_0, Z_0, Dir)$, then L is an ICFAL.

Proof. Let $G = (V_N, \Sigma, P, S, \#)$ be an ICFAG, where $V_N = \{[q, A, p] \mid q, p \in Q, A \in \Gamma\}$. P is the set of productions:
(1) $S \rightarrow [q_0, Z_0, q]$ for each q in Q;
(2) $[q, A, q_3] \vec{d} [q_1, B, q_2][q_2, C, q_3]$ for each q, q_1, q_2 and q_3 in Q, and each A, B and C in Γ/Σ, such that $\delta(q, \varepsilon, A)$ contains (d, q_1, BC);
(3) $[q, A, q_2] \vec{d} a[q_1, C, q_2]$ for each q, q_1 and q_2 in Q, each a in Σ, A, C in Γ/Σ, such that $\delta(q, a, A)$ contains (d, q_1, C);
(4) $[q, A, q_1] \rightarrow a$ for each q, q_1 in Q, A in Γ/Σ and a in Σ, such that $\delta(q, a, A)$ contains (T, q_1, ε).

It is easy to show that $S \overset{*}{\Rightarrow}_{G} w$ if and only if $(q_0, w, (Z_0, (0, 0), \phi), \phi, \phi, \phi, yes) \vdash^{*}_{M} (q, \varepsilon, (\varepsilon, \varepsilon, \varepsilon), set0, set1, \phi, yes)$ for some q in Q and $set0, set1$ in 2^J.

Example 4.4. Consider $M = (\{q_0, q_1, q_2\}, \{a, b\}, \{A, B, C\}, \delta, q_0, A, Dir)$ with $\delta(q_0, \varepsilon, A) = \{(R, q_1, BC)\}$, $\delta(q_0, a, A) = \{(R, q_0, A)\}$, $\delta(q_1, b, B) = \{(D, q_1, B), (T, q_2, \varepsilon)\}$ and $\delta(q_2, a, C) = \{(R, q_2, C), (T, q_2, \varepsilon)\}$, which generates "T"-shaped arrays composed of as and bs as shown in Fig. 2. To construct an ICFAG $G = (V_N, V_T, P, S, \#)$ generating $L(M)$, let $V_N = \{S\} \cup \{[p, X, p'] \mid p, p' \in \{q_0, q_1, q_2\}, X \in \{A, B, C\}\}$ and $V_T = \{a, b\}$. To construct the set of productions easily, we must realize that some nonterminal symbols may not appear in any derivation starting with the symbol S. Thus, we can save some effort if we start with the productions for S, then add productions only for those nonterminal symbols that appear on the right of some productions already in the set. The productions for S are $S \rightarrow [q_0, A, q_0]$, $S \rightarrow [q_0, A, q_1]$ and $S \rightarrow [q_0, A, q_2]$. Next we add productions for each of the nonterminals $[q_0, A, q_0]$, $[q_0, A, q_1]$ and

$[q_0, A, q_2]$; there is only one production for $[q_0, A, q_0]$: $[q_0, A, q_0] \vec{R} a[q_0, A, q_0]$ which is required by $(R, q_0, A) \in \delta(q_0, a, A)$. Next, the production for $[q_0, A, q_1]$ is $[q_0, A, q_1] \vec{R} a[q_0, A, q_1]$ which is also required by $(R, q_0, A) \in \delta(q_0, a, A)$. The productions for the remaining nonterminals and the relevant moves of the PDAA are:

(1) $[q_0, A, q_2] \vec{R} a[q_0, A, q_2]$ since $(R, q_0, A) \in \delta(q_0, a, A)$,

(2) $[q_0, A, p] \vec{R} [q_1, B, p'][p', C, p]$ for each $p, p' \in \{q_0, q_1, q_2\}$ since $(R, q_1, BC) \in \delta(q_0, \varepsilon, A)$,

(3) $[q_1, B, q_0] \vec{D} b[q_1, B, q_0], [q_1, B, q_1] \vec{D} b[q_1, B, q_1]$ and $[q_1, B, q_2] \vec{D} b[q_1, B, q_2]$ since $(D, q_1, B) \in \delta(q_1, b, B)$,

(4) $[q_2, C, q_0] \vec{R} a[q_2, C, q_0], [q_2, C, q_1] \vec{R} a[q_2, C, q_1]$ and $[q_2, C, q_2] \vec{R} a[q_2, C, q_2]$ since $(R, q_2, C) \in \delta[q_2, a, C)$,

(5) $[q_1, B, q_2] \rightarrow b$ since $(T, q_2, \varepsilon) \in \delta(q_1, b, B)$ and

(6) $[q_2, C, q_2] \rightarrow a$ since $(T, q_2, \varepsilon) \in \delta(q_1, a_1, C)$.

It should be noted that there are no productions for the nonterminals $[q_0, C, q_0]$, $[q_0, C, q_1], [q_0, C, q_2], [q_1, C, q_0], [q_1, C, q_1]$ and $[q_1, C, q_2]$ and no terminal array can be derived from each of the nonterminals $[q_2, C, q_0], [q_2, C, q_1], [q_1, B, q]$ and $[q_1, B, q_1]$. Deleting all productions involving one of these ten nonterminals on either the right or left, we end up with the following productions:

$S \rightarrow [q_0, A, q_2]$,

$[q_0, A, q_2] \vec{R} a[q_0, A, q_2]$

$[q_1, A, q_2] \vec{D} b[q_1, B, q_2]$

$[q_2, C, q_2] \vec{R} a[q_2, C, q_2]$

$[q_1, B, q_2] \rightarrow b$

$[q_2, C, q_2] \rightarrow a$

$[q_0, A, q_2] \vec{R} [q_1, B, q_2] [q_2, C, q_2]$.

By Lemma 4.1 and Lemma 4.3, we obtain the following theorem:

Theorem 4.5. $\mathscr{L}(\text{PDAA}) = \mathscr{L}(\text{ICFAG})$.

5. RECOGNITION FOR NOISY ARRAYS

Up to now, we have only discussed the recognition for non-noisy patterns. However, noisy patterns can be "smoothed" before being recognized. As in Ref. 14, eight pattern primitives which are line segments with eight different orientations, $d_1 = \uparrow$, $d_2 = \nearrow$, $d_3 = \rightarrow$, $d_4 = \searrow$, $d_5 = \downarrow$, $d_6 = \swarrow$, $d_7 = \leftarrow$ and $d_8 = \nwarrow$ are selected. For example, the 3-primitive chains $d_1 d_2 d_1$, $d_4 d_4 d_6$ and $d_2 d_3 d_3$ are smoothed into $d_1 d_1 d_1$, $d_5 d_5 d_5$ and $d_3 d_3 d_3$ respectively. Several typical results from such data preparation are shown in Fig. 3.

For example, as in Fig. 4, the noisy patterns t and p can be smoothed into the new patterns t' and p' respectively.

$$l \geqslant 0 \; m \geqslant 1$$

$$\overline{aa.....a}\,\overline{baa.....a}$$

$$\left.\begin{array}{c} b \\ . \\ . \\ . \\ b \end{array}\right\} n \geqslant 0$$

Fig. 2. A T-shaped array.

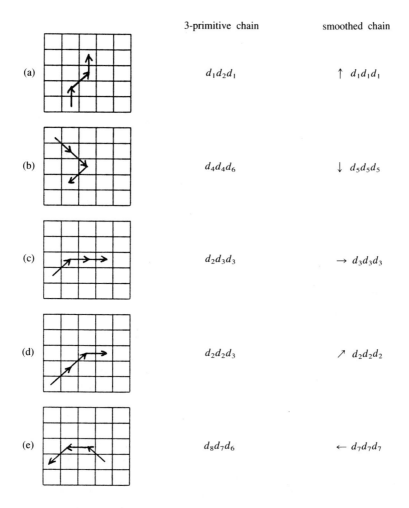

3-primitive chain   smoothed chain

(a) $d_1 d_2 d_1$ $\uparrow \; d_1 d_1 d_1$

(b) $d_4 d_4 d_6$ $\downarrow \; d_5 d_5 d_5$

(c) $d_2 d_3 d_3$ $\rightarrow d_3 d_3 d_3$

(d) $d_2 d_2 d_3$ $\nearrow \; d_2 d_2 d_2$

(e) $d_8 d_7 d_6$ $\leftarrow d_7 d_7 d_7$

Fig. 3. Primitive selections.

```
            aaaa
        aaa aaaa
    aa      a                       aaaaaaaaaaaaaa
            a                             a
            a                             a
            a                             a
          a                               a
          a                               a
          a                               a
        a                                 a
        a                                 a
        a                                 a
          a                               a
          a                               a
                                          a

    (a) A noisy pattern t.              (b) The smoothed pattern t'.
```

```
    aaaaaaaaaaa                       aaaaaaaaaaaaaa
    aa              a                 a               a
    a               a                 a               a
    a               a                 a               a
    a                   a             a               a
    a                   a             a               a
    aaaa        aaaaaa                aaaaaaaaaaaaaa
     a      aaaa                      a
     a                                a
     a                                a
     a                                a
       a                              a
       a                              a

    (c) A noisy pattern p.              (d) The smoothed pattern p'.
```

Fig. 4.   Some examples of primitive selections.

6.   CONCLUSIONS AND DISCUSSIONS

In this paper, we have presented pushdown array automata which are equipped with memories in order to parse the input arrays completely but not redundantly. In fact, ICFAGs are not entirely context-free; they are sensitive to the #s. This is the main reason why so many properties of the one-dimensional CFLs and PDA cannot be extended to the two-dimensional ICFALs and PDAA directly. For instance, $\{a^n b^n | n > 0\}$ is a CFL[15] but not an ICFAL.[16] Furthermore, due to the decision for directions, some ICFALs consisting of arrays with even simple patterns cannot be accepted by any DPDAA. The future research is to investigate a new PDAA which can widely accept ICFALs deterministically. Also it will be interesting to explore the relations between PDAA and another closely related model known as the Lindenmayer system.[17]

APPENDIX 1

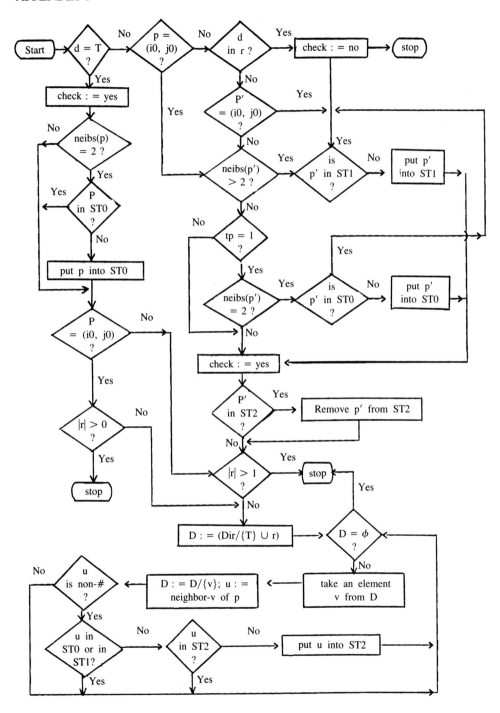

Flowchart PDAA Checking Parsable

APPENDIX 2

The array
$$\begin{matrix} aaa \\ a \\ aaa \\ a \\ a \end{matrix}$$
is accepted by M_3 through the following sequence of moves (where $(i_0, j_0) = (0, 0)$).

$(q,\ \begin{matrix} \text{ⓐ}aa \\ a \end{matrix},\ (S, (0, 0), \phi),\ \phi,\ \phi,\ \phi,\ yes) \vdash_{M_3}$
$$\begin{matrix} aaa \\ a \\ a \end{matrix}$$

$(q,\ \begin{matrix} \text{ⓐ}aa \\ a \end{matrix},\ (AB, (0, 0)(0, 1), \{R\}\{L\}),\ \{(0, 1)\},\ \phi,\ \{(1, 0)\},\ yes) \vdash_{M_3}$
$$\begin{matrix} aaa \\ a \\ a \end{matrix}$$

$(q,\ \begin{matrix} \cancel{a}aa \\ \text{ⓐ} \end{matrix},\ (AB, (1, 0)(0, 1), \{U\}\{L\}),\ \{(0, 1)\},\ \phi,\ \phi,\ yes) \vdash_{M_3}$
$$\begin{matrix} aaa \\ a \\ a \end{matrix}$$

$(q,\ \begin{matrix} \cancel{a}aa \\ \cancel{a} \\ \text{ⓐ} \end{matrix},\ (AB, (2, 0)(0, 1), \{U\}\{L\}),\ \{(0, 1)\},\ \phi,\ \phi,\ yes) \vdash_{M_3}$
$$\begin{matrix} aaa \\ a \\ a \end{matrix}$$

$(q,\ \begin{matrix} \cancel{a}aa \\ \cancel{a} \\ \cancel{a} \end{matrix},\ (A'B, (3, 0)(0, 1), \{U\}\{L\}),\ \{(0, 1)\},\ \{(3, 0)\},\ \phi,\ yes) \vdash_{M_3}$
$$\begin{matrix} \text{ⓐ}aa \\ a \\ a \end{matrix}$$

¢aa
¢
$(q, \quad ¢ \quad , (BCB, (3, 0)(4, 0)(0, 1), \{U, D\}\{U\}\{L\}), \{(0, 1), (4, 0)\}, \{(3, 0)\},$
ⓐaa $\{(3, 1)\}, yes) \vdash_{M_3}$
a
a

¢aa
¢
$(q, \quad ¢ \quad , (BCB, (3, 1)(4, 0)(0, 1), \{L\}\{U\}\{L\}), \{(0, 1), (4, 0)\}, \{(3, 0)\},$
¢ⓐa $\phi, yes) \vdash_{M_3}$
a
a

¢aa
¢
$(q, \quad ¢ \quad , (BCB, (3, 2)(4, 0)(0, 1), \{L\}\{U\}\{L\}), \{(0, 1), (4, 0)\}, \{(3, 0)\},$
¢¢ⓐ $\phi, yes) \vdash_{M_3}$
a
a

¢aa
¢
$(q, \quad ¢ \quad , (CB, (4, 0)(0, 1), \{U\}\{L\}), \{(0, 1), (4, 0)\}, \{(3, 0)\}, \phi, yes) \vdash_{M_3}$
¢¢¢
ⓐ
a

¢aa
¢
$(q, \quad ¢ \quad , (CB, (5, 0)(0, 1), \{U\}\{L\}), \{(0, 1), (4, 0)\}, \{(3, 0)\}, \phi, yes) \vdash_{M_3}$
¢¢¢
¢
ⓐ

¢ⓐa
¢
$(q, \quad ¢ \quad , (B, (0, 1), \{L\}), \{(0, 1), (4, 0)\}, \{(3, 0)\}, \phi, yes) \vdash_{M_3}$
¢¢¢
¢
¢

111

$¢¢@$
$¢$
$(q, ¢ \quad , (B, (0, 2), \{L\}), \{(0, 1), (4, 0)\}, \{(3, 0)\}, \phi, yes) \vdash_{M_3}$
$¢¢¢$
$¢$
$¢$

$¢¢¢$
$¢$
$(q, ¢ \quad , (\varepsilon, \varepsilon, \varepsilon), \{(0, 1), (4, 0)\}, \{(3, 0)\}, \phi, yes).$
$¢¢¢$
$¢$
$¢$

APPENDIX 3

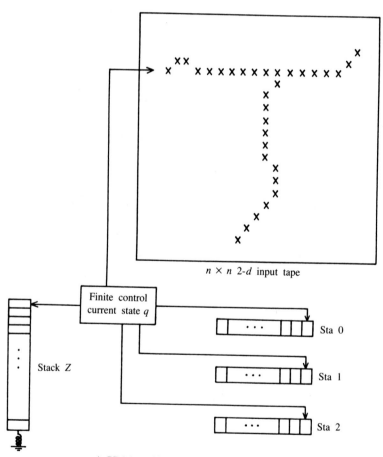

$n \times n$ 2-d input tape

A PDAA architecture as defined in Sect. 3.

REFERENCES

1. C. R. Cook and P. S. P. Wang, "A Chomsky hierarchy of isotonic array grammars and languages", *Computer Graphics and Image Processing* **8** (1978) 144–152.
2. A. Mercer and A. Rosenfeld, "An array grammar programming system", *C. ACM* **16** (1973) 299–305.
3. D. L. Milgram and A. Rosenfeld, "Array automata and array grammars", *IFIP Congress 71*, North-Holland Pub. Co., Amsterdam, 1971, Booklet TA-2, pp. 166–173.
4. A. Rosenfeld, "Coordinate grammars revisited: Generalized isometric grammars", *Int. J. Pattern Recognition and Artificial Intelligence* **3** (1989).
5. A. R. Smith III, "Cellular automata and formal languages", *Proc. 11th IEEE Symp. on Switching and Automata Theory*, 1970, pp. 144–152.
6. A. R. Smith III, "Two-dimensional formal languages and pattern recognition by cellular automata", *Proc. 12th IEEE Symp. on Switching and Automata Theory*, 1971, pp. 216–224.
7. P. S. P. Wang, "Sequential/Parallel matrix array languages", *J. Cybernetics* **5**, 4 (1975) 19–36.
8. P. S. P. Wang, "Some new results on isotonic array grammars", *Information Processing Letters* **10** 3 (1980) 129–131.
9. P. S. P. Wang and X. W. Dai, "A grammatical inference algorithm for digitized array patterns", *Proc. ICPR '86*, Paris, 1986, pp. 129–131.
10. P. S. P. Wang and H. J. Lin, "A pumping lemma for two-dimensional array languages", *Proc. ICPR '86*, Paris, 1986, pp. 126–128.
11. H. J. Lin and P. S. P. Wang, "Pushdown array automata", *Proc. International Computer Symposium*, Taipei, Taiwan, R. O. C., 1988, pp. 276–281.
12. A. Rosenfeld, *Picture Languages: Formal Models for Picture Recognition*, Academic Press, New York, 1979.
13. P. S. P. Wang, "An application of array grammars to clustering analysis for syntactic patterns", *Pattern Recognition* **17**, 4 (1984) 441–451.
14. K. S. Fu, *Syntactic Pattern Recognition and Applications*, Prentice-Hall, 1982, Chapter 10, pp. 349–410.
15. J. E. Hopcroft and J. D. Ullman, *Introduction to Automata Theory, Languages, and Computation*, Addison Wesley, 1979.
16. P. S. P. Wang, "Hierarchical structures and complexities of parallel isometric languages", *IEEE Trans. on Pattern Analysis and Machine Intelligence* **5**, 1 (1983) 92–99.
17. R. Siromoney, "Array languages and Lindenmayer systems—A survey", *The Book of L*, Eds. G. Rozenberg and A. Salomaa, Springer-Verlag, 1986, pp. 413–426.

Hwei Jen Lin received her B.S. degree from National Chiao Tung University, Taiwan in 1981, her M.S. degree from Northeastern University, Boston in 1984, and her Ph.D. degree in Computer Science and Mathematics from Northeastern University in 1989.

Dr. Lin is now a lecturer at the Department of Mathematics of Northeastern University. She has several publications in *ICPR '86* (Paris), *International Workshop on Structural Pattern Recognition '88* (Nancy) and *ICS '88* (Taipei). Her research interests lie in pattern recognition and automata theory.

Patrick S. P. Wang is a visiting scientist at MIT Artificial Intelligence Laboratory, on leave from Northeastern University. He received his Ph.D. degree in computer science from Oregon State University, his M.S.I.C.S. degree from Georgia Institute of Technology, his M.S.E.E. degree from National Taiwan University and his B.S.E.E. degree from National Chiao Tung University.

Before joining Northeastern University as tenured full Professor of Computer Science, he had been with WANG Laboratories, GTE Laboratories, Boston University and University of Oregon as software engineering specialist, senior member of technical staff, adjunct Associate Professor and Assistant Professor, respectively. He is now also teaching part-time at Harvard University.

Prof. Wang has edited four books and published over sixty technical papers in imaging technology, pattern recognition and artificial intelligence. One of his most recent inventions concerning Pattern Recognition Systems has been granted by the US Patent Bureau. He has attended and organized numerous international conferences for IEEE, ACM, ICS, AAAI, CLCS and the International Association for Pattern Recognition. He is also a reviewer for grants proposals of the NSF Intelligent Systems Division, and for several computer journals including *IEEE-PAMI, Computer Vision, Graphics, and Image Processing, Information Sciences* and *Information Processing Letters*. Prof. Wang is now an editor-in-charge of the *International Journal of Pattern Recognition and Artificial Intelligence*.

As a senior member of IEEE, Prof. Wang is also a member of ACM, AAAI, the Pattern Recognition Society and a governing board member and the newsletter editor of the Chinese Language Computer Society (CLCS), Washington, D.C. His research interests include software engineering, programming languages, pattern recognition, artificial intelligence, image technology, and automation.

Prof. Wang has also written several articles on the operas of Puccini and Wagner, and on Beethoven's and Mozart's symphonies.

THE SIMULATION OF TWO-DIMENSIONAL ONE-MARKER AUTOMATA BY THREE-WAY TURING MACHINES

AKIRA ITO

Technical College, Yamaguchi University, Ube, 755 Japan

KATSUSHI INOUE and ITSUO TAKANAMI

Faculty of Engineering, Yamaguchi University, Ube, 755 Japan

Received 23 April 1989

We denote a two-dimensional deterministic (nondeterministic) one-marker automaton by 2-DM$_1$ (2-NM$_1$), and a three-way two-dimensional deterministic (nondeterministic) Turing machine by TR2-DTM (TR2-NTM). In this paper, we show that the necessary and sufficient space for TR2-NTMs to simulate 2-DM$_1$s (2-NM$_1$s) is $n \log n$ (n^2), and the necessary and sufficient space for TR2-DTMs to simulate 2-DM$_1$s (2-NM$_1$s) is $2^{O(n \log n)}$ ($2^{O(n^2)}$), where n is the number of columns of rectangular input tapes.

Keywords: Two-dimensional one-marker automata; Three-way two-dimensional Turing machines; Space complexity.

1. INTRODUCTION

Intuitively, a 2-dimensional (multi-)marker automaton is a 2-dimensional finite automaton which can make marks on its input with the restriction that a bound number of these marks can exist at any given time. This automaton has been widely investigated. For example, 2-markers are strictly more powerful than 1-markers and 1-markers are strictly more powerful than 0-markers, a 1-marker can recognize connected pictures, nondeterministic 1-markers are strictly more powerful than deterministic ones, and so on.[1-3]

In this paper, we characterize 2-dimensional *1-marker* automata in terms of the spaces that *3-way* 2-dimensional Turing machines, which can move left, right, or down, but not up on rectangular input tapes, require and which suffice to simulate 1-marker automata. Our research will give a quantitative estimate of the power of 1-marker automata.

We denote a 2-dimensional deterministic (nondeterministic) 1-marker automaton by 2-DM$_1$ (2-NM$_1$), and a three-way 2-dimensional deterministic (nondeterministic) Turing machine by TR2-DTM (TR2-NTM). The results are shown in Table 2, where n is the number of columns of rectangular input tapes. Compare those with the case of a 2-dimensional deterministic (nondeterministic) finite automaton which is denoted by 2-DF (2-NF) in Table 1.

We can know, for example, from the first columns of both tables that the increase of markers from 0 to 1 causes an *exponential increase* of spaces for the simulations.

International Journal of Pattern Recognition and Artificial Intelligence Vol. 3 No. 3 & 4 (1989) 393–404
© World Scientific Publishing Company

Table 1. Necessary and sufficient space for Ys to simulate 0-marker Xs.

X \ Y	TR2-DTM	TR2-NTM
2-DF	$\Theta(n \log n)$	$\Theta(n)$
2-NF	$\Theta(n^2)$	$\Theta(n)$

Table 2. Necessary and sufficient space for Ys to simulate 1-marker Xs.

X \ Y	TR2-DTM	TR2-NTM
2-DM$_1$	$2^{\Theta(n \log n)}$	$\Theta(n \log n)$
2-NM$_1$	$2^{\Theta(n^2)}$	$\Theta(n^2)$

In this paper, the detailed definitions of 2-dimensional marker automata and (space-bounded) 3-way 2-dimensional Turing machines are omitted. If necessary, see Refs. 2 and 6.

2. PRELIMINARIES

Definition 2.1. Let Σ be a finite set of symbols. A *2-dimensional tape* over Σ is a 2-dimensional rectangular array of elements of Σ. The set of all 2-dimensional tapes over Σ is denoted by $\Sigma^{(2)}$.

For a tape $x \in \Sigma^{(2)}$, we let $l_1(x)$ be the number of rows of x and $l_2(x)$ be the number of columns of x. If $1 \leq i \leq l_1(x)$ and $1 \leq j \leq l_2(x)$, we let $x(i, j)$ denote the symbol in x with coordinates (i, j). Furthermore, we define

$$x[(i, j), (i', j')],$$

when $1 \leq i \leq i' \leq l_1(x)$ and $1 \leq j \leq j' \leq l_2(x)$, as the two-dimensional tape z satisfying the following:
(i) $l_1(z) = i' - i + 1$ and $l_2(z) = j' - j + 1$,
(ii) for each k, r [$1 \leq k \leq l_1(z)$, $1 \leq r \leq l_2(z)$], $z(k, r) = x(k + i - 1, r + j - 1)$.
When a 2-dimensional tape x is given to any 2-dimensional automaton as an input, x is surrounded by the boundary symbol $\#$.

Definition 2.2. Let x be in $\Sigma^{(2)}$ and $l_2(x) = n$. When $l_1(x)$ is divided by n, we call

$$x[((j - 1)n + 1, 1), (j \cdot n, n)]$$

an *n-block of x*, for each $j(1 \leq j \leq l_1(x)/n)$.

Definition 2.3. For any 2-dimensional automaton M with input alphabet Σ, define $T(M) = \{x \in \Sigma^{(2)} \mid M \text{ accepts } x\}$. Furthermore, define

$$\mathcal{L}[2\text{-}DM_1] = \{T \mid T = T(M) \text{ for some } 2\text{-}DM_1M\} \text{ and}$$
$$\mathcal{L}[2\text{-}NM_1] = \{T \mid T = T(M) \text{ for some } 2\text{-}NM_1M\}.$$

We similarly define $\mathcal{L}[TR2\text{-}DTM(L(m, n))]$ ($\mathcal{L}[TR2\text{-}NTM(L(m, n))]$) as the class of sets accepted by $L(m, n)$ space-bounded TR2-DTMs (TR2-NTMs).

By using an ordinary technique, we can easily show that the following theorem holds.

Theorem 2.4. For any function $L(n) \geq \log n$, $\mathcal{L}[TR2\text{-}NTM(L(n))] \subseteq \mathcal{L}[TR2\text{-}DTM(2^{O(L(n))})]$.

3. SUFFICIENT SPACES

In this section, we investigate the sufficient spaces (i.e. upper bounds) for 3-way Turing machines to simulate 1-marker automata. We first show that $n \log n$ space is sufficient for TR2-NTMs to simulate $2\text{-}DM_1$s.

Theorem 3.1. $\mathcal{L}[2\text{-}DM_1] \subseteq \mathcal{L}[TR2\text{-}NTM(n \log n)]$.

Proof. Suppose that a $2\text{-}DM_1$ M is given. Let the set of states of M be S. We partition S into two disjoint subsets S^+ and S^- which correspond to the sets of states when M is holding and not holding the marker in the finite control respectively. (Rigorously, neither S^+ nor S^- contains the states in which the input head of M is positioned on the same cell where the marker is placed.) We assume that the initial state q_0 and the unique accepting state q_a of M are both in S^+. In order to make our proof clear, we also assume that M begins to move with its input head on the rightmost bottom boundary symbol # of an input tape and, when M accepts an input, it enters the accepting state at the rightmost bottom boundary symbol.

Suppose that an input tape x with $l_1(x) = m$ and $l_2(x) = n$ is given to M. For M and x, we define three types of mappings $f^{\uparrow-}_i : S^- \times \{0, 1, \ldots, n + 1\} \rightarrow S^- \times \{0, 1, \ldots, n + 1\} \cup \{l\}$, $f^{\uparrow+}_i : S^+ \times \{0, 1, \ldots, n + 1\} \rightarrow S^+ \times \{0, 1, \ldots, n + 1\} \cup \{l\}$, and $f^{\downarrow-}_i : S^- \times \{0, 1, \ldots, n + 1\} \rightarrow S^- \times \{0, 1, \ldots, n + 1\} \cup \{l\}$ ($i = 0, 1, \ldots, m + 1$) as follows.

$f^{\uparrow-}_i(q^-, j) =$ $(q^{-\prime}, j')$: Suppose that we make M start from the configuration $(q^-, (i - 1, j))$ with no marker on the input x (i.e. we take away the marker from the input tape by force). After that, if M reaches the ith row of x in some time, the configuration corresponding to the first arrival is $(q^{-\prime}, (i, j'))$;

         l : Starting from the configuration $(q^-, (i - 1, j))$ with no marker on the input tape, M never reaches the ith row of x.

$f^{\uparrow+}_i(q^+, j) =$ $(q^{+\prime}, j')$: Suppose that we make M start from the configuration $(q^+, (i - 1, j))$. After that, if M reaches the ith row of x with its marker held in the finite control in some time (so, when M puts down the marker on the way, it must return to this position again and pick up the marker), the

$$f^{\downarrow-}{}_i(q^-, j) =$$

configuration corresponding to the first arrival is $(q^{+\prime}, (i, j'))$;

l : Starting from the configuration $(q^+, (i - 1, j))$ with no marker on the tape, M never reaches the ith row of x with its marker held in the finite control.

$(q^{-\prime}, j')$: Suppose that we make M start from the configuration $(q^-, (i + 1, j))$ with no marker on the input tape (i.e. we take away the marker from the input tape by force). After that, if M reaches the ith row of x in some time, the configuration corresponding to the first arrival is $(q^{-\prime}, (i, j'))$;

l : Starting from the configuration $(q^-, (i + 1, j))$ with no marker on the tape, M never reaches the ith row of x.

Below, we show that there exists a TR2-NTM $(n \log n)$ M' such that $T(M') = T(M)$. Roughly speaking, while scanning from the top row down to the bottom row of the input, M' guesses $f^{\downarrow-}{}_i$, constructs $f^{\uparrow-}{}_{i+1}$ and $f^{\uparrow+}{}_{i+1}$, checks $f^{\downarrow-}{}_{i-1}$, and finally at the bottom row of the input, M' decides by using $f^{\uparrow-}{}_{m+1}$ and $f^{\uparrow+}{}_{m+1}$ whether or not M accepts x (see Fig. 1). In order to record these mappings for each i, $O(n)$ blocks of $O(\log n)$ size suffice, so in total $O(n \log n)$ cells of the working tape suffice. More precisely, the working tape must be used as a "multi-track" tape. In the following discussion, we omit the detailed construction of the working tape of M'.

First, set $f^{\uparrow}{}_0$, $f^{\uparrow+}{}_0$ to the fixed value l.

For $i = 0$ to $m + 1$, repeat the following. [$f^{\uparrow-}{}_i, f^{\uparrow+}{}_i$ are already computed at the $(i - 1)$th row.]

(0) Go to the ith row; when $i = 0$, assume the boundary symbols on the first row.

(1) Guess $f^{\downarrow-}{}_i$; if $i = m + 1$, set $f^{\downarrow-}{}_{m+1}$ to the fixed value l.

(2) [Compute $f^{\uparrow-}{}_{i+1}$ from $f^{\uparrow-}{}_i$] When $i \neq m + 1$, do the following: assume that there is no marker on the input tape. For each $(q^-, j) \in S^- \times \{0, 1, \ldots, n + 1\}$, start to simulate M from the configuration $(q^-, (i, j))$. While M moves only at the ith row, behave just as M does. On the way of the simulation, if M goes up to the $(i - 1)$th row at the kth column and enters the internal state p^-, then search the table $f^{\uparrow-}{}_i$ to know the behavior of M above the ith row. If the value $f^{\uparrow-}{}_i(p^-, k)$ is "l", write "l" into the block corresponding to $f^{\uparrow-}{}_{i+1}(q^-, j)$; if the value $f^{\uparrow-}{}_i(p^-, k)$ is "$(p^{-\prime}, k')$", restart the simulation of M from the configuration $(p^{-\prime}, (i, k'))$. While continuing to move in this way, if M goes down to the $(i + 1)$th row, then write the pair of the internal state and column number just after that movement into the block corresponding to $f^{\uparrow-}{}_{i+1}(q^-, j)$ of the working tape. If M never goes down to the $(i + 1)$th row (including the case when M enters a loop), then write "l" into the correspondent block.

(3) [Compute $f^{\uparrow+}{}_{i+1}$ from $f^{\uparrow-}{}_i, f^{\uparrow+}{}_i$ and $f^{\downarrow-}{}_i$] When $i \neq m + 1$, do the following: for each $(q^+, j) \in S^+ \times \{0, 1, \ldots, n + 1\}$, starting from the configuration $(q^+, (i, j)$, simulate M until M goes down to the $(i + 1)$th row with the marker in the finite control. On the way of the simulation, if M would go up to the $(i - 1)$th row

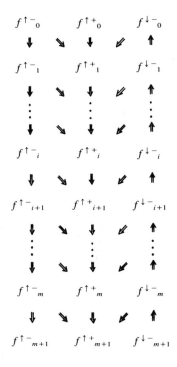

$$f^{\uparrow-}_0 \qquad f^{\uparrow+}_0 \qquad f^{\downarrow-}_0$$

$$f^{\uparrow-}_1 \qquad f^{\uparrow+}_1 \qquad f^{\downarrow-}_1$$

$$f^{\uparrow-}_i \qquad f^{\uparrow+}_i \qquad f^{\downarrow-}_i$$

$$f^{\uparrow-}_{i+1} \qquad f^{\uparrow+}_{i+1} \qquad f^{\downarrow-}_{i+1}$$

$$f^{\uparrow-}_m \qquad f^{\uparrow+}_m \qquad f^{\downarrow-}_m$$

$$f^{\uparrow-}_{m+1} \qquad f^{\uparrow+}_{m+1} \qquad f^{\downarrow-}_{m+1}$$

Fig. 1.   Interdependency of the mappings.

with the marker held, then search the table $f^{\uparrow+}_i$ to know the behavior of M above the ith row. If this value of $f^{\uparrow+}_i$ is "l", write "l" into the block corresponding to $f^{\uparrow+}_{i+1}(q^-, j)$; otherwise, restart the simulation of M from the configuration on the ith row determined by the table value. If M puts the marker down on the ith row of the input tape, then record the column number of this position in some track of the working tape and start the simulation of M which has no marker in the finite control. After that, if M goes down to the $(i + 1)$th row or goes up to the $(i - 1)$th row, then search the respective table $f^{\downarrow-}_i$ or $f^{\uparrow-}_i$ to find the configuration in which M returns to the ith row again. (If M never returns to the ith row, write "l" into the block corresponding to $f^{\uparrow+}_{i+1}(q^+, j)$). From this configuration, restart the simulation of M. After that, if M returns to the position where it put down the marker previously and picks it up, then continue the simulation of M; otherwise write "l" into the block corresponding to (q^+, j). At some point of the simulation, if M goes down to the $(i + 1)$th row with the marker held in the finite control, write the pair of the internal state which M would enter just after that time and the row number of this head position into the block corresponding to $f^{\uparrow+}_{i+1}(q^+, j)$. If M never goes down to the $(i + 1)$th row with the marker held in the finite control, then write "l" into the correspondent block.

(4) [Check the validity of $f^{\downarrow-}_{i-1}$ by $f^{\downarrow-}_i$] When $i \neq 0$, do the following: in order to check that the table $f^{\downarrow-}_{i-1}$ guessed on the previous row is consistent with the table $f^{\downarrow-}_i$ (guessed at the present row), first newly compute a mapping $\underline{f^{\downarrow-}_{i-1}}$,

which is uniquely determined from $f^{\downarrow -}{}_i$ and the content of the ith row of the input. [Assume that there is no marker on the input tape. For each $(q^-, j) \in S^- \times \{0, 1, \ldots, n + 1\}$, M' starts to simulate M from the configuration $(q^-, (i, j))$. While M moves only at the ith row, M' behaves just as M does. On the way of the simulation, if M goes down to the $(i + 1)$th row at the kth column and enters the internal state p^-, then M' searches the table $f^{\downarrow -}{}_i$ to know the behavior of M below the ith row. If the value $f^{\downarrow -}{}_i(p^-, k)$ is "l", M' writes "l" into the block corresponding to $f^{\downarrow -}{}_{i-1}(q^-, j)$; if the value $f^{\downarrow -}{}_i(p^-, k)$ is "$(p^{-\prime}, k')$", M' restarts the simulation of M from the configuration $(p^{-\prime}, (i, k'))$. While continuing to move in this way, if M goes up to the $(i - 1)$th row, then M' writes the pair of the internal state and column number just after that movement into the block corresponding to $f^{\downarrow -}{}_{i-1}(q^-, j)$ of the working tape. If M never goes up to the $(i - 1)$th row (including the case when M enters a loop), then M' writes "l" into the correspondent block.] After this computation, check that $f^{\downarrow -}{}_{i-1}$ is identical to the mapping $f^{\downarrow -}{}_{i-1}$ guessed at the previous row. If the equality holds, then continue the process; otherwise, reject and halt.

After the above procedure, on the $(m + 1)$th row, M' begins to simulate M from the initial configuration $(q^+{}_0, (m + 1, n + 1))$ to decide whether or not M accepts the input after all. When M goes up to the mth row with or without the marker, we can know how M returns again to the $(m + 1)$th row, from $f^{\uparrow -}{}_{m+1}$ or $f^{\uparrow +}{}_{m+1}$ respectively. If M never returns to the $(m + 1)$th row again, then M' rejects and halts. If M returns to the $(m + 1)$th row, then M' continues the simulation. M' accepts the input x only if M' finds that M enters the accepting configuration $(q^+{}_a, (m + 1, n + 1))$. It will be obvious that $T(M) = T(M')$. ∎

From Theorem 2.4 and Theorem 3.1, we get the following.

Corollary 3.2. $\mathcal{L}[\text{2-DM}_1] \subseteq \mathcal{L}[\text{TR2-DTM}(2^{O(n\log n)})]$.

We next show that n^2 space is sufficient for TR2-NTMs to stimulate 2-NM$_1$s. The basic idea and outline of the proof are the same as those of Theorem 3.1.

Theorem 3.3. $\mathcal{L}[\text{2-NM}_1] \subseteq \mathcal{L}[\text{TR2-NTM}(n^2)]$.

Proof. Suppose that a 2-NM$_1$ M and an input x with $l_1(x) = m$ and $l_2(x) = n$ are given. We take the same assumptions and notations for the states of M, i.e. initial and accepting configurations of M, as in the proof of Theorem 3.1.

From M and x, we define three types of mappings $g^{\uparrow -}{}_i : S^- \times \{0, 1, \ldots, n + 1\} \to 2^{S^- \times \{0,1,\ldots,n+1\}}$, $g^{\uparrow +}{}_i : S^+ \times \{0, 1, \ldots, n + 1\} \to 2^{S^+ \times \{0,1,\ldots,n+1\}}$, and $g^{\downarrow -}{}_i : S^- \times \{0, 1, \ldots, n + 1\} \to 2^{S^- \times \{0,1,\ldots,n+1\}}$ $(i = 0, 1, \ldots, m + 1)$ as follows.

$g^{\uparrow -}{}_i(q^-, j) \ni (q^{-\prime}, j')$: Suppose that we take away the marker of M from the input tape. Then, there exists a sequence of moves in which M starts from the configuration $(q^-, (i - 1, j))$ and reaches the ith row of x in the configuration $(q^{-\prime}, (i, j))$ for the first time.

$g^{\uparrow+}{}_i(q^+, j) \ni (q^{+\prime}, j')$: There exists a sequence of moves in which M starts from the configuration $(q^+, (i-1, j))$ and reaches the ith row of x in the configuration $(q^{+\prime}, (i, j'))$ for the first time with its marker in the finite control (so, when M puts down the marker on the way, there exists a sequence of moves in which M returns to this position and picks up the marker).

$g^{\downarrow-}{}_i(q^-, j) \ni (q^{-\prime}, j')$: Suppose that we take away the marker from the input tape. Then, there exists a sequence of moves in which M starts from the configuration $(q^-, (i+1, j))$ and M reaches the ith row of x in the configuration $(q^{-\prime}, (i, j'))$ for the first time.

Note that, in order to record these mappings for each i, $O(n^2)$ cells of working tape suffice in total. Roughly speaking, a TR2-NTM M' accepting $T(M)$ acts as follows: while scanning from the top row down to the bottom row of the input, M' guesses $g^{\downarrow-}{}_i$, constructs $g^{\uparrow-}{}_{i+1}$ and $g^{\uparrow+}{}_{i+1}$, checks $g^{\uparrow-}{}_{i-1}$, and finally at the bottom row of the input, M' decides whether or not M accepts x by using $g^{\uparrow-}{}_{m+1}$ and $g^{\uparrow+}{}_{m+1}$.

First, set $g^{\uparrow-}{}_0 = \varnothing$ and $g^{\uparrow+}{}_0 = \varnothing$.

For $i = 0$ to $m+1$ repeat the following:

(0) Go to the ith row.

(1) Guess $g^{\downarrow-}{}_i$; when $i = m+1$, set $g^{\downarrow-}{}_{m+1} = \varnothing$.

(2) Compute $g^{\uparrow-}{}_{i+1}$ from $g^{\uparrow-}{}_i$ (for $i \neq m+1$). Details are omitted. See (3) below.

(3) [Compute $g^{\uparrow+}{}_{i+1}$ from $g^{\uparrow-}{}_i$, $g^{\uparrow+}{}_i$, and $g^{\downarrow-}{}_i$ (for $i \neq m+1$)] For each $(q^+, j) \in S^+ \times \{0, 1, \ldots, n+1\}$, M' does the following to compute $g^{\uparrow+}{}_{i+1}(q^+, j)$: M' starts to simulate M from the configuration $(q^+, (i, j))$. Since M is nondeterministic, M' tries to examine the whole possibilities of the moves of M in a systematic way. To this end, M' will construct the list $H^+(q^+, j)$ which consists of state and column-position pairs and which implies the set of all the configurations (with the marker in the finite control) on the ith row which are reachable from $(q^+, (i, j))$ after some steps, with the restriction that M does not move below the ith row with the marker. Note that the size of the set is $O(n)$. M' constructs the list $H^+(q^+, j)$ as follows. Initially, $H^+(q^+, j) = \{(q^+, j)\}$. M' updates the list by performing all the possible one step simulations of M for each unexamined configuration contained in the list as follows:

(i)   While M moves along the ith row with the marker in the finite control, M simply adds the pair of the state and column-position of such a configuration to $H^+(q, j)$.

(ii) If M would go up to the $(i-1)$th row at some column j_1 with the marker held in the finite control and would enter some state q_1, then search for $g^{\uparrow+}{}_i(q_1, j_1)$ and add it to $H^+(q^+, j)$.

(iii) If M would put down the marker at the kth column on the ith row and would enter the state p^-, then M' must know all the configurations in which M returns to the same position and picks up the marker. To this end, M' calls a subroutine which examines the whole moves of M with no marker after the configuration $(p^-, (i, k))$. In the subroutine, M' constructs another list $H^-(p^-, k)$ of size $O(n)$ which will contain all the possible configurations (without the marker) on the ith row which are reachable from the configuration $(p^-, (i, k))$ after some steps with the assumption that the marker is placed on the kth column of the ith row. Initially, $H^-(p^-, k) = \{(p^-, k)\}$. M' updates $H^-(p^-, k)$ by performing one step simulation of M for each configuration contained in $H^-(p^-, k)$ as follows:

(a) While M moves along the ith row, M' simply adds these configurations to $H^-(p^-, k)$.

(b) If M would go down to the $(i + 1)$th row or would go up to the $(i - 1)$th row, then search the respective table $g^{\downarrow -}_i$ or $g^{\uparrow -}_i$ to find all the configurations in which M again returns to the ith row and add those to $H^-(p^-, k)$.

After at most $O(n)$ updates, $H^-(p^-, k)$ does not change any more. The subroutine then terminates. At this time, M' searches the list $H^-(p^-, k)$ for each configuration c in which M returns to the position where M had put down the marker previously (i.e. the k-column of the ith row), and M' adds to list $H^+(q^+, j)$ all the configurations which are reachable from c by one step simulation of M and which hold the marker in the finite control.

After at most $O(n)$ updates of $H^+(q^+, j)$, M' can construct the desired list $H^+(q', j)$. At this time, performing one step simulation of M from each configuration contained in $H^+(q^+, j)$, M' tests if there exists a configuration in which M goes down to the $(i + 1)$th row with the marker held in the finite control, and adds to $g^{\uparrow +}_{i+1}(q^+, j)$ the configuration just after that movement. This completes all of the task for (q^+, j).

(4) Check the validity of $g^{\downarrow -}_{i-1}$ by $g^{\downarrow -}_i$ (for $i \neq 0$). Details are omitted. See (3) above.

After the above procedure, by using the two mappings $g^{\uparrow -}_{m+1}$ and $g^{\uparrow +}_{m+1}$, M' checks that there exists a sequence of moves of M from the initial configuration $(q^+_0, (m + 1, n + 1))$ to the accepting configuration $(q^+_a, (m + 1, n + 1))$ and decides whether M accepts the input x. If M' finds that M accepts x, then M' also accepts x. Otherwise, M' rejects x. It will be obvious that $T(M) = T(M')$. ■

From Theorem 2.4 and Theorem 3.3, we get the following.

Corollary 3.4. $\mathcal{L}[\text{2-NM}_1] \subseteq \mathcal{L}[\text{TR2-DTM}(2^{O(n^2)})]$.

4. NECESSARY SPACES

In this section, we show that the algorithms described in the previous section are optimal in some sense. That is, those spaces are required (i.e. the lower bounds) for 3-way Turing machines when the spaces depend only on one variable n (= the number of columns of the input tapes).

Lemma 4.1. Let $T_1 = \{x \in \{0, 1\}^{(2)} | \exists n \geq 1(l_2(x) = n$ & (each row of x contains exactly one "1") & $\exists k \geq 2[(x$ has k n-blocks) & (the last n-block is equal to some other n-block)]]\}$. Then,

(1) $T_1 \in \mathscr{L}(2\text{-DM}_1]$, but

(2) $T_1 \notin \mathscr{L}(\text{TR2-DTM}(2^{L(n)}))]$ (so, $T_1 \notin \mathscr{L}(\text{TR2-NTM}(L(n)))])$ for any function L such that $\lim_{n \to \infty} [L(n)/n \log n] = 0$.

Proof.

(1) We construct a 2-DM$_1$ M accepting T_1 as follows. Given an input x with $l_2(x) = n$, M first checks that each row of x contains exactly one "1" by horizontal sweep on each row and that x consists of k n-blocks for some $k \geq 2$ by a zigzag of 45°-direction from top to bottom. Then, M tests whether some n-block is identical to the last n-block (i.e. the kth n-block) from the first block to the next-to-last block by utilizing its own marker (see Fig. 2): In some n-block and some row of this block, say the jth block and ith row, M first puts the marker on the position where the input tape symbol is "1", then M starts to zigzag from the rightmost cell of the ith row of this block until it reaches the bottom boundary. M then goes back to the "1" position on the ith row of the last block. From this position, M vertically moves up until it encounters the marker put previously by itself or arrives at the top boundary. If M meets the marker again, then the ith rows of the two blocks are identical and M proceeds to check the $(i + 1)$th rows of the two blocks. If M does not meet the marker again, M can conclude that the jth n-block and the last n-block are different and must go to the next n-block to test the equality. M accepts x, if M finds that some n-block is identical to the last block (this fact is recognized from the fact that when M reaches the bottom boundary, this is the rightmost position there). It is clear that $T(M) = T_1$.

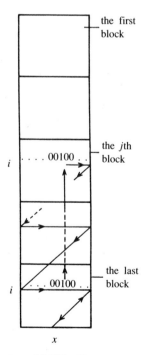

Fig. 2. Action of 2-DM$_1$ M on a tape x in T_1.

123

(2) Suppose to the contrary, there exists a TR2-DTM($2^{L(n)}$) M accepting T_1. Let s and t be the number of states in the finite control and storage tape symbols of M respectively. We assume without loss of generality that if M accepts an input, then M enters an accepting state at the bottom boundary. For each $n \geqslant 1$, let

$$V(n) = \{x \in T_1 \mid \exists\, n \geqslant 1[l_2(x) = n \ \& \ (x \text{ has exactly } (2^{n \log n} + 1) \ n\text{-blocks})]\}.$$

For each $x \in V(n)$, let

$$B(x) = \{b \in \{0,\ 1\}^{(2)} \mid \exists\, i(1 \leqslant i \leqslant 2^{n \log n}) \ [b \text{ is the } i\text{th } n\text{-block of } x)]\},$$

and let $S(n) = \{B(x) \mid x \in V(n)\}$. Note that for each $x \in V(n)$, there is a sequence of configuration of M which leads M to an accepting state. Let conf(x) be the configuration just after M leaves the second-to-last n-block of x.

Proposition 4.2. For any two tapes $x, y \in V(n)$, if $B(x) \neq B(y)$, then conf(x) $\neq$ conf(y).

Proof. Suppose to the contrary that conf(x) = conf(y) for some x, y in $V(n)$ such that $B(x) \neq B(y)$. Without loss of generality, we assume that there exists an n-*block* b such that $b \in B(x)$ and $b \notin B(y)$. From this n-block b, we make up a new tape z consisting of $(2^{n \log n} + 1)$ n-blocks such that the first $2^{n \log n}$ blocks are equal to those of y and the last n-block is b. Clearly, z is not in T_1. On such a tape z, M eventually enters an accepting state, because conf(x) = conf(y) and M accepts x, which contradicts the assumption that M does not accept a tape not in T_1. ∎

Proof of Lemma 4.1(2) (continued). There are at most

$$E(n) = (n + 2) \cdot s \cdot 2^{L(n)} \cdot t^{2^{L(n)}}$$

different configurations of M when crossing into the last n-block of tapes in $V(n)$. On the other hand, there exist

$$2^{2^{n \log n}}$$

different elements in $S(n)$. Since $\lim_{n \to \infty} [L(n)/n \log n] = 0$, it follows that there exists an integer n such that $|S(n)| > E(n)$ holds. For such n, there exist two tapes x, y in $V(n)$ such that $B(x) \neq B(y)$ and conf(x) = conf(y). This contradicts Proposition 4.2. Therefore, we can conclude that no TR2-DTM($2^{L(n)}$) accepts T_1. ∎

From Lemma 4.1, we can get the following theorem for 2-DM$_1$.

Theorem 4.3. To simulate 2-DM$_1$s, (1) TR2-NTMs require Ω ($n \log n$) space and (2) TR2-DTMs require $2^{\Omega(n \log n)}$ space.

Lemma 4.4. Let $T_2 = \{x \in \{0,\ 1\}^{(2)} \mid \exists\, n \geqslant 1[l_2(x) = n \ \& \ \exists\, k \geqslant 2[(x \text{ has } k \ n\text{-blocks}) \ \& \ (\text{the last } n\text{-block is equal to some other } n\text{-block})]]\}$. Then,

(1) $T_2 \in \mathscr{L}(2\text{-NM}_1]$, but
(2) $T_2 \notin \mathscr{L}[\text{TR2-DTM}(2^{L(n)})]$ (so, $T_2 \notin \mathscr{L}[\text{TR2-NTM}(L(n))]$) for any function L such that $\lim_{n\to\infty} [L(n)/n^2] = 0$.

Proof.   It is shown in Ref. 3 that Part (1) holds. By using the same technique as in the proof of Lemma 4.1(2), we can show that Part (2) holds.   ■

From Lemma 4.4, we can get the desired result for 2-NM$_1$ as follows.

Theorem 4.5.   To simulate 2-NM$_1$s,
(1) TR2-NTMs require Ω (n^2) space and
(2) TR2-DTMs require $2^{\Omega(n^2)}$ space.

5.   DISCUSSION

In this paper, we have investigated how much space is required and suffices for 3-way Turing machines to simulate 2-dimensional 1-marker automata on any vertically long input tapes and have given the satisfactory answers to this question.

By a slight improvement of the algorithms in the proofs of Theorem 3.1 and Theorem 3.3 when the number of rows are greater than the number of columns of input tapes, and the extended argument of the proofs of Lemma 3.4 and Lemma 3.5 in Ref. 6, we can get the following results: the necessary and sufficient spaces for TR2-NTMs to simulate 2-DM$_1$s and 2-NM$_1$s are

$$n \cdot \min\{\log m, \ \log n\} \quad \text{and} \quad n \cdot \min\{m, \ n\} \quad (m \geq 2),$$

respectively, which are the most general expressions as the two-variable space-complexity function $L(m, n)$. The formal proofs will appear in a subsequent paper.

REFERENCES

1. M. Blum and C. Hewitt, "Automata on a 2-dimensional tape", *Proc. 8th IEEE Symposium of Switching and Automata Theory*, 1967, pp. 155–160.
2. A. Rosenfeld, *Picture Languages—Formal models for Picture Recognition*, Academic Press, 1979.
3. K. Inoue and A. Nakamura, "Some properties of two-dimensional nondeterministic finite automata and parallel sequential array acceptors", *Trans. Institute of Electronics and Communication Engineers of Japan*. **60-D** (1977) 990–997.
4. K. Morita, H. Umeo and K. Sugata, "Accepting abilities of offside-free two-dimensional marker automata—The simulation of four-way automata by three-way tape-bounded Turing machines", *Tech. Reports of the Institute of Electronics and Communication Engineers of Japan* **AL79**, 19 (1979) 1–10.
5. K. Inoue and A. Nakamura, "Some properties of two-dimensional on-line tessellation acceptors", *Information Sciences* **13** (1977) 95–121.
6. K. Inoue and I. Takanami, "A note on deterministic three-way tape-bounded two-dimensional Turing machines", *Information Sciences* **20** (1980) 41–55.

Akira Ito received the B.S. and M.S. degrees in electronics engineering from Yamaguchi University. Since 1983, he has been an Assistant of the Technical College, Yamaguchi University. His current interests are automata theory and digital image processing.

Katsushi Inoue received the B.E. and M.E. degrees in electrical engineering from Hiroshima University, in 1969 and 1971 respectively, and the Ph.D. degree in electrical engineering from Nagoya University in 1977. From 1971 to 1973, he joined Musashino Electrical Communication Laboratory, NTT, Musashino. From 1973 to 1977, he was an Assistant Professor of Hiroshima University and from 1977 to 1987, he was an Associate Professor of Yamaguchi University. He is presently a Professor in the Faculty of Engineering, Yamaguchi University. His main interests are automata theory, computer geometry and parallel processing.

Itsuo Takanami received the M.E. and D.E. degrees in electrical and communication engineering from Tohoku University, Sendai, in 1967 and 1970 respectively. In March 1970 he joined Tohoku University, where from 1971 to 1972 and from 1972 to 1974 he was an Assistant and an Associate Professor respectively. He is presently a Professor in the Faculty of Engineering, Yamaguchi University. His current interests are automata theory, parallel processing and multi-valued logic circuits.

SYSTOLIC PYRAMID AUTOMATA, CELLULAR AUTOMATA AND ARRAY LANGUAGES

KAMALA KRITHIVASAN and MEENA MAHAJAN

Department of Computer Science and Engineering
Indian Institute of Technology, Madras 600 036, India

Received 30 April 1989
Revised 15 May 1989

Systolic pyramid automata accepting square arrays are defined. Homogeneous and semi-homogeneous pyramid automata are shown to have equal power though regular pyramid automata are more powerful. Languages accepted by these automata are compared with languages generated by array grammars and languages accepted by one-way 2-D cellular automata. Hexagonal pyramid automata are also considered and are shown to accept some languages generated by hexagonal array grammars.

Keywords: Systolic automata; Pyramid automata; Cellular automata; Array grammars; Hexagonal array languages.

1. INTRODUCTION

It is known that systolic systems with simple interconnection networks (like tree-structured, linear, orthogonal or hexagonally interconnected) can solve nontrivial problems like matrix multiplication, sorting, etc.[1]

A systolic system is called pure if there is an integer k such that every path from an input node to an output node possesses delay k.[2] The study of pure systolic systems began in Ref. 3, where systolic tree automata were studied as language recognition devices. Hexagonally connected networks are more powerful than tree-like structures, and in Refs. 4 and 5, these systems are studied as language recognition devices. Many properties of these systolic trellis automata are studied in Refs. 6 and 7.

A natural extension of string languages is array languages which consist of rectangular arrays of terminals. In Ref. 8, many formal models generating interesting classes of pictures are presented. Some models have been defined in Refs. 9–11 to generate rectangular arrays which describe picture languages.

In Ref. 8, cellular pyramid automata are defined and they accept square arrays of terminals. There are processors in different levels and in level n there are $2^n \times 2^n$ processors. Each processor has four sons in the next level, one father in the previous level, and four brothers in the same level. The square array of size $2^n \times 2^n$ is fed in at the proper level and is said to be accepted if the root (processor at level 1) attains a final state. Many of its properties are discussed and its power is compared with cellular array acceptors. The main drawback in this model is that only arrays of size $2^n \times 2^n$ (n is an integer) are accepted.

127

We define in this paper systolic pyramid automata (Fig. 1) as a natural extension of systolic trellis automata.[4] The basic structure of a pyramid automaton is a pyramid. It consists of packed levels of processors. At the topmost level there is only one processor which we can call the root and the topmost level is denoted as level 1. At level m we have an $m \times m$ array of processors. In general, each processor has four sons and four fathers. The input is a square array of terminals entered through the external input pins at the bottom level. Information flows from the bottom level to the top level. The square array is accepted if the processor at the top level reaches a final state.

In Ref. 12 we have defined array automata to accept the models defined in Ref. 10. These are sequential automata and take a lot of time for recognition. We find that many languages generated by models in Ref. 10 can be accepted by systolic pyramid automata, which are basically parallel automata, and hence acceptance is faster.

A variation on these types of pyramid, the hexagonal pyramid automaton, is also defined. Here each level consists of nodes arranged in a regular hexagonal array, and each node in general has seven sons and seven fathers. The input is a regular hexagonal array with n elements on a side, and is fed to the processors at level n of the pyramid. Acceptance is

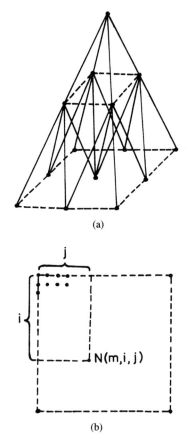

(a)

(b)

Fig. 1.   Structure of the systolic pyramid automaton.
(a) A pyramid (up to level 3).   (b) $m \times m$ processors at level m.

as defined earlier. It is seen that several languages of hexagonal arrays, defined in Ref. 13, can be accepted by this type of automaton.

Section 2 contains the basic definitions about systolic pyramid automata. In Sect. 3, we show that any language consisting of square arrays generated by a subclass of (R : R)AG can be accepted by a systolic pyramid automaton. We give examples of (CF : R)AL which can be accepted by systolic pyramid automata. Section 4 compares languages accepted by systolic pyramid automata and by one-way two-dimensional cellular automata. In Sect. 5 we consider hexagonal pyramid automata. The paper ends with concluding remarks in Sect. 6.

2. DEFINITIONS AND EXAMPLES

In this section we give definitions about systolic pyramid automata.

Definition 2.1. An infinite pyramid is an infinite directed graph (with orientation of edges from sons to fathers) which satisfies the following conditions:
(1) There is exactly one node (called the root) with no father.
(2) Every node N has four sons, the northwest, northeast, southwest and southeast, denoted by N_{nw}, N_{ne}, N_{sw} and N_{se} respectively, and always $(N_{sw})_{ne} = (N_{se})_{nw} = (N_{nw})_{se} = (N_{ne})_{sw}$, $(N_{ne})_{se} = (N_{se})_{ne}$, $(N_{se})_{sw} = (N_{sw})_{se}$, $(N_{nw})_{sw} = (N_{sw})_{nw}$ and $(N_{ne})_{nw} = (N_{nw})_{ne}$.

An infinite labeled pyramid T is an infinite pyramid with nodes labeled by symbols from a finite alphabet Δ.

If T is an infinite (labeled) pyramid, then for $j = 1, 2, \ldots$, $\text{LEVEL}_T(j)$ denotes the set of all (labeled) nodes of T whose distance from the root is $j - 1$. At each level we have a square array of processors. At level m, the processor at the intersection of row i and column j is denoted by $N_T(m, i, j)$, $1 \leqslant i, j \leqslant m$ and its label $\lambda_T(m, i, j)$. Figure 1(a) shows the structure of a pyramid and Fig. 1(b) shows the square array of processors at level m.

To any infinite labeled pyramid T and to any integer $k \geqslant 1$ we take the pyramid T_k of height k to be the maximal subgraph of T with the set of nodes $\bigcup\limits_{i=1}^{k} \text{LEVEL}(i)$. The nodes in $\text{LEVEL}(k)$ in T_k are called the input nodes of T_k.

Definition 2.2. An infinite labeled pyramid is said to be regular (semihomogeneous) if the label of any node is uniquely determined by the labels of its fathers (by the label of any of its fathers).

Definition 2.3. A systolic pyramid automaton is a construct $K = (1, \Delta, \Sigma, \Gamma, \Gamma_0, f, g)$ where Δ, Σ and Γ are finite alphabets referred to as the labeling, terminal and operating alphabets respectively. $\Gamma_0 \subseteq \Gamma$ is the alphabet of accepting symbols. $1 : (\Delta \cup \{\#\}) \times (\Delta \cup \{\#\}) \times (\Delta \cup \{\#\}) \times (\Delta \cup \{\#\}) \to \Delta$ is referred to as the labeling function. $f : \Delta \times \Sigma \to \Gamma$ is the input function. $g : \Delta \times \Gamma \times \Gamma \times \Gamma \times \Gamma \to \Gamma$ is the transition function.

With every pyramid $K = (1, \Delta, \Sigma, \Gamma, \Gamma_0, f, g)$ we can associate a regular pyramid T (the so-called underlying pyramid of K) where T is the pyramid in which the label of each node is uniquely determined by those of its four fathers as per the labeling function 1. If a father is missing the label is taken to be #.

An input array of size $n \times n$ is fed to the external input pins of processors on the level n. They compute in parallel the values of their input functions and send their results to their fathers. At any level $j < n$, all processors receive inputs on their internal input pins at the same time. They compute in parallel the values of the corresponding transition functions and again send the results along output interconnections.

If an array w is fed to K, then in time $n - 1$ the processor at the root is activated and w is accepted if and only if the output is in Γ_0.

$$L(K) = \{w \in {}_+^+ \Sigma {}_+^+ \mid \text{OUTPUT}(K, w, 1, 1, 1) \in \Gamma_0\}$$

where OUTPUT$(K, w, m, i, j\}$ is the output emitted by the node $N(m, i, j)$ of K when array w is fed as input, and ${}_+^+ \Sigma {}_+^+$ denotes the set of all square arrays over Σ.

Definition 2.4. An infinite labeled pyramid T is said to be a homogeneous pyramid if all nodes are labeled by the same label. In this cse, 1 and Δ can be omitted from the description of the pyramid automaton.

It can be shown by methods similar to those used in Ref. 4 that semihomogeneous and homogeneous systolic pyramid automata are equally powerful though less powerful than regular pyramid automata.

Example 1. Local Property Detection

The following homogeneous pyramid automaton accepts an input array if

$$\begin{array}{ccc} a & b & c \\ b & a & d \\ c & m & n \end{array}$$

occurs as a subarray.

$$\Sigma = \{a, b, c, \ldots\},$$

$$\Gamma = \Sigma \cup \left\{ \begin{bmatrix} \alpha & \beta \\ \gamma & \delta \end{bmatrix} \mid \alpha, \beta, \gamma, \delta \in \{0, 1\} \right\} \cup \{A, 0\},$$

$$\Gamma_0 = \{A\}.$$

f is the identity function. g is defined as follows:

$$g\begin{pmatrix} y_1 & y_2 \\ y_3 & y_4 \end{pmatrix} = \begin{bmatrix} z_1 & z_2 \\ z_3 & z_4 \end{bmatrix} \text{ where } z_1 = 1 \text{ if } \begin{bmatrix} y_1 & y_2 \\ y_3 & y_4 \end{bmatrix} = \begin{bmatrix} a & b \\ b & a \end{bmatrix}$$

$$z_2 = 1 \text{ if } \begin{bmatrix} y_1 & y_2 \\ y_3 & y_4 \end{bmatrix} = \begin{bmatrix} b & c \\ a & d \end{bmatrix}$$

$$z_3 = 1 \text{ if } \begin{bmatrix} y_1 & y_2 \\ y_3 & y_4 \end{bmatrix} = \begin{bmatrix} b & a \\ c & m \end{bmatrix}$$

$$z_4 = 1 \text{ if } \begin{bmatrix} y_1 & y_2 \\ y_3 & y_4 \end{bmatrix} = \begin{bmatrix} a & d \\ m & n \end{bmatrix}.$$

$$g\begin{pmatrix} x_1 & x_2 \\ x_3 & x_4 \end{pmatrix} = A \quad \text{if each } x_i \text{ is of the form} \begin{bmatrix} \alpha & \beta \\ \gamma & \delta \end{bmatrix} \quad \text{where } \alpha, \ \beta, \ \gamma,$$

$\delta \in \{0, 1\}$ and for x_1, $\alpha = 1$; for x_2, $\beta = 1$; for x_3, $\gamma = 1$; for x_4, $\delta = 1$.

$$g\begin{pmatrix} P & Q \\ R & S \end{pmatrix} = A \quad \text{if one of } P, Q, R, S \text{ is } A$$

$$= 0 \quad \text{in all other cases.}$$

Example 2. The following homogeneous systolic pyramid automaton accepts an input array if

$$\begin{matrix} a & b & c \\ b & a & d \\ c & m & n \end{matrix}$$

occurs as a subarray within two mismatches.

$\Sigma = \{a, b, c, \dots \}$

$\Gamma = \Sigma \cup \{A, O\} \cup$

$$\left\{ \begin{bmatrix} \alpha & \beta \\ \gamma & \delta \end{bmatrix} \mid \alpha, \ \beta, \ \gamma, \ \delta \in \{0, 1\} \times \{0, 1/4, 1/2, 3/4, 1, 5/4, 3/2\} \right\}$$

$\Gamma_0 = \{A\}$

f is the identity function.

g is defined as follows:

$$g\begin{pmatrix} y_1 & y_2 \\ y_3 & y_4 \end{pmatrix} = \begin{bmatrix} z_1 & z_2 \\ z_3 & z_4 \end{bmatrix} \quad \text{where } z_1 = (u_1, v_1),$$

$$u_1 = 1 \quad \text{if } \begin{bmatrix} y_1 & y_2 \\ y_3 & y_4 \end{bmatrix} = \begin{bmatrix} a & b \\ b & a \end{bmatrix} \quad \text{within 2 mismatches.}$$

If there are no mismatches, $v_1 = 0$.

If the mismatch occurs at y_1, it is given a weight 1. If the mismatch occurs at y_2 or y_3, it is given a weight $1/2$. If the mismatch occurs at y_4, it is given a weight $1/4$. v_1 is the sum of the weights due to mismatches.

$z_2 = (u_2, v_2)$ where $u_2 = 1$ if $\begin{bmatrix} y_1 & y_2 \\ y_3 & y_4 \end{bmatrix} = \begin{bmatrix} b & c \\ a & d \end{bmatrix}$ within two mismatches

131

and v_2 is a number calculated in a similar manner as v_1.

$z_3 = (u_3, \ v_3)$ where $u_3 = 1$ if $\begin{bmatrix} y_1 & y_2 \\ y_3 & y_4 \end{bmatrix} = \begin{bmatrix} b & a \\ c & m \end{bmatrix}$ within two mismatches

and v_3 is a number calculated in a similar manner as v_1 and v_2.

$z_4 = (u_4, \ v_4)$ where $u_4 = 1$ if $\begin{bmatrix} y_1 & y_2 \\ y_3 & y_4 \end{bmatrix} = \begin{bmatrix} a & d \\ m & n \end{bmatrix}$ within two mismatches

and v_4 is calculated by giving due weight to the mismatches.

$g\begin{pmatrix} X_1 & X_2 \\ X_3 & X_4 \end{pmatrix} = A$ if each X_i is of the form $\begin{bmatrix} (u_1, \ v_1) & (u_2, \ v_2) \\ (u_3, \ v_3) & (u_4, \ v_4) \end{bmatrix}$ and for

$X_1, u_1 = 1$; for $X_2, u_2 = 1$; for $X_3, u_3 = 1$; for $X_4, u_4 = 1$; and the sum of the second components corresponding to these elements is ≤ 2.

$$g\begin{pmatrix} P & Q \\ R & S \end{pmatrix} = A \text{ if one of } P, Q, R, S \text{ is } A,$$

$$= 0 \text{ in all other cases.}$$

Note that if the given pattern is $\begin{matrix} p_{11} & p_{12} & p_{13} \\ p_{21} & p_{22} & p_{23}, \\ p_{31} & p_{32} & p_{33} \end{matrix}$

and if a mismatch occurs at p_{11}, p_{13}, p_{31} or p_{33}, it is given a weight 1. If it occurs at p_{12}, p_{21}, p_{23} or p_{32}, it is given a weight $1/2$, because it will be calculated twice. If the mismatch occurs at p_{22} it is given a weight of $1/4$ since it is calculated four times.

3.   CLOSURE PROPERTIES AND COMPARISON WITH ARRAY LANGUAGES

In this section, we consider a few closure properties of systolic pyramid automata and compare its power with the power of array grammars.

Theorem 3.1.   The family of languages accepted by systolic pyramid automata is closed under union and intersection.

Proof.   Let K and K' be two systolic pyramid automata.

$$K = (1, \ \Delta, \ \Sigma, \ \Gamma, \ \Gamma_0, \ f, \ g), \ K' = (1', \ \Delta', \ \Sigma, \ \Gamma', \ \Gamma_0', \ f', \ g').$$

$\bar{K}$ accepting $L(K) \cup L(K')$ is constructed as follows:

$$\bar{K} = (\bar{1}, \ \Delta \times \Delta', \ \Sigma, \ \Gamma \times \Gamma', \ \Gamma \times \Gamma_0' \cup \Gamma_0 \times \Gamma', \ \bar{f}, \ \bar{g}).$$

The label of the (m, i, j)th node in $\bar{K}$ is (a, b) where the labels of the (m, i, j)th node in K and K' are a and b respectively.

$$\overline{f}_{(a,b)}(x) = (f_a(x),\ f'_b(x))$$

$$\overline{g}_{(a,b)}\begin{pmatrix} (x_1,\ y_1) & (x_2,\ y_2) \\ (x_3,\ y_3) & (x_4,\ y_4) \end{pmatrix} = \begin{pmatrix} g_a\begin{pmatrix} x_1 & x_2 \\ x_3 & x_4 \end{pmatrix},\ g'_b\begin{pmatrix} y_1 & y_2 \\ y_3 & y_4 \end{pmatrix} \end{pmatrix}.$$

By taking $\overline{\Gamma}_0 = \Gamma_0 \times \Gamma_0'$, we can prove closure under intersection.

We usually denote the set of all rectangular arrays over Σ as Σ^{++}. Let ${}_+^+\Sigma_+^+$ denote the set of all square arrays over Σ. If L is an array language (consisting of rectangular arrays of terminals), then the complement of L is defined as $\Sigma^{++} - L$. We define a new operation called square complementation as follows.

Definition 3.2. If L is a language of square arrays over Σ, then the square complementation $\lfloor L \rfloor$ of L is defined as $\lfloor L \rfloor = {}_+^+\Sigma_+^+ - L$.

Theorem 3.3. The family of languages accepted by systolic pyramid automata is a Boolean algebra.

Proof. We have already proved closure under union and intersection. Closure under square complementation can be proved by interchanging the final and the nonfinal states.

We shall next state a few more closure properties which have meaning when the square array is considered as a digitised picture. The formal definitions of these operations are given in Ref. 10. The names themselves are self-explanatory. We omit the proofs as they are straightforward.

Theorem 3.4. The family of languages accepted by systolic pyramid automata are closed under the following picture operations.
(i)   reflection about the rightmost vertical,
(ii) reflection about the base,
(iii) rotation through 90°,
(iv) rotation through 180°,
(v)   transpose.

Definition 3.5. Let $\Sigma = \{0,\ 1\}$. The conjugate of an array w over Σ is obtained by replacing 0 in w by 1 and 1 by 0.

Theorem 3.6. Let $\Sigma = \{0,\ 1\}$. The family of languages over Σ accepted by systolic pyramid automata is closed under conjugation.

The closure of homogeneous systolic pyramid automata languages under the operations of array homomorphism and inverse array homomorphism is considered in a separate paper.[14]

We compare the power of systolic pyramid automata with that of array grammars to generate some picture languages which are rectangular arrays. The reader is referred to Ref. 10 for the definition. Regular matrix grammars[10] can be accepted by systolic trellis automata if we input the entire matrix of size $m \times n$, column by column, at level m. Each column is a regular set and this can be accepted by the trellis automaton while the overall computation can be done at the root. But in the rectangular arrays generated by these models, there is no connection between the length and breadth of the array. In Ref. 11, we defined an array model which generates rectangular arrays, where there is a proportion between the length and breadth of the array. We have seen that systolic pyramid automata accept only square arrays. We now explore the connection between languages accepted by systolic pyramid automata and the languages generated by the models defined in Ref. 11. First we consider a few examples.

Example 3. L_1 consists of squares describing the token L (Fig. 2). This is accepted by a homogeneous systolic pyramid automaton

$$K_1 = (\Sigma, \Gamma, \Gamma_0, f, g).$$

$\Sigma = \{x, \cdot\}$, $\Gamma = \{x, \cdot, p\}$, $\Gamma_0 = \{p\}$, f is the identity function and g is defined by

$$g\begin{pmatrix} x & \cdot \\ x & \cdot \end{pmatrix} = g\begin{pmatrix} \cdot & \cdot \\ x & x \end{pmatrix} = x, \; g\begin{pmatrix} x & \cdot \\ x & x \end{pmatrix} = g\begin{pmatrix} x & \cdot \\ p & x \end{pmatrix} = p, \; g\begin{pmatrix} \cdot & \cdot \\ \cdot & \cdot \end{pmatrix} = \cdot$$

```
                                                              X  ·  ·  ·  ·  ·
                                      X  ·  ·  ·  ·           X  ·  ·  ·  ·  ·
                      X  ·  ·  ·      X  ·  ·  ·  ·           X  ·  ·  ·  ·  ·
          X  ·  ·     X  ·  ·  ·      X  ·  ·  ·  ·           X  ·  ·  ·  ·  ·
  X  ·     X  ·  ·    X  ·  ·  ·      X  ·  ·  ·  ·           X  ·  ·  ·  ·  ·
  X  X     X  X  X    X  X  X  X      X  X  X  X  X           X  X  X  X  X  X
```

Fig. 2. The token L.

Example 4. L_2 is the set of Kirsch's right triangles (Fig. 3). This is accepted by the homogeneous systolic pyramid automaton $K_2 = (\Sigma, \Gamma, \Gamma_0, f, g)$ where $\Sigma = \{V, H, W, R, B, L, I, \cdot\}$, $\Gamma = \Sigma \cup \{q\}$, $\Gamma_0 = \{q\}$, f is the identity function, and g is defined as follows:

$$g\begin{pmatrix} \cdot & \cdot \\ \cdot & \cdot \end{pmatrix} = \cdot, \; g\begin{pmatrix} \cdot & W \\ H & L \end{pmatrix} = W, \; g\begin{pmatrix} \cdot & H \\ V & B \end{pmatrix} = V$$

$$g\begin{pmatrix} H & L \\ B & R \end{pmatrix} = g\begin{pmatrix} I & L \\ B & R \end{pmatrix} = R, \; g\begin{pmatrix} I & I \\ I & I \end{pmatrix} = g\begin{pmatrix} H & I \\ I & I \end{pmatrix} = I$$

$$g\begin{pmatrix} H & I \\ B & B \end{pmatrix} = g\begin{pmatrix} I & I \\ B & B \end{pmatrix} = B, \; g\begin{pmatrix} H & L \\ I & L \end{pmatrix} = g\begin{pmatrix} I & L \\ I & L \end{pmatrix} = L$$

$$g\begin{pmatrix} \cdot & H \\ H & I \end{pmatrix} = H, \; g\begin{pmatrix} \cdot & \cdot \\ \cdot & H \end{pmatrix} = \cdot, \; g\begin{pmatrix} \cdot & W \\ V & R \end{pmatrix} = q.$$

```
                                                          .   .   .   .   .   W
                                      .   .   .   .   W    .   .   .   .   H   L
                  .   .   .   W       .   .   .   H   L    .   .   .   H   I   L
          .   .   W       .   .   H   L       .   .   H   I   L       .   .   H   I   I   L
  .   W       .   H   L       .   H   I   L       .   H   I   I   L       .   H   I   I   I   L
  V   R       V   B   R       V   B   B   R       V   B   B   B   R       V   B   B   B   B   R
```

Fig. 3. Kirsch's right triangles.

Example 5. L_3 is the set of arrays representing token I (Fig. 4). This is accepted by the homogeneous systolic pyramid automaton $K_3 = (\Sigma, \Gamma, \Gamma_0, f, g)$ where $\Sigma = \{x, \cdot\}$ and f is the identity function. $\Gamma = \{x, \cdot, t, b, m, m', a\}$, $\Gamma_0 = \{a\}$ and g is given as follows:

$$g\begin{pmatrix} x & x \\ \cdot & \cdot \end{pmatrix} = g\begin{pmatrix} x & x \\ \cdot & x \end{pmatrix} = g\begin{pmatrix} x & x \\ x & \cdot \end{pmatrix} = t$$

$$g\begin{pmatrix} \cdot & \cdot \\ x & x \end{pmatrix} = g\begin{pmatrix} \cdot & x \\ x & x \end{pmatrix} = g\begin{pmatrix} x & \cdot \\ x & x \end{pmatrix} = b$$

$$g\begin{pmatrix} \cdot & x \\ \cdot & x \end{pmatrix} = g\begin{pmatrix} x & \cdot \\ x & \cdot \end{pmatrix} = m, \quad g\begin{pmatrix} \cdot & \cdot \\ \cdot & \cdot \end{pmatrix} = \cdot$$

$$g\begin{pmatrix} t & t \\ m & m \end{pmatrix} = g\begin{pmatrix} t & t \\ m & \cdot \end{pmatrix} = g\begin{pmatrix} t & t \\ \cdot & m \end{pmatrix} = g\begin{pmatrix} t & t \\ \cdot & \cdot \end{pmatrix} = t$$

$$g\begin{pmatrix} m & m \\ b & b \end{pmatrix} = g\begin{pmatrix} m & \cdot \\ b & b \end{pmatrix} = g\begin{pmatrix} \cdot & m \\ b & b \end{pmatrix} = g\begin{pmatrix} \cdot & \cdot \\ b & b \end{pmatrix} = b$$

$$g\begin{pmatrix} \cdot & m \\ \cdot & m \end{pmatrix} = g\begin{pmatrix} m & \cdot \\ m & \cdot \end{pmatrix} = \cdot, \quad g\begin{pmatrix} m & m \\ m & m \end{pmatrix} = m'$$

$$g\begin{pmatrix} t & t \\ \cdot & m' \end{pmatrix} = g\begin{pmatrix} t & t \\ m' & \cdot \end{pmatrix} = t$$

$$g\begin{pmatrix} \cdot & m' \\ b & b \end{pmatrix} = g\begin{pmatrix} m' & \cdot \\ b & b \end{pmatrix} = b$$

$$g\begin{pmatrix} \cdot & m' \\ \cdot & m' \end{pmatrix} = g\begin{pmatrix} m' & \cdot \\ m' & \cdot \end{pmatrix} = m$$

$$g\begin{pmatrix} t & t \\ b & b \end{pmatrix} = a.$$

We next give the definition of array grammars as given in Ref. 11.

```
                                                    X  X  X  X  X  X  X  X  X
                                                    .  .  .  .  X  .  .  .  .
                            X  X  X  X  X  X  X      .  .  .  .  X  .  .  .  .
                            .  .  .  X  .  .  .      .  .  .  .  X  .  .  .  .
            X  X  X  X  X   .  .  .  X  .  .  .      .  .  .  .  X  .  .  .  .
            .  .  X  .  .   .  .  .  X  .  .  .      .  .  .  .  X  .  .  .  .
  X  X  X   .  .  X  .  .   .  .  .  X  .  .  .      .  .  .  .  X  .  .  .  .
  .  X  .   .  .  X  .  .   .  .  .  X  .  .  .      .  .  .  .  X  .  .  .  .
  X  X  X   X  X  X  X  X   X  X  X  X  X  X  X      X  X  X  X  X  X  X  X  X
```

Fig. 4. The token I.

Definition 3.7. If

$$X = \begin{matrix} a_{11} & \cdots & a_{1n} \\ \cdot & & \cdot \\ \cdot & & \cdot \\ \cdot & & \cdot \\ a_{m1} & & a_{mn} \end{matrix} \quad \text{and} \quad Y = \begin{matrix} b_{11} & \cdots & b_{1n'} \\ \cdot & & \cdot \\ \cdot & & \cdot \\ \cdot & & \cdot \\ b_{m'1} & & b_{m'n'} \end{matrix}$$

the column concatenation $X \oplus Y$ is defined only when $m = m'$ and is given by

$$\begin{matrix} a_{11} & \cdots & a_{1n} & b_{11} & \cdots & b_{1n'} \\ \cdot & & \cdot & \cdot & & \cdot \\ \cdot & & \cdot & \cdot & & \cdot \\ \cdot & & \cdot & \cdot & & \cdot \\ a_{m1} & & a_{mn} & b_{m1} & & b_{mn'} \end{matrix}$$

and the row concatenation $X \ominus Y$ is defined only when $n = n'$ and is given by

$$\begin{matrix} a_{11} & \cdots & a_{1n} \\ \cdot & & \cdot \\ \cdot & & \cdot \\ \cdot & & \cdot \\ a_{m1} & \cdots & a_{mn} \\ b_{11} & \cdots & b_{1n} \\ \cdot & & \cdot \\ \cdot & & \cdot \\ \cdot & & \cdot \\ b_{m'1} & \cdots & b_{m'n}. \end{matrix}$$

We use $\oplus$ to denote either $\oplus$ or $\ominus$. Also, when there is no ambiguity the operator $\oplus$ is left out.

Definition 3.8. If M and M' are two sets of matrices, then the column product $M \oslash M'$ is given by $\{X \oslash Y \mid X$ in M, Y in $M'\}$ and the row product $M \ominus M'$ is given by $\{X \ominus Y \mid X$ in M, Y in $M'\}$.

Notation: $I*$ denotes the set of all horizontal sequences of letters from I and $I^+ = I* - \{\varepsilon\}$ where ε is the identity element (of length 0). I_* denotes the set of all vertical sequences of letters over I, and $I_+ = I_* - \{\varepsilon\}$. Also, $(x)^{i+1} = (x)^i \oslash x$, $(x)_{i+1} = (x)_i \ominus x$ where $x \in I^{++}$. In the special case where x is a string (horizontal or vertical) the operator $\oplus$ has the same meaning as "$\cdot$".

Definition 3.9. Let $G = (V, I, P, S)$ be an array (rewriting) grammar (AG), where $V = V_1 \cup V_2$ and V_1 is a finite set of nonterminals, V_2 a finite set of intermediates, I a finite set of terminals. $P = P_1 \cup P_2 \cup P_3$, P_1 is the finite set of nonterminal rules, P_2 the finite set of intermediate rules, and P_3 the finite set of terminal rules. $S \in V_1$ is the start symbol.

P_1 is a finite set of ordered pairs (u, v) (written $u \to v$), with u and v in $(V_1 \cup V_2)_+$ or u and v in $(V_1 \cup V_2)^+$.

P_1 is context-free (CF) if every (u, v) pair in P_1 is such that $u \in V_1$ with v in $(V_1 \cup V_2)_+$ or $(V_1 \cup V_2)^+$ and regular if $u \in V_1$ and v is of the form $U \oplus V$, U in V_1 and V in V_2 or U in V_2 and V in V_1.

Instead of enumerating the rules in P_2, we give the language generated by each intermediate in V_2. Each intermediate in V_2 generates either a language (called intermediate matrix language) whose terminals are a finite number of arrays with the same number of rows or the transpose of such a language. P_2 is called CF or R accordingly as the intermediate matrix languages generated are CF or R.

P_3, the finite set of terminal rules, has ordered pairs (u, v), with u in V_1 and v in I^{++}.

An array grammar is called a (CF : R) AG if the nonterminal rules are CF and the intermediate languages are regular. Similarly for (CF : CF), (R : R) and (R : CF).

Notation: We write $\alpha \underset{P_1}{\Rightarrow} \beta$ or $\alpha \underset{P_2}{\Rightarrow} \beta$ or $\alpha \underset{P_3}{\Rightarrow} \beta$ when a rule in P_1 or P_2 or P_3 is used in the derivation. When the meaning is clear, we omit P_1, P_2 and P_3. $\overset{*}{\Rightarrow}$ is the reflexive transitive closure of $\Rightarrow$.

Starting with the start symbol S, nonterminal rules are applied without restriction just as in string grammars (except that $\oplus$ acts both horizontally and vertically) till all the nonterminals are replaced, introducing parentheses whenever necessary, since the operator $\oplus$ is not associative. Now each intermediate A in V_2 is replaced by an element from M_A (the intermediate matrix language generated by A) subject to the conditions imposed by the row and column concatenation operator. The replacements start from the innermost parentheses and proceed outwards. The derivation comes to a dead end if the condition for row or column concatenation is not satisfied.

Definition 3.10. $L(G) = \{A \mid S \overset{*}{\Rightarrow} A, A$ in $I^{++}\}$. $M \subseteq I^{++}$ is an $(X : Y)$ array language if there exists an $(X : Y)$AG G such that $M = L(G)$. $(X = $ CF or R, $Y = $ CF or R).

Example 3 can be generated by an $(R : R)$AG whereas Examples 4 and 5 can be generated by $(CF : R)$AG. The grammars are given in Ref. 11. Array grammars can generate nonsquare arrays also whereas systolic pyramid automata accept only square arrays. We shall prove our main result after two more definitions.

Definition 3.11. An (R : R)AG is said to be uniform if it satisfies the following conditions:

(a) All intermediates generate rows and columns of the same finite thickness.

(b) All non-terminal rules belong to exactly one of the following forms, where X, $Y \in V_1$, B, $C \in V_2$.

  (i) $X \to (Y \ominus B) \oslash C$
       $X \to (Y \oslash B) \ominus C$
       i.e. growth from top left corner.

  (ii) $X \to (B \ominus Y) \oslash C$
       $X \to B \ominus (Y \oslash C)$
       i.e. growth from bottom left corner.

  (iii) $X \to B \ominus (C \oslash Y)$
        $X \to B \oslash (C \ominus Y)$
        i.e. growth from bottom right corner.

  (iv) $X \to (B \oslash Y) \ominus C$
       $X \to B \oslash (Y \ominus C)$
       i.e. growth from top right corner.

These rules ensure that the same number of rows and columns are added to the array on the r. h. s. of the terminal rule, and that too in a uniform manner. Thus if the starting point is a square array, then every step in the derivation yields a square array. This makes it possible for the systolic pyramid automaton to recognise the language, since the automaton has squares of decreasing size at each level, and must be able to completely process and eliminate one row and one column from the array at each step of the computation.

Remark. Despite the apparently misleading form, rules of type (ii) and (iv) are regular and not linear. This is because we are considering a 2-D language. Thus rules in (ii) can be depicted as $X \to \dfrac{B}{Y}\bigg| C$, $X \to \dfrac{B}{Y\,|\,C}$. A linear rule would have had row (or column) concatenation on both sides of the array, as in $X \to (A \ominus Y) \ominus B$, or $X \to (A \oslash Y) \oslash B$.

$$\text{i.e. } X \to A \,|\, Y \,|\, B \text{ or } X \to \dfrac{\dfrac{A}{Y}}{B}.$$

Definition 3.12. An (R : R)AG is called a simple (R : R)AG if there is only one terminal rule.

Lemma 3.13. Every (R : R)AL is a union of a finite number of simple (R : R)ALs. The proof is obvious.

Theorem 3.14. Let G be a uniform (R : R)AG with square arrays on the r. h. s. of terminal rules. Then $L(G)$ can be accepted by a systolic pyramid automaton.

Proof. Without loss of generality we assume that the uniform (R : R)AG is simple as we have already proved closure under union for languages accepted by systolic pyramid automata.

We shall make two more assumptions which make the proof simpler. In the general case, the proof has to be modified a little. One assumption is that the terminal rule is of

the form $S' \to \begin{matrix} a & b \\ c & d \end{matrix}$, (i.e. r. h. s. is of size 2×2). If the r. h. s. of a terminal rule is of

a larger size, the grammar can be modified by introducing more intermediates so that the terminal rule has r. h. s. of size 2×2. If it is of smaller size (i.e. 1×1, i.e. a single letter), then the following proof itself can be easily modified. The second assumption is that the horizontal and vertical intermediates generate single rows or single columns. In uniform (R : R)AG, they can also generate rows of columns of the same finite thickness. In this case the modification required will be explained towards the end of the proof.

Let $G = (N, I, P, S)$ be the (R : R)AG. Let $A_1, \ldots, A_k$ be the horizontal intermediates, i.e. intermediates generating a horizontal language. Let $B_1, \ldots, B_r$ be the vertical intermediates generating a vertical language. Let the arrays be generated as shown in Fig. 5 (i.e. the rules are of type (i) described above). There are three more possibilities which can be similarly dealt with. These are cases when the first block is the lower left, lower right and upper right corner respectively. Let $A_1, \ldots, A_k$ generate regular sets $R_{H1}, \ldots, R_{Hk}$. Let R_{Hi} be accepted by an FSA with initial state q_{Hi} and other states $q_{Hi_1}, \ldots$ etc. Let $B_i, \ldots, B_r$ generate vertical regular sets $R_{V1}, \ldots, R_{Vr}$. R_{Vj} is accepted by FSA with initial state q_{Vj} and other states q_{Vj_1}, etc. The states of the FSAs are disjoint.

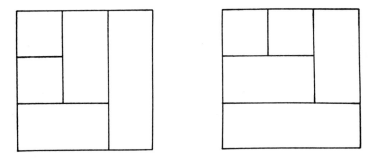

Fig. 5. Generation of arrays by array grammar.

The systolic pyramid automaton $K = (1, \Delta, \Sigma, \Gamma, \Gamma_0, f, g)$ accepting $L(G)$ is constructed as follows. The labels of the nodes are given by the following rule: at any level the topleft corner node has label S. All other top row nodes have label V. All other left column nodes have label H. All other nodes have label X. $\Delta = \{S, V, H, X\}$, $\Sigma = I$, $\Gamma = N \cup \Sigma \cup (\Sigma \times N) \cup (\Sigma \times Q_{H1} \times Q_{H2} \times \ldots \times Q_{Hk}) \cup (\Sigma \times Q_{V1} \times \ldots \times Q_{Vr})$ where Q_{Vj} is the set of states for the FSA accepting R_{Vj}, and Q_{Hi} is the set of states for the FSA accepting R_{Hi}. f and g are defined below:

$$f_S(a) = (a, S)$$

$$f_H(a) = (a, q_{H1}, \ldots, q_{Hk})$$

$$f_V(a) = (a, q_{V1}, \ldots, q_{Vr})$$

$$f_X(a) = a$$

$$g_S\begin{pmatrix} (a, S) & (b, q_{V1}, \ldots, q_{Vr}) \\ (c, q_{H1}, \ldots, q_{Hk}) & d \end{pmatrix} = S'$$

if $S' \to \begin{matrix} a & b \\ c & d \end{matrix}$ is the terminal rule of G.

$$g_V\begin{pmatrix} \alpha & (a, q_{V1i_1}, q_{V2i_2}, \ldots, q_{Vri_r}) \\ \beta & b \end{pmatrix}$$

$$= (b, \delta(q_{V1i_1}, a), \delta(q_{V2i_2}, a), \ldots, \delta(q_{Vri_r}, a)) \text{ for some } \alpha, \beta \in \Gamma \text{ and } a, b \in \Sigma.$$

$$g_H\begin{pmatrix} \alpha & \beta \\ (a, q_{H1j_1}, \ldots, q_{Hkj_k}) & b \end{pmatrix}$$

$$= (b, \delta(q_{H1j_1}, a), \delta(q_{H2j_2}, a), \ldots, \delta(q_{Hkj_k}, a)) \text{ for some } \alpha, \beta \in \Gamma \text{ and } a, b \in \Sigma.$$

$$g_X\begin{pmatrix} a & b \\ c & d \end{pmatrix} = d \qquad a, b, c, d \in \Gamma.$$

$$g_S\begin{pmatrix} S_1 & (a, q_{V1j_1}, \ldots, q_{Vri_r}) \\ (b, q_{H1j_1}, \ldots, q_{Hkj_k}) & e \end{pmatrix} = S_2$$

if $S_2 \to (S_1 \ominus A_n) \oplus B_m$ is a rule in P and $\delta(\delta(q_{Vmi_m}, a), e)$ is a final state for R_{Vm} and $\delta(q_{Hnj_n}, b)$ is a final state for R_{Hn}, or $S_2 \to (S_1 \oplus B_m) \ominus A_n$ is a rule in P and $\delta(\delta(q_{Hnj_n}, b), e)$ is a final state for R_{Hn} and (q_{Vmi_m}, a) is a final state for R_{Vm}, for some m, n.

The array is accepted if S is output at the root.

The fact that this systolic automaton accepts $L(G)$ is seen as follows: Suppose an $n \times n$ array is generated by the grammar by building up of blocks as in Fig. 5. When an array

$$W = \begin{matrix} a_{11} & \cdots & a_{1n} \\ \cdot & & \\ a_{n1} & \cdots & a_{nn} \end{matrix}$$

is input at the nth level of the systolic pyramid automaton, the states of the processors at this level will be

(a_{11}, S) $\qquad$ $(a_{12}, q_{V1}, \ldots, q_{Vr})$ $\cdots$ $(a_{1n}, q_{V1}, \ldots, q_{Vr})$

$(a_{21}, q_{H1}, \ldots, H_k)$ $\qquad\qquad a_{22}$ $\qquad\qquad \cdots \qquad\qquad a_{2n}$

$\qquad\qquad\qquad .$

$\qquad\qquad\qquad .$

$\qquad\qquad\qquad .$

$(a_{n1}, q_{H1}, \ldots, q_{Hk})$ $\qquad\qquad a_{n2}$ $\qquad\qquad \cdots \qquad\qquad a_{n_n}$

At any level the states of the processors will be of the form

$$
\begin{array}{ccc}
q_{11} & \cdots & q_{1i} \\
. & & \\
. & & \qquad \text{where } q_{11} \in N \\
. & & \\
q_{i1} & \cdots & q_{ii}
\end{array}
$$

$$
\begin{aligned}
q_{1p} &\in (\Sigma \times Q_{V1} \times \ldots \times Q_{Vr}) & 2 \leq p \leq i \\
q_{s1} &\in (\Sigma \times Q_{H1} \times \ldots \times Q_{Hk}) & 2 \leq s \leq i \\
q_{mn} &\in \Sigma & 2 \leq m, n \leq i
\end{aligned}
$$

By induction, we can show that at the ith level we get $q_{11}(\in N)$ as the state of the processor $(i, 1, 1)$ if and only if $q_{11} \overset{*}{\Rightarrow} w'$ in G where w' is the topleft $(n - i + 1) \times (n - i + 1)$ subarray of W. Since $\Gamma_0 = \{S\}$, an $n \times n$ array is accepted by the systolic pyramid automaton if and only if it is generated by the (R : R)AG.

If the intermediate languages generate columns and rows of thickness p say, then this should be taken care of by labeling the left column nodes as $S, H_1, H_2, \ldots, H_p, H_1,$ $H_2, \ldots$ and top row nodes as $S, V_1, V_2, \ldots, V_p, V_1, V_2, \ldots$ and defining the g mappings properly.

The set of Kirsch's right triangles and token I can be generated by (CF : R)AG. The grammars for these are given in Ref. 11.

The nonterminal rules in these grammars can be called linear as only one nonterminal occurs on the right hand side of any nonterminal rule. All such languages can be accepted by systolic pyramid automata if they generate square arrays only. The labels of the nodes of the pyramid have to be determined carefully by looking at the way the arrays are built. A formal proof will be unwieldy and is hence omitted. This result looks quite natural considering the fact that all linear languages are accepted by systolic trellis automata.

There are (CF : R) and (R :R) languages that generate nonsquare arrays. Hence there are (CF : R) languages that cannot be accepted by systolic pyramid automata. On the other hand, there are languages accepted by systolic pyramid automata which cannot be generated by (CF : CF)AG. One such example is the language consisting of squares of as of size $2^n \times 2^n$ ($n \geq 0$).

We also note that in the proof of Theorem 3.14 the systolic automaton constructed is a semihomogeneous one. Hence any uniform (R : R)AL can be accepted by a homogeneous systolic pyramid automaton.

4.   TWO-DIMENSIONAL CELLULAR AUTOMATA AND SYSTOLIC PYRAMID AUTOMATA

In this section, we compare the power of one-way 2-D cellular automata and systolic pyramid automata.

A two-dimensional cellular automaton is an array of cells, each of which, at any given time, is in some state. The cells operate in a sequence of discrete time steps, at each of which every cell reads the states of its four horizontal and vertical neighbors and changes to a (possibly) new state. Thus formally, a two-dimensional cellular automaton K is defined by specifying a pair (Q, δ) where Q is the set of states and δ is the transition function that maps quintuples of states into a state $\delta : Q^5 \rightarrow Q$ (we take K to be deterministic). A configuration of K is simply a mapping from $I \times I$ (pairs of integers) into Q that specifies the state of each cell K. Sometimes other neighborhoods are also considered. But we shall consider this 5-neighborhood which is known as the von Neumann neighborhood. The initial configuration is a set of cells not in the quiescent state (a special state similar to the blank symbol). The initial configuration is accepted if a predesignated cell enters a final state after some time.

A one-dimensional cellular automaton 1D-CA is a linear array of cells and the state of each cell at any instant depends on its own state and the states of its left and right neighbors. An initial configuration is a string of cells in the nonquiescent state. The initial configuration is accepted if the leftmost cell in this string reaches a final state. A one-dimensional cellular automaton is said to be one-way (OCA) if the state of any cell depends on its own state and that of its right neighbor only. An OCA is said to be real-time if a string of length n is accepted in time $n - 1$. In Ref. 15, it is shown that real-time OCA are equivalent to homogeneous trellis automata. The main idea is that the time-space diagram of a real-time OCA computation is equivalent to a trellis computation, see Fig. 6.

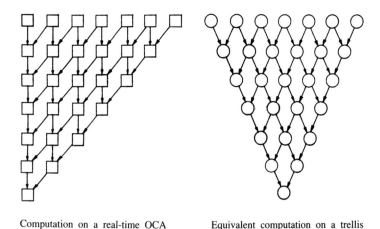

Computation on a real-time OCA   Equivalent computation on a trellis

Fig. 6.   Trellis computation and real-time OCA computation.

A one-way 2-D cellular automaton is one where the state of a cell depends on the states of its left and upper neighbors and its own state only. The initial configuration of the cellular automaton is taken to be an $m \times n$ array of cells in the nonquiescent state. We also take the bottom-right cell to be the special cell. The initial configuration is accepted if this cell reaches a final state. We call the one-way 2-D cellular automaton real-time if when started with an $m \times n$ array of cells in the nonquiescent state, the special cell reaches a final state in time $m + n - 2$. This is the minimum time taken by any signal from the topleft cell to reach the accepting cell.

Definition 4.1. Let L be a language of arrays. We define $L^\#$ as $L^\# = \{w^\# \mid w$ is an $m \times n$ array $\in L$ and $w^\#$ is an $(m + n - 1)$ array obtained from w by adding $n - 1$ rows of #s at the top and $m - 1$ columns of #s to the left$\}$.

Theorem 4.2. If a language L is accepted by a real-time one-way 2-D cellular automaton then $L^\#$ can be accepted by a homogeneous systolic pyramid automaton.

Proof. Let the cellular automaton be given by (Q, δ). The equivalent homogeneous systolic pyramid automaton is constructed as follows: $K = (\Sigma, \Gamma, \Gamma_0, f, g)$, $\Sigma = \Gamma = Q = $ set of states of the cellular automaton, Γ_0 is the set of final states in Q, f is the identity function and g will be defined below. The input is fed at level $m + n - 1$ where the top $(n - 1)$ rows and the left $(m - 1)$ columns receive the input symbol # (equivalent to quiescent state). The lower right $m \times n$ processors receive the real input. $g\begin{pmatrix} \# & \# \\ \# & \# \end{pmatrix} = \#$ and $g\begin{pmatrix} a & b \\ c & d \end{pmatrix} = \delta\begin{pmatrix} & b \\ c & d \end{pmatrix}$ where d is the state of a cell and b and c are states of its upper and left neighbors.

It is easy to see that an $m \times n$ array is accepted by the one-way 2-D cellular automaton if and only if an $(m + n - 1) \times (m + n - 1)$ array with top $(n - 1)$ rows and left $(m - 1)$ columns having special symbol # is accepted by the systolic pyramid automaton. The reason behind this is obvious. The configuration of the cellular automaton is maintained up to the $\max(m, n)$th level; afterwards at level j say, we have a $j \times j$ array. This is computed at time $t = m + n - j - 1$. In the configuraton of the cellular automaton at time $t = m + n - j - 1$, the top $m - j$ rows and left $n - j$ columns do not affect the final outcome. At level j, the $j \times j$ array of processors store the states of the bottomright $j \times j$ cells of the one-way 2-D cellular automaton. In an obvious manner the systolic automaton simulates the one-way 2-D cellular automaton.

Theorem 4.3. A language accepted by a homogeneous systolic pyramid automaton can be accepted by a real-time one-way 2-D cellular automaton.

Proof. Let L be the language accepted by the homogeneous systolic pyramid automaton $K = (\Sigma, \Gamma, \Gamma_0, f, g)$. Without loss of generality we take f to be the identity function $(\Sigma \subseteq \Gamma)$. The one-way 2-D cellular automaton M is constructed as follows. The set of states Q of M is $\Gamma \cup \{\Gamma \times \Gamma \times \Gamma\} \cup \{\#\}$ where # is the quiescent state. If an $n \times n$ array is fed into the systolic automaton, the processor at level 1 reaches final state at time $t = n - 1$. In the case of the one-way 2-D cellular automaton, the initial configuration

(which is the input) occurs at time $t = 0$. At time $t = 1, 3, \ldots$ the states are from
$(\Gamma \times \Gamma \times \Gamma) \cup \{\#\}$. At time $t = 2, 4, \ldots$ the states are from $\Gamma \cup \{\#\}$. At
time $t = 2$, the top row and left column assume state $\#$; at time $t = 4$, the top two rows
and left two columns are $\#$s. The transitions are as defined below.

$$\delta\begin{pmatrix} & c \\ a & b \end{pmatrix} = [a, b, c] \text{ if not all } a, b, c = \#, \text{ for } a, b, c \in \Gamma \cup \{\#\}$$

$$= \# \text{ otherwise.}$$

$$\delta\begin{pmatrix} & \gamma \\ \alpha & \beta \end{pmatrix} = g\begin{pmatrix} s & r \\ p & q \end{pmatrix} \text{ if } \alpha = [n, p, s], \beta = [p, q, r], \gamma = [s, r, y]$$

$$= \# \text{ if } \beta = [\#, q, \#], \alpha = \gamma = \#$$

$$= \# \text{ if } \alpha = \#, \beta = [\#, q, r], \gamma = [\#, r, y]$$

$$= \# \text{ if } \alpha = [n, p, \#], \beta = [p, q, \#], \gamma = \#.$$

The mappings are defined in such a way that the one-way 2-D cellular automaton
simulates, in two steps, the behavior of the systolic pyramid automaton in one step. At
time $t = 2n - 2$, the top $n - 1$ rows and left $n - 1$ columns assume the state $\#$ and the
bottomright corner cell reaches the final state. Thus we see that the one-way 2-D cellular
automaton accepts in real-time the language accepted by the homogeneous systolic
pyramid automaton.

5. HEXAGONAL PYRAMID AUTOMATA

Hexagonal cellular automata (HCA) have been defined in Ref. 16 as a generalisation of
the 2-D rectangular CA. In an HCA, cells are placed on each point of an equiangular
triangular grid. Each cell thus has six neighbors arranged in a regular hexagon with itself
as center. In the pyramid version, we define hexagonal pyramid automata (HPA) in a
manner similar to the pyramid automata defined earlier, except that in each level nodes are
arranged in a regular hexagon rather than in a square array. At the topmost level, there is a
single node, the root. At the ith level, $i > 1$, nodes are arranged in a regular hexagonal
structure with i nodes on a side (size i). The nodes in level i are thus concentric hexagons
of sizes $1, 2, \ldots, i$ (see Fig. 7). Each node N has seven sons in the next level: one
denoted N_m vertically below it, and six others $N_a, N_b, N_c, N_d, N_e, N_f$ arranged in a
regular hexagon (in clockwise order) around N_m. Adjacent nodes share four sons, as
described below.

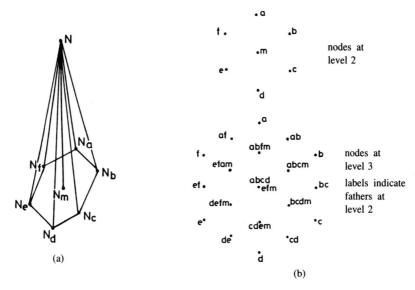

Fig. 7. Structure of the hexagonal pyramid automaton.
(a) Sons of a node in an HPA. (b) Shared sons and fathers in an HPA.

$$(N_m)_m = (N_a)_d = (N_b)_e = (N_c)_f = (N_d)_a = (N_e)_b = (Nf)_c$$
$$(N_m)_a = (N_a)_m = (N_f)_b = (N_b)_f$$
$$(N_m)_b = (N_b)_m = (N_a)_c = (N_c)_a$$
$$(N_m)_c = (N_c)_m = (N_b)_d = (N_d)_b$$
$$(N_m)_d = (N_d)_m = (N_c)_e = (N_e)_c$$
$$(N_m)_e = (N_e)_m = (N_d)_f = (N_f)_d$$
$$(N_m)_f = (N_f)_m = (N_e)_a = (N_a)_e$$
$$(N_a)_b = (N_b)_a \qquad (N_b)_c = (N_c)_b$$
$$(N_c)_d = (N_d)_c \qquad (N_d)_e = (N_e)_d$$
$$(N_e)_f = (N_f)_e \qquad (N_f)_a = (N_a)_f$$

Note that unlike the square array pyramid automata defined in Sect. 2, HPA have vertically aligned nodes at consecutive levels. Consecutive levels correspond to our most natural idea of hexagons of increasing size, with the result that at consecutive levels, a complete periphery is added to the structure at preceding levels. This is in contrast to the square arrays, which increase in size (while retaining square shape) by the addition of only one row and one column, not an entire border.

The operation of the HPA is very similar to that of the pyramid automata defined in Sect. 2. A regular hexagon of size n is fed as input to the nodes at level n. These nodes send up their output values along all output arcs at the same time. So at $t = 1$, nodes at level $n - 1$ have all their inputs defined and can compute their outputs. These outputs will be sent up at time $t = 2$. Carrying on like this, the root will output a symbol at $t = n$. The input hexagon is accepted if this symbol is an accepting symbol.

The formal definition is similar to Definition 2.3 and is omitted here. As in Sect. 2, we can similarly define labeled HPA, and classify them as regular, semihomogeneous or homogeneous. The main concepts in labeling carry over for this pyramid. Thus, for example, the "roof" labeling for trellis automata has been defined in Ref. 4. The equivalent "roof" labeling for an HPA is shown in Fig. 8. There are fourteen types of nodes: $E_i(i = 1$ to 6) along the edges of the pyramid, $F_i(i = 1$ to 6) along the faces of the pyramid, X at internal nodes and R at the root. This labeling can be obtained by a semihomogeneous labeling function, where the label of a node is uniquely determined by the label of any of its fathers.

The HPA can be studied with respect to accepting power for languages of hexagonal arrays. Since the input to the HPA must be a regular hexagon, we will consider only languages of regular hexagonal arrays. Hexagonal arrays and hexagonal patterns are found in the literature on picture processing and scene analysis.[16-20] These arrays have been studied as formal models,[13] where the authors introduce array grammars to generate languages of hexagonal arrays. The main point to be noted is that unlike strings, hexagons cannot be concatenated to give hexagons, so the grammatical models use arrowhead concatenation which is illustrated in Fig. 9.

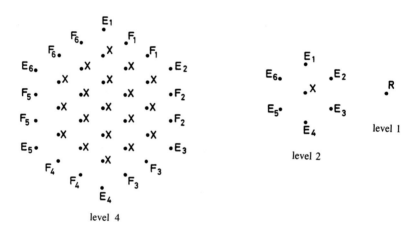

Fig. 8.   Roof labeling for an HPA.

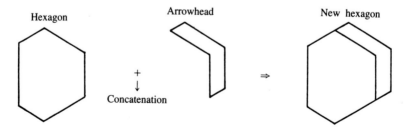

Fig. 9.   Arrowhead concatenation.

A hexagonal kolam array grammar (HKAG) has 3 disjoint sets of alphabets—nonterminals, intermediates and terminals. There are 3 types of rewriting rules:

(i)   In the first type, called nonterminal rules, the left hand side (l. h. s.) has one nonterminal and the right hand side (r. h. s.) has exactly one nonterminal along with zero or more intermediates. Treating the intermediates as terminals, these rules are either left linear or linear.

(ii) The second type has a single terminal rule with a nonterminal on the l. h. s. and a hexagonal array of terminals on the r. h. s..

(iii) In the third type, comprising of intermediate rules, usually the intermediate languages are specified rather than having to enumerate the intermediate rules. These languages consist of arrowheads made up of terminal symbols.

The derivation proceeds as follows:

Initially, nonterminal rules are applied in sequence, with arrows indicating direction of concatenation, and parentheses inserted at each step. This results in a string with intermediates and one nonterminal. In the second phase, the nonterminal is replaced by a hexagonal array of terminals, using the terminal rule. In the last phase, starting from the innermost parentheses, each intermediate is replaced by an arrowhead of appropriate size (appropriate with respect to concatenation) from the corresponding intermediate language. This arrowhead is concatenated to the existing hexagon to get a new hexagon.

The grammar is called regular (R) or linear (L) accordingly as the first phase (applying nonterminal rules) is left linear or linear. (Note: In this context, a linear rule is one which involves arrowheads of opposite directions, like $S \rightarrow ((S' \uparrow a) \downarrow b)$. This parallels the linear rule $S \rightarrow aS'b$ of string grammars.) Further, a regular grammar may be R : R or R : CF or R : CS accordingly, as all intermediate languages are regular, or all are context-free, or all are context-sensitive. Similarly, we have (L : R), (L : CF) and (L : CS) grammars.

Example 6. G_1 is an R : R grammar.

$G_1 = (V, I, P, S, \mathcal{L})$ where

$V = V_1 \cup V_2$

$V_1 = \{S, S_1\}$ nonterminals

$V_2 = \{a, b, c, x, y, z\}$ intermediates

$I = \{G, Y\}$ terminals

$P = P_1 \cup P_2$

$P_1 = \{S \rightarrow (((S_1 \nearrow a) \searrow b) \downarrow c),\ S_1 \rightarrow (((S \nearrow x) \searrow y) \downarrow z)\}$ nonterminal rules

$$P_2 = \left\{ S \rightarrow \begin{matrix} & & G & & \\ & G & & G & \\ & & G & & \\ & G & & G & \\ & & G & & \end{matrix} \right\}$$ terminal rule

$$\mathscr{L} = \{L_a, L_b, L_c, L_x, L_y, L_z\}$$

set of intermediate languages

$L_a = L_c = \{G^n\langle G\rangle G^n\}$ where the letters of the arrowhead are written clockwise and the letter within $\langle\ \rangle$ appears at the vertex of the arrowhead.

$$L_b = \{G^n\langle G\rangle G^{n+1}\}, \ L_y = \{Y^n\langle Y\rangle Y^{n+1}\}$$
$$L_x = L_z = \{Y^n\langle Y\rangle Y^n\}$$

A typical derivation is shown below:

Phase 1 $S = (((S_i \nearrow a) \nwarrow b) \downarrow c)$
           $= (((([[[S \nearrow x] \nwarrow y] \downarrow z] \nearrow a)\nwarrow b)\downarrow c)$

Phase 2
$$= (((([[\ \begin{matrix} & G & \\ G & & G \\ & G & \\ G & & G \\ & G & \end{matrix}\ \ \nearrow x] \nwarrow y] \downarrow z] \nearrow a] \nwarrow b) \downarrow c)$$

Phase 3
$$= (((([[\ \begin{matrix} & & Y & \\ & G & & Y \\ G & & G & \\ & G & & Y \\ G & & G & \\ & G & & \end{matrix}\ \nwarrow y] \downarrow z] \nearrow a) \nwarrow b) \downarrow c)$$

$$\Rightarrow (((([\ Y \begin{matrix} & & Y & \\ & Y & & Y \\ & & G & Y \\ & G & & G \\ G & & G & \\ & G & & \end{matrix}\ Y \downarrow z] \nearrow a) \nwarrow b) \downarrow c)$$

$$\Rightarrow (((Y \begin{matrix} & & Y & \\ & Y & & Y \\ Y & & G & Y \\ & G & & G \\ G & & G & \\ Y & & G & Y \\ & Y & & Y \\ & & Y & \end{matrix}\ Y \nearrow a) \nwarrow b) \downarrow c)$$

148

```
                G
           G         G
        G      Y        G
     G      Y      Y       G
        Y       G      Y
     G      G       G      G
 *
 ⇒      Y       G      Y
     G      G       G      G
        Y       G      Y
     G      Y      Y       G
        G      Y       G
           G      G
              G
```

The language generated by this grammar can be recognised by an HPA as follows. H' is the input (initial configuration) of the acceptor HPA. The acceptor merely reverses the steps in the derivation and checks whether the hexagon resulting at level 2 is H_0, the r. h. s. of the terminal rule. To do this, we use an HPA with the roof labeling. The transitions are defined below.

$$\Sigma = \{G,\ Y\}$$
$$\Gamma = \{G,\ Y,\ \bar{G},\ \bar{Y},\ D,\ A,\ N\}$$

$$\Gamma_0 = \{A\}$$

$$g_{E_i}\begin{pmatrix} & G & \\ G & & G \\ & Y & \\ Y & & Y \\ & G & \end{pmatrix} = \bar{G}$$

$$g_{E_i}\begin{pmatrix} & \bar{G} & \\ \bar{G} & & \bar{G} \\ & G & \\ G & & G \\ & Y & \end{pmatrix} = G$$

$$g_{E_i}\begin{pmatrix} & \bar{G} & \\ \bar{G} & & \bar{G} \\ & G & \\ G & & G \\ & G & \end{pmatrix} = D$$

$$g_{E_i}\begin{pmatrix} & a & \\ f & & b \\ & g & \\ e & & c \\ & d & \end{pmatrix} = N \qquad \text{for any other } a,\, b,\, c,\, d,\, e,\, f,\, g \in \Gamma.$$

Similarly for other E_i:

$$g_{F_i}\begin{pmatrix} & G & \\ Y & & G \\ & Y & \\ G & & Y \\ & G & \end{pmatrix} = \bar{G}$$

$$g_{F_i}\begin{pmatrix} & \bar{G} & \\ G & & \bar{G} \\ & G & \\ Y & & G \\ & Y & \end{pmatrix} = G$$

$$g_{F_i}\begin{pmatrix} & a & \\ f & & b \\ & g & \\ e & & c \\ & d & \end{pmatrix} = N \qquad \text{for any other } a,\, b,\, c,\, d,\, e,\, f,\, g \in \Gamma.$$

Similarly for other F_i:

$$g_X\begin{pmatrix} & a & \\ f & & b \\ & g & \\ e & & c \\ & d & \end{pmatrix} = g \qquad \text{for all } a,\, b,\, c,\, d,\, e,\, f,\, g \in \Gamma.$$

$$g_R\begin{pmatrix} & D & \\ D & & D \\ & G & \\ D & & D \\ & D & \end{pmatrix} = A$$

$$g_R\begin{pmatrix} & a & \\ f & & b \\ & d & \\ e & & c \\ & g & \end{pmatrix} = N \qquad \text{for any other } a,\, b,\, c,\, d,\, e,\, f,\, g \in \Gamma.$$

There is another formal model for generating languages of hexagonal arrays, based on L-systems. L-systems were originally defined for string languages to describe the growth of biological systems. These systems have been extended to rectangular arrays[21] and hexagonal arrays.[13]

The controlled table hexagonal arrays[13] are either 0-L (context-independent) or 1-L (context-dependent, dependent on one neighbor). The starting point (axiom) is a hexagon and there are three types of tables corresponding to the three directions of concatenation $\nearrow$, $\nwarrow$ and $\downarrow$. (Six directions may also be considered). Each table consists of 0-L rules in normal form $a \to bc$ or 1-L rules in normal form $ab \to acd$ with neighborhood context. Application of a table means that the set of rules in the table acts in parallel along the entire edge defined by the arrowhead. The sequence of application of tables in the arrowhead directions is controlled by regular, context-free or context-sensitive languages. Consider the example given below.

Example 7. $G_2 = (V, H_0, \rho, C)$

$V = \{O, B\}$ is the set of terminals,

$$H_0 = \begin{matrix} & & B & & \\ & B & & B & \\ & & O & & \\ & B & & B & \\ & & B & & \end{matrix} \quad \text{is the axiom,}$$

$\rho = \{T_1, T_2, T_3\}$ is the set of tables, and

$C = \{(T_1 T_2 T_3)^n \mid n \geqslant 0\}$ is the control language regulating the application of tables.

$$T_1 = \{OB \nearrow OOB, BB \nearrow BBB\}$$

$$T_2 = \{BO \nwarrow BOO, BB \nwarrow BBB\}$$

$$T_3 = \{ \begin{matrix} O \downarrow O & & B \downarrow B \\ B \quad O & & B \quad B \\ B & & B \end{matrix} \}$$

The first three members of this language are shown in Fig. 10. The sequence of application of tables for generating H_1 is shown in Fig. 11. This language can be accepted by an HPA with roof labeling. The transitions are defined below.

$$\Sigma = \{B, O\}$$
$$\Gamma \ \{B, O, Y\}$$
$$\Gamma_0 = \{Y\}$$

$$g_{E_i} \begin{pmatrix} & B & \\ B & & B \\ & O & \\ O & & O \\ & O & \end{pmatrix} = B, \quad g_{F_i} \begin{pmatrix} & B & \\ O & & B \\ & O & \\ O & & O \\ & O & \end{pmatrix} = B,$$

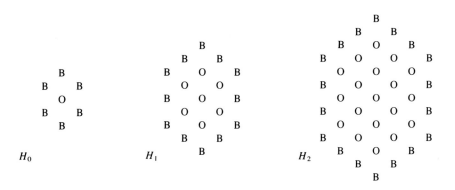

Fig. 10.   The first three members of $L(G_2)$.

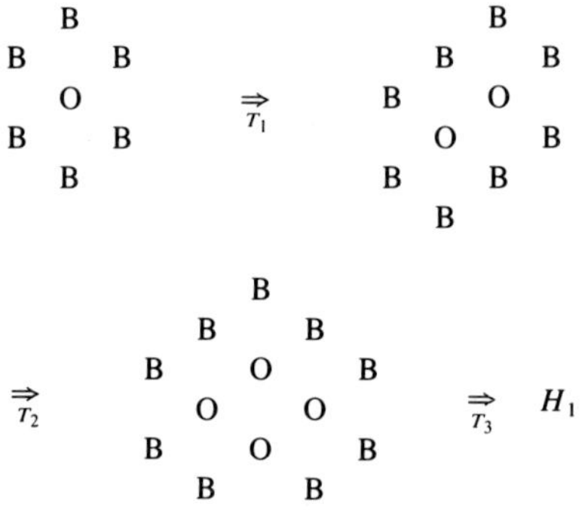

Control string $= T_1 T_2 T_3$

Fig. 11.   Derivation of H_1 in $L(G_2)$.

and similarly for other E_i and F_i:

$$
g_X \begin{pmatrix} & a & \\ f & & b \\ & O & \\ e & & c \\ & d & \end{pmatrix} = O, \qquad
g_R \begin{pmatrix} & B & \\ B & & B \\ & O & \\ B & & B \\ & B & \end{pmatrix} = Y.
$$

At each level of the HPA, the size of the hexagon being considered decreases by 1. It is as if the borders of the hexagons are shrinking uniformly. Thus for acceptance, the HPA can only consider grammars which uniformly expand all borders of the hexagon. Uniform HKAG can be defined similar to uniform (R : R)AG. However the result of

Theorem 3.14 does not extend here identically, because the original array in this case is centered in the input array, and not at any particular corner. But controlled table L-array languages with some uniformity restrictions as follows can be accepted by the HPA.
(a) The r. h. s of the terminal rule is a regular hexagon.
(b) The rules are 0-L , i.e. context-free, or 1-L i.e. neighborhood dependent on only one neighbor.
(c) All rules expand the borders of the hexagon by the same finite thickness.
(d) The control language contains strings $a_1a_2a_3 \ldots$ such that each substring $a_{3i+1}a_{3i+2}a_{3i+3}$ contains a table each from $\mathcal{T}_1$, $\mathcal{T}_2$, $\mathcal{T}_3$, where the set $\mathcal{T}_1$ (respectively $\mathcal{T}_2$, $\mathcal{T}_3$) is the set of tables appending arrowheads in the $\nearrow$ direction (respectively $\nwarrow$ and $\downarrow$ direction).

These restrictions ensure that the growth of a hexagon belonging to the language takes place uniformly, with the hexagon going through all smaller sizes of regular hexagons before reaching its full size. Hence this growth can be traced over successive levels of the HPA and suitable transitions ensuring acceptance can be defined.

6.   CONCLUSION

Systolic pyramid automata are capable of doing a number of computations. We can construct a systolic pyramid automaton which accepts only symmetric matrices. We can construct a systolic pyramid automaton consisting of pairs of elements (a, b) and define acceptance in such a way that the matrix is accepted if and only if the first component of the (i, j)th element is the same as the second component of the (j, i)th element. This amounts to finding the transpose of a matrix.

In Ref. 8 cellular pyramid automata are defined. Also there are levels of square arrays of processors. But at level n there is a $2^n \times 2^n$ array of processors. Each processor has one father, four sons and four brothers (processors at the same level). In Ref. 8 it is explained how cellular pyramid acceptors can be used for local property detection, for example, finding the number of occurrences of a symbol in a matrix. A UPCA is a pyramid cellular automaton where a processor cannot communicate with its brothers and information flows from bottom to top. It is mentioned in Ref. 8 that for UPCA, detecting arbitrary local patterns (pattern matching problem) is harder. But we find that using a systolic pyramid automaton, finding whether a local pattern occurs in an input array of size $n \times n$, can be done in time $n - 1$. This can be done by using mappings which decide whether a particular pattern occurs in the lowest few levels and if it occurs, by sending a flag to the root.

We have seen the relationship between homogeneous systolic pyramid automata and one-way 2-D cellular automata in Sect. 4. Whatever computation is done by one-way 2-D systolic arrays defined in Ref. 22, can be done by one-way 2-D cellular automata with slight modifications. We find that the same computation can be done in a systolic pyramid automaton by feeding the input in an appropriate manner. This is in agreement with the results obtained in Sect. 4. Note that the computation takes the same amount of time in both cases.

All operations which can be done on a tree of processors[1] can be done on systolic pyramid automata—like the census functions which include addition, multiplication, logical 'AND' and 'OR', minimum and maximum. But it should be noted that the computation is slower in this case. For example, to find the maximum of n elements it takes $O(\log n)$ time in a tree of processors organization. Here, to find the maximum of n^2 elements it takes time $n - 1$, i.e. to find the maximum of n elements it takes $O(\sqrt{n})$ time.

In the systolic pyramid automaton model, the information flows from bottom to top. It would be of interest to design VLSI algorithms using this type of architecture where both-way communications are allowed. In Ref. 23 data movement techniques for a pyramid computer are discussed. The pyramid computer defined there is similar to the cellular pyramid automaton of Ref. 8 where both-way communications are allowed. Algorithms for graphs and other problems are given using that architecture. It can be seen that for problems where the input is viewed as a digitized picture input, the systolic pyramid architecture defined in this paper (and Ref. 24) will be better than the pyramid architecture defined in Ref. 23, especially for problems like pattern matching (exact and approximate), component labeling, nearest neighbors, etc. The main reason is that each subarray is examined simultaneously in this case, whereas only non-overlapping subarrays are examined in the pyramid computer in Ref. 23. A topic for further research would be to develop efficient algorithms using this systolic pyramid architecture for these problems and to discuss their complexity.

The sequential machine characterization of systolic pyramid automata, and stability and decidability results as considered for trellis automata in Ref. 6, are reported in Ref. 14.

REFERENCES

1. J. D. Ullman, *Computational Aspects of VLSI*, Computer Science Press, 1984.
2. K. Culik II, J. Gruska and A. Salomaa, "Systolic automata for VLSI on balanced trees", *Acta Informatica* **18** (1983) 335–344.
3. K. Culik II, A. Salomaa and D. Wood, "Systolic tree acceptors", *R.A.I.R.O. Theoretical Informatics* **18** (1984) 53–69.
4. K. Culik II, J, Gruska and A. Salomaa, "Systolic trellis automata, Part I", *Int. J. Computer Mathematics* **15** (1984) 145–212.
5. K. Culik II, J. Gruska and A. Salomaa, "Systolic trellis automata, Part II", *Int. J. Computer Mathematics* **16** (1984) 3–22.
6. K. Culik II, J. Gruska and A. Salomaa, "Systolic trellis automata: stability, decidability and complexity', *Information and Control* **71** (1986) 218–230.
7. O. H. Ibarra and S. M. Kim, "Characterizaton and computational complexity of systolic trellis automata", *Theoretical Computer Science* **29** (1984) 123–153.
8. A. Rosenfeld, *Picture Languages*, Academic Press, 1979.
9. N. Nirmal and K. Krithivasan, "Table matrix L-systems", *Int. J. Computer Mathematics* **10** (1982) 247–265.
10. G. Siromoney, R. Siromoney and K. Krithivasan, "Abstract families of matrices and picture languages', *Computer Graphics and Image Processing* **1** (1972) 284–307.
11. G. Siromoney, R. Siromoney and K. Krithivasan, "Picture languages with array rewriting rules", *Information and Control* **22** (1973) 447–470.
12. K. Krithivasan and R. Siromoney, "Array automata and operations on array languages", *Int. J. Computer Mathematics* **4** (1974) 3–30.

13. G. Siromoney and R. Siromoney, "Hexagonal arrays and rectangular blocks", *Computer Graphics and Image Processing* **5** (1976) 353–381.
14. K. Krithivasan, "Systolic pyramid automata—properties and characterisations", DST Technical Report, Dept. of Computer Science and Engg., I. I. T., Madras, May 1988.
15. C. Choffrut and K. Culik II, "On real-time cellular automata and trellis automata", *Acta Informatica* **21** (1984) 393–407.
16. K. Krithivasan and M. Mahajan, "Hexagonal cellular automata", in *A Perspective in Theoretical Computer Science—Commemorative Volume for Gift Siromoney*, Ed. R. Narasimhan, World Scientific, Singapore 1989, pp. 134–164.
17. R. Narasimhan and V. S. N. Reddy, in *Some Experiments in Scene Generation using COMPAX in Graphics Languages*, Eds. F. Nake and A. Rosenfeld, North-Holland, Amsterdam, 1972, pp. 111–120.
18. K. Preston, Jr., "Applications of cellular automata in biomedical image processing", in *Computer Techniques in Biomedicine and Medicine*, Ed. Enoch Haga, Auerbach, Philadelphia, 1973.
19. A. Rosenfeld and J. L. Pfaltz, "Distance functions on digital pictures", *Pattern Recognition* **1** (1968) 33–61.
20. P. V. Sankar, "A vertex coding scheme for interpreting ambiguous trihedral solids", Technical Report 127, Tata Institute of Fundamental Research, Bombay, Nov. 1974.
21. G. Siromoney, R. Siromoney and K. Krithivasan, "Array grammars and kolam", *Computer Graphics and Image Processing* **3** (1984) 63–82.
22. O. H. Ibarra, M. A. Palis and S. M. Kim, "Designing systolic algorithms using sequential machines", *Proceedings of FOCS 1984*, pp. 46–55.
23. R. Miller and Q. F. Stout, "Data movement for the pyramid computer", *SIAM Journal of Computing* **16** (1987) 38–60.
24. K. Krithivasan, "Parallel recognition of array languages", *SIAM Conf. on Discrete Mathematics*, San Francisco, CA, June 1988.

Kamala Krithivasan obtained her B.Sc. and M.Sc. degrees in mathematics from Madras Christian College (1967) and Madras University (1969) respectively. She received her Ph.D. degree in 1975 from Madras University for her work in array languages. In 1975, she joined the Department of Computer Science and Engineering, Indian Institute of Technology, Madras. At present she is an Associate Professor in that department. During 1986–87, she visited the University of Maryland under the Fulbright scholarship. She has authored many papers in the area of formal languages and automata, especially in array languages. Currently her interests are in cellular automata, graph grammars and path planning problems.

Meena Mahajan obtained her B.Tech and M.Tech degrees in computer science from the Indian Institute of Technology (IIT), Bombay in 1986 and 1988 respectively. At present she is working at IIT, Madras for her Ph.D. degree in the area of formal languages and automata, under the guidance of Dr. Kamala Krithivasan.

COORDINATE GRAMMARS REVISITED: GENERALIZED ISOMETRIC GRAMMARS

AZRIEL ROSENFELD

Center for Automation Research
University of Maryland, College Park, MD 20742, USA

Received 10 December 1987
Revised 11 May 1988

In a "coordinate grammar", the rewriting rules replace sets of symbols having been given coordinates by sets of symbols whose coordinates are given functions of the coordinates of the original symbols. It was shown in 1972 that coordinate grammars are "too powerful"; even if the rules are all of finite-state types and the functions are all computable by finite transducers, the grammar has the power of a Turing machine. This paper shows that if we require the functions to be shift-invariant and the rules to be of bounded diameter, then such grammars do have a useful hierarchy of types; in fact, when we require that their sentential forms always remain connected, they turn out to be equivalent to "isometric grammars".

Keywords: Coordinate grammars; Isometric grammars; Picture languages; Array grammars.

1. INTRODUCTION

In a "coordinate grammar", or "grammar with coordinates", each symbol has coordinates (e.g. d-tuples of integers) associated with it. A rewriting rule in such a grammar replaces a tuple of symbols, say $A_1, \ldots, A_m$, by another tuple of symbols, say $B_1, \ldots, B_n$, where the coordinates of the B's are computed from those of the A's by a set of partial functions associated with the given rule.

It was shown in Ref. 1 that such grammars are "too powerful", in the sense that even if the forms of the rules and the nature of the coordinate-computing functions are greatly restricted, they already have the power of a Turing machine. Specifically, it was shown for the one-dimensional case ($d = 1$) that even if the rules are all of finite-state type (e.g. right linear: a single nonterminal symbol is replaced either by a single terminal symbol, or by a terminal symbol located to the right of a new nonterminal symbol) and the functions are all computable by one-way finite transducers, it is still possible to compute any partial recursive function.

It was suggested in Ref. 1 that coordinate grammars might be made more interesting by imposing a boundedness constraint on the coordinate computing functions, i.e. requiring that the new symbols are all within a bounded distance of the old symbols. However, this idea was not pursued.

This paper reopens the subject of coordinate grammars and shows that if we introduce boundedness constraints, we do obtain a reasonable hierarchy of grammar types. In fact, it shows that boundedness-constrained coordinate grammars are closely related to "isometric grammars",[2] which (in one dimension) have a hierarchy very similar to that of conventional grammars.

157

International Journal of Pattern Recognition and Artificial Intelligence Vol. 3 No. 3 & 4 (1989) 435–444
© World Scientific Publishing Company

Sections 2–4 of this paper define the class of coordinate grammars that we will consider (we call them C-grammars, for brevity) and discuss some of their properties, treating primarily the one-dimensional case ($d = 1$). Section 5 introduces conditions on one-dimensional C-grammars that insure that all sentential forms are connected strings; this is done in order to allow comparison between C-grammars and conventional string grammars, and in fact to show that connectedness-preserving C-grammars are equivalent to isometric grammars. Section 6 discusses various extensions and restrictions of these concepts, including the special cases of monotonic and "finite-state" C-grammars, as well as the extension to d dimensions ($d > 1$).

2. RESTRICTIONS ON COORDINATE GRAMMARS

In this section we introduce the restrictions on the coordinates and coordinate-computing functions that will be imposed on the coordinate grammars considered in this paper.

In a general coordinate grammar, the coordinates can in principle be arbitrary real numbers, so that symbols can be located anywhere in (d-dimensional) Euclidean space. However, since we are primarily interested in discrete patterns of symbols (strings, arrays, . . .), it is reasonable to require that the coordinates be *integers*, and we shall do so from now on.

The coordinates associated with a symbol can be arbitrarily large, since we want to be able to generate arbitrarily large strings, etc. However, we shall require that the sets of coordinates involved in a given rewriting rule be of *bounded diameter*—i.e. that in any given rule $(A_1, \ldots, A_m) \rightarrow (B_1, \ldots, B_n)$, all the A's must be within a bounded distance of one another and all the B's must be within a bounded distance of the A's.

In a general coordinate grammar, the applicability of a rule can depend on the absolute coordinates of the A's. This is not true for other types of grammars, where any instance of the left-hand side of a rule can be replaced by the right-hand side, no matter where it occurs. We shall require from now on that our rules be *shift-invariant*—in other words, that the applicability of any rule $(A_1, \ldots, A_m) \rightarrow (B_1, \ldots, B_n)$ depends only on the positions of the A's relative to one another, but not on their absolute positions.

When we require that all rules be shift-invariant and of bounded diameter, it is no longer necessary to explicitly associate coordinates with each symbol, or to explicitly compute coordinates when a rule is applied. Rather, we can regard the rule $(A_1. \ldots, A_m) \rightarrow (B_1, \ldots, B_n)$ as applicable to certain specific arrangements of the A's, wherever they occur, and we apply the rule to such an arrangement by erasing the A's and creating B's in the appropriate positions (relative to where the A's were). Without loss of generality, we shall assume from now on that each rule applies to just one specific arrangement of A's. Viewed in this way, our restricted class of coordinate grammars can be regarded as replacing "templates" of symbols (i.e. arrangements of symbols in given relative positions) by templates of symbols.

It should be pointed out that rewriting one-dimensional "templates" is quite different from rewriting strings. In a string grammar, when we replace the string $\alpha \equiv A_1 \cdots A_m$ by the string $\beta \equiv B_1 \cdots B_n$, the B's are not put into specified positions relative to the

A's. Rather, given the string $\rho\alpha\sigma$, we rewrite it as $\rho\beta\sigma$, irrespective of whether the number of B's is less than, equal to, or greater than the number of A's. If we regard the symbols as having coordinates, this implies that the coordinates of the symbols in ρ (or σ, or both) may have to change when we replace α by β. This does not happen in a coordinate grammar, where the coordinates of symbols not explicitly occurring in a rule are not affected by applying the rule. On the other hand, in a coordinate grammar, if we replace $A_1 \cdots A_m$ by $B_1 \cdots B_n$ where $n > m$, we do not push apart the other symbols to make room for the extra B's; they are written in the positions specified by the rule, and may overwrite other symbols that already exist in those positions. Conversely, if $n < m$, the other symbols are not pushed together to make up for the missing A's; the positions in which A's were erased and B's were not written are left blank. (For this reason, we will make explicit use of a "blank symbol" $\#$ when we formally define our coordinate grammars in Sect. 3.) Note that as a result, application of a rule may cause the non-blank symbols to become disconnected. In Sect. 4 we will define conditions on a coordinate grammar that insure preservation of connectedness.

3. C-GRAMMARS

Based on the informal discussion Sect. 2, we are now ready to formally define a C-grammar (in one dimension) as a 5-tuple $G \equiv (V, V_T, \Pi, s, \#)$, where

V is a finite, nonempty set of symbols, called the *vocabulary*,

$\varnothing \subsetneqq V_T \subsetneqq V$ is called the *terminal vocabulary*,

$s \in V - V_T$ is called the *start symbol*,

$\# \in V - V_T$ is called the *blank symbol*,

Π is a finite, nonempty set of pairs (α, β) where α, β are non-null tuples of elements of V, located in specified relative positions, as described below. These pairs are called the *rules* of G, and are written in the form $\alpha \to \beta$, denoting the fact that α can be replaced by β.

In more detail, the relative positions of the symbols in a rule are specified by writing the rule in the form

$$\alpha \equiv (A_1, \ldots, A_m | i_1, i_2, \ldots, i_m) \text{ where } 0 = i_1 < i_2 < \cdots < i_m \leqslant k,$$

$$\beta \equiv (B_1, \ldots, B_n | j_1, \ldots, j_n) \text{ where } -k \leqslant j_1 < \cdots < j_n \leqslant k.$$

Here k (the same for all rules) defines the bound on the rule diameters; i_r is the position of A_r relative to A_1 (i.e. if A_1 has integer coordinate t, then A_r has coordinate $t + i_r$); and j_r is the position of B_r relative to A_1.

In order to define the language of G, we must first define patterns and derivations. A *pattern* is a mapping from the integers into V which maps all but finitely many integers into #. We say that the pattern τ is *directly derivable* in G from the pattern σ if there exists a rule $\alpha \to \beta$ of G such that:

(a) The symbols of α occur in σ in the specified relative positions—in other words, for some t we have $\sigma(t + i_r) = A_r$, $1 \leqslant r \leqslant m$,

(b) τ is the result of deleting these occurrences of the symbols of α and inserting the symbols of β in the specified relative positions—in other words, if we change the symbols at positions $t + i_r$ to #, $1 \leqslant r \leqslant m$, and then change the symbols at. positions $t + j_r$ to B_r, $1 \leqslant r \leqslant n$, the resulting pattern is τ.

We say that τ is *derivable* in G from σ if there exists a finite sequence of patterns $\sigma \equiv \sigma_0$, $\sigma_1, \ldots, \sigma_h \equiv \tau$ such that σ_i is directly derivable in G from σ_{i-1}, $1 \leqslant i \leqslant h$. $L(G)$, the *language* of G, is the set of patterns τ such that

(i) The non-# symbols in τ (i.e. the non-# images of integers under τ) are all in V_T,

(ii) τ is derivable in G from a pattern of the form $\#^\infty s \#^\infty$—i.e. a pattern that maps one integer into s and all other integers into #.

Note that the non-# symbols in τ need not be connected; in the next section we will discuss conditions on G that imply connectedness. The language of a C-grammar will be called a *C-language*.

Any C-language has a C-grammar in which terminal symbols are never rewritten by any rule—in other words, for any rule $\alpha \to \beta$, if $A_u \in V_T$, $1 \leqslant u \leqslant m$, then there exists v, $1 \leqslant v \leqslant n$, such that $j_v = i_u$ and $B_v = A_u$. In fact, let G be any C-grammar; then we can define a C-grammar G' such that $L(G') = L(G)$ and terminal symbols are not rewritten by the rules of G'. Specifically, we define G' to have nonterminal vocabulary $(V - V_T) \cup V'_T$ and terminal vocabulary V_T, where V'_T is a set of primed copies of the symbols in V_T. For each rule $\alpha \to \beta$ of G we have the rule $\alpha' \to \beta'$ in G', where the primes denote the fact that each symbol in V_T is replaced by the corresponding symbol in V'_T. In addition, G' has the rules $a' \to a$ for all $a \in V_T$. Evidently any pattern in $L(G)$ is in $L(G')$, since in G' we can derive the corresponding pattern with primed terminal symbols, and then change them to unprimed symbols using the $a' \to a$ rules. Conversely, any pattern in $L(G')$ is in $L(G)$, since the only rules of G' that produce symbols in V_T are the $a' \to a$ rules, so that the corresponding pattern with primed terminal symbols must be derivable in G' using the other rules. We shall assume from now on that terminal symbols are never rewritten.

We conclude this section by giving three trivial examples of C-grammars. If the rules of G are $(s|0) \to (a, s|0, 1)$ and $(s|0) \to (a|0)$, $L(G)$ is the set of all strings of a's (embedded in an infinite string of #'s); if the rules are $(s|0) \to (a, s|0, 2)$ and $(s|0) \to (a|0)$, $L(G)$ is the set of patterns of a's alternating with #'s); if the rules are $(s|0) \to (a, t|0, 1)$, $(t|0) \to (t|1)$ and $(t|0) \to (a|0)$, $L(G)$ is the set of pairs of a's an arbitrary distance ($\geqslant 1$) apart.

4.   A STANDARD FORM FOR C-GRAMMARS

In an arbitrary C-grammar, the A's and B's in a given rule need not be in the same positions: i_u need not be one of the j's, and j_v need not be one of the i's. Note that if i_u is not one of the j's, then when the rule is applied, A_u is replaced by a $\#$, even though the rule did not specify that a $\#$ was to be written in position i_u (relative to the position of A_1). Conversely, if j_v is not one of the i's, then when the rule is applied, B_v is written in place of whatever symbol ($\#$ or non-$\#$) was located in position j_v (relative to A_1), even though that symbol is not mentioned in the rule.[a]

In fact, however, any C-language $L(G)$ has a C-grammar G^* in which, in every rule, the A's and B's are in the same set of positions (and in particular, $m = n$). We can define G^* as follows:

(a) Let $\alpha \to \beta$ be a rule of G. For each $u(1 \leqslant u \leqslant m)$ such that i_u is not one of the j's, insert a $\#$ into the tuple of B's in position i_u. Evidently, applying the resulting modified rule to any pattern has exactly the same effect as applying the original rule $\alpha \to \beta$.

(b) For each $v(1 \leqslant v \leqslant n)$ such that j_v is not one of the i's, and each symbol X in V, create a new rule by inserting an X into the tuple of A's in position j_v. (Note that this replaces the original rule by pq new rules, where p is the number of v's such that j_v is not one of the i's, and q is the number of symbols in V.)

Evidently, after performing steps (a) and (b), each of the pq new rules has the same number of A's as B's, and the B's are in the same positions as the A's (relative to A_1). Moreover, whenever the original rule $\alpha \to \beta$ applies to a given pattern, exactly one of the new rules applies (namely, the one for which the symbols in the j_v positions are the ones that actually occur in the given pattern), and applying it produces the same result as applying $\alpha \to \beta$.

We say that a C-grammar is in *standard form* if for any rule $\alpha \to \beta$ we have

$$\begin{aligned} \alpha &\equiv (A_1, \ldots, A_m | h_1, \ldots, h_m) \\ \beta &\equiv (B_1, \ldots, B_m | h_1, \ldots, h_m) \end{aligned} \quad \text{where } -k \leqslant h_1 < \cdots < 0 < \cdots < h_m \leqslant k.$$

Here 0 is one of the h's, say h_i, and h_j is the position of A_j and B_j relative to A_i (and B_i). The preceding paragraph shows that any C-language has a C-grammar in standard form.

We can now establish a relationship between ordinary (string) languages and C-languages. It is shown in Ref. 2 that the string languages (i.e. the languages generated by "type 0" grammars) are the same as the languages generated by "isometric grammars". In an isometric grammar, the rules are of the form $\alpha \to \beta$ where α and β are strings having the same length. (The rules must also satisfy additional restrictions in order to insure that the set of non-$\#$ symbols remains connected, but the nature of these restrictions need not concern us for the moment.) Let G be a C-grammar in standard form such that, in every rule $\alpha \to \beta$, the h's are *consecutive* integers, i.e. $h_{i+1} = h_i + 1$, $1 \leqslant i < m$. Evidently, the rules of such a grammar can be regarded as isometric string rewriting rules. Thus isometric grammars can be regarded as a special class of

---

[a] Grammars having rules of this type are of limited power because they (sometimes) rewrite symbols "blindly"; but the effects of allowing/forbidding rules of this type will not be explored here.

C-grammars. Since every string language is the language of an isometric grammar, we have thus proved

Proposition 4.1.   Every string language is a C-language.   ∎

(More precisely: for any string language L, there exists a C-language L' such that σ is a string in L iff $\#^\infty \sigma \#^\infty$ is a pattern in L'.)

Evidently, a C-language need not be a string language, since it can generate patterns in which the non-$\#$'s are not connected. In the next section we will consider restrictions on a C-grammar that insure that the non-$\#$'s in the patterns it generates always remain connected. We will then be able to show that if a C-grammar satisfies these restrictions, its language can be regarded as a string language.

5.   CONNECTEDNESS PRESERVATION

In this section we define a set of conditions on the rules of a C-grammar (which we assume to be in standard form) that insure that when we apply a rule to a pattern in which the non-$\#$'s are connected, they remain connected. [Connectedness of the non-$\#$'s in a one-dimensional pattern σ means that there exist integers p, q such that $\sigma(i) \neq \#$ iff $p \leq i \leq q$. We also require that the set of non-$\#$'s be nonempty, i.e. $p \leq q$. We will not treat connectedness for d-dimensional patterns in detail (see Sect. 6.3), but roughly speaking it means that if u, v are d-tuples which are the positions of non-$\#$'s, then there exists a sequence $u \equiv u_0, u_1, \ldots , u_r \equiv v$ of d-tuples (a "path") such that u_i is a neighbor of u_{i-1}, $1 \leq i \leq r$, and all the u's are the positions of non-$\#$'s.] Note that, in particular, in an initial pattern $\#^\infty s \#^\infty$, the non-$\#$'s are connected. Thus if the rules of G preserve connectedness, any pattern derivable from $\#^\infty s \#^\infty$, and in particular any pattern in $L(G)$, has connected non-$\#$'s.

For a given rule $\alpha \to \beta$, let $S = \{h_i | A_i = \#$ and $B_i \neq \#\}$ and $T = \{h_i | A_i \neq \#$ and $B_i = \#\}$. Our conditions on the rule can be stated [for arbitrary d] in terms of S and T as follows:

(a) For each $h_i \in S$, B_i is connected in β to some non-$\#$ B_j such that $h_j \notin S$. [When $d = 1$, to insure connectedness of B_i to B_j in β, where (say) $h_i < h_j$, all the integers between h_i and h_j must be h's and the corresponding B's must all be non-$\#$; otherwise, B_i might not be connected to B_j, since $\#$'s might occur between them.]

(b) For each $h_i \in T$, any pair of neighbors of h_i that are non-$\#$ in α or that are not h's must be connected in α by a path not containing any symbol in T (except possibly for its endpoints). [When $d = 1$, h_i has only one pair of neighbors ($h_i - 1$ and $h_i + 1$), and since $h_i \in T$, these neighbors cannot be connected as required by (b); hence the neighbors of h_i cannot have the properties in (b), i.e. at least one of them must be an h and must be $\#$ in α.]

We shall also assume that β always contains non-$\#$'s. [Note that by (a) it follows that α also contains non-$\#$'s.]

We now prove that if (a) and (b) hold, and we apply $\alpha \to \beta$ to a pattern σ in which the non-$\#$'s are connected, they remain connected in the resulting pattern τ. It suffices to show that if u, v are the positions of any non-$\#$ symbols in τ, then they are connected by non-$\#$'s in τ. Suppose first that neither u nor v is in S; then they were non-$\#$ in σ, and so were connected in σ. If there is a path ρ joining them in σ that contains no elements of T, it still consists of non-#'s in τ, and we are done. If not, let h_i be any element of T on ρ; then the predecessor and successor of h_i on ρ are neighbors of h_i that are either non-# in α or are not h's. By (b), the predecessor and successor are connected in α by a path ρ_i not containing any symbol in T (except possibly for its endpoints). Thus we can drop h_i from ρ and join its predecessor and successor using ρ_i; this eliminates one element of T from ρ without adding any new elements of T to ρ. By doing this for each element of T on ρ, we obtain a path joining u and v in σ that contains no elements of T.

Finally, suppose that u or v (or both) is in S. By (a), if $u \in S$, it is connected in β (hence in τ) to some non-# u' that is not in S; and similarly for v. By the preceding paragraph, u' and v' (or u' and v, or u and v') are connected in τ, hence u and v are connected in τ, completing the proof.

If the rules of a C-grammar G satisfy (a) and (b), the patterns in $L(G)$ all have connected non-#'s, so $L(G)$ can be regarded as a set of strings. It remains to show that this set of strings is a string language. To this end, we shall show that $L(G)$ has a C-grammar in which the h's in any rule are consecutive integers, so that the rules can be regarded as isometric string rewriting rules, and that these isometric rules preserve connectedness; thus $L(G)$ can be regarded as an isometric string language.

We first observe that any C-language has a C-grammar in standard form in which, in any rule, the h's are consecutive integers. Indeed, given a standard form C-grammar, we simply fill the gaps in each rule with all possible vocabulary symbols, as we did in step (b) in Sect. 4. Evidently, whenever the rule $\alpha \rightarrow \beta$ applies, exactly one of these augmented rules applies (namely, the one such that the filled-in symbols are actually present), and applying it has the same effect (since the filled-in symbols are the same on both sides of the rule). Thus $L(G)$ does not change if we assume that in every rule of G, the h's are connective integers.

Let G satisfy (a) and (b), and suppose G has rules $\alpha \rightarrow \beta$ in which the non-#'s in α are not connected. Since (a) and (b) imply that any derivable pattern has connected non-#'s, no such rule can ever apply. Hence if we discard these rules, $L(G)$ does not change. We can thus assume that in every rule $\alpha \rightarrow \beta$ of G, the non-#'s in α are connected, so that α is of the form $\#^r \alpha' \#^s$ where r, $s \geq 0$ and α' is a string of non-#'s.

We next prove that, for any rule $\alpha \rightarrow \beta$ of G, the non-#'s in β are connected. We have already assumed that non-#'s exist in β. By (b), every # in β that was non-# in α has a neighbor that was # in α. Since the non-#'s in α are a connected string α', only the first and last symbols of α' have # neighbors, so only they can become # in β, and the remaining symbols of α' give rise to a string β' of non-#'s in β that were non-# in α. By (a), every non-# in β either was itself non-# in α (so is in β'), or is connected in β to a non-# in β'. Thus the non-#'s in β are connected.

Finally, we prove that if h_1 is non-# in α, it is also non-# in β (and similarly for h_m). By (b), since $h_1 - 1$ is not an h, $h_1 + 1$ must be an h and must be # in α. But the non-#'s in α are connected; hence there can be no other non-#'s in α, i.e. α is of the form $A \#^s$ (where $s \geq 1$). Now there are non-#'s in β, so that by (a) there is a non-# in β that was non-# in α; hence h_1 is non-# in β.

We have thus proved that G, regarded as an isometric string grammar, satisfies the conditions[2] that insure preservation of connectedness. This completes the proof of

Proposition 5.1. Every C-language having a grammar that satisfies (a) and (b) is a string language. ∎

6. RESTRICTIONS AND EXTENSIONS

6.1. Monotonicity

We say that a C-grammar (in standard form) is *monotonic* if no rule creates #'s, i.e. if $B_i = \#$ implies $A_i = \#$, $1 \leqslant i \leqslant m$. Since in Ref. 2 the isometric languages that never create #'s are the same as the monotonic string languages, it follows immediately that every monotonic string language is a monotonic C-language. Conversely, since monotonicity is compatible with (a) and (b), every monotonic C-language having a grammar that satisfies (a) and (b) is a monotonic string language. Note that for monotonic C-grammars $T = \varnothing$; hence (b) is vacuous, and (a) is sufficient to guarantee that connectedness is preserved. (We also need to assume that in any rule $\alpha \to \beta$, α contains non-#'s; this guarantees that β also contains non-#'s.)

For C-grammars that are not in standard form, if any A_i is not a B_j, a # is created; thus if we want monotonicity we must require that every A_i be a B_j. On the other hand, if any B_j is not an A_i, if the B_j is non-# we can put any A in the jth position, but if it is # we can only put a # in the jth position. Thus we can define monotonicity for C-grammars that are not in standard form by requiring that every A_i be a B_j, and that every # B_j be a # A_i. The standard form of such a grammar is evidently monotonic.

6.2. Finite-Stateness

It is shown in Ref. 2 that the isometric grammars in which the left side of each rule consists of a single non-# together with #'s, and the right side consists of non-#'s, generate exactly the finite-state languages. Evidently any such grammar can be regarded as a C-grammar, and evidently it preserves connectedness of the non-#'s. On the other hand, consider a C-grammar in standard form in which all but one of the A's are #'s and all the B's are non-#'s. If this grammar is to preserve connectedness of the non-#'s, by (a) of Sect. 5 the (non-#) B's cannot have gaps between them, so that the rule must in fact be in isometric form. Thus the languages of such C-grammars are exactly the finite-state languages. Finally, consider a C-grammar in non-standard form in which each rule rewrites only one non-# and creates only non-#'s. Since such a grammar is monotonic, as we saw in Sect. 6.1 all the A's must be B's; and to insure that the rule rewrites only the non-#, all the B's must be A's, so that such a grammar must be in standard form.

6.3. Higher Dimensions

The definition of a C-grammar given in Sect. 3 extends straightforwardly to d dimensions. Instead of using single integers to represent the relative displacements of the symbols in a rule, we use d-tuples of integers. Otherwise, the definitions of a C-grammar, a derivation, and a C-language remain exactly the same, as does the definition of standard form in Sect. 4 (but now using d-tuples).

It follows that (two-dimensional) array grammars, which rewrite arrays of symbols as geometrically identical arrays of symbols, are a special case of two-dimensional C-grammars, so that every array language is a C-language.

In Sect. 5 we gave general conditions on a C-grammar that insure that the non-#'s remain connected. To prove that every 2-D C-language for which the conditions hold is an array language, we only need to make sure that when we "fill in" the gaps in the rules (so that they rewrite connected arrays), the conditions in Ref. 2 for any array grammar to preserve connectedness hold for the filled-in rules. We will not give the details of the proof here.

Finally, the concepts of monotonicity and finite-stateness generalize straightforwardly to d dimensions; again, we omit the details.

It would be of interest to study the relationships between C-grammars and other types of grammars that generate d-dimensional arrays, as well as the various types of array acceptors. For references to the literature on such grammars and acceptors see the author's bibliographies entitled "Picture Processing 19xx", which appear annually in the journal *Computer Vision, Graphics, and Image Processing*, under the heading "formal models".

6.4. Hierarchies

Coordinate grammars whose rules have bounded diameter can generate patterns of arbitrary size, but they do so inefficiently, requiring long derivations to generate large patterns. An interesting possible generalization would be a "hierarchy" of C-grammars which generate patterns at different scales (i.e. with different-sized units of length in their coordinate systems), where the terminal symbols in a large-scale pattern (at coordinates which are multiples of a large unit) become initial symbols for generating patterns at the next smaller scale (using coordinates which are multiples of a smaller unit). Such C-grammar hierarchies would be very appropriate for generating patterns that have hierarchical structures, as is frequently desirable in pattern recognition applications.

6.5. Parallelism

In this paper we have considered only "sequential" coordinate grammars, in which at each step of a derivation, only one rule is applied and only one instance of its left hand side is rewritten. It would be of interest to consider parallel rule application in C-grammars, as is done for isometric and array grammars in Ref. 2.

7. CONCLUDING REMARKS

C-grammars are a generalization of isometric grammars (in one or more dimensions) that are capable of generating non-connected patterns; they become the same as isometric grammars when we restrict them to generate only connected patterns. Like isometric grammars, they have a nontrivial Chomsky-like hierarchy, at least as regards Chomsky types 0, 1 and 3. They are a natural mechanism for generating classes of patterns in which connectedness would be an artificial restriction—e.g. labeled dots in the (discrete) plane. Their properties and capabilities deserve further study.

ACKNOWLEDGEMENTS

The support of the U. S. Air Force Office of Scientific Research under Grant AFOSR-86-0092 is gratefully acknowledged, as is the help of Sandy German in preparing this paper. The author thanks Rameshkumar Sitaraman for greatly improving Sect. 5 of this paper.

REFERENCES

1. D. L. Milgram and A. Rosenfeld, "A note on 'grammars with coordinates'" in *Graphic Languages*, Eds. F. Nake and A. Rosenfeld, North-Holland, Amsterdam, 1972, pp. 187–191.
2. A. Rosenfeld, *Picture Languages*, Academic Press, New York, 1979, Sec. 8.1.3.

Azriel Rosenfeld is a tenured Research Professor and Director of the Center for Automation Research, a department-level unit of the University of Maryland in College Park. He also holds Affiliate Professorships in the Departments of Computer Science and Psychology and in the College of Engineering. He holds a Ph.D. in mathematics from Columbia University (1957), rabbinic ordination (1952) and a Doctor of Hebrew Literature degree (1955) from Yeshiva University, and an honorary Doctor of Technology degree from Linköping University, Sweden (1980), and is a certified Manufacturing Engineer (1988).

He is a Fellow of the Institute of Electrical and Electronics Engineers (1971), and won its Emanuel Piore Award in 1985; he was a founding Director of the Machine Vision Association of the Society of Manufacturing Engineers (1985–8), and won its President's Award in 1987; he was a founding member of the IEEE Computer Society's Technical Committee on Pattern Analysis and Machine Intelligence (1965), served as its Chairman (1985–7), and received the Society's Meritorious Service Award in 1986; he was a founding member of the Governing Board of the International Association for Pattern Recognition (1978–85), served as its President

He is a widely known researcher in the field of computer image analysis. He wrote the first textbook in the field (1969); was a founding editor of its first journal (1972); and was co-chairman of its first international conference (1987). He has published over 20 books and over 400 book chapters and journal articles, and has directed over 30 Ph.D. dissertations.

(1980–2), and won its first K. S. Fu Award in 1988; he is a Fellow of the Washington Academy of Sciences (1988), and won its Mathematics and Computer Science Award in 1988; he is a Corresponding Member of the National Academy of Engineering of Mexico (1982) and a Foreign Member of the Academy of Science of the German Democratic Republic (1988).

RELATIONSHIPS BETWEEN
COORDINATE GRAMMARS AND
PATH CONTROLLED GRAPH GRAMMARS

AKIRA NAKAMURA and KUNIO AIZAWA

Department of Applied Mathematics, Hiroshima University
Higashi-Hiroshima, 724, Japan

Received 20 April 1989
Revised 12 May 1989

We define a graph grammar called node-replacement graph grammar with path controlled embedding (nPCE grammars) which use a sequence of edges instead of the single edge to embed a newly replaced graph into the host graph, then show some relationships between two-dimensional "coordinate grammars" and nPCE grammars. We also suggest an extension of PCE grammars to describe "disconnected coordinate languages".

Keywords: Coordinate grammars; Disconnected languages; Graph grammars; Picture languages.

1. INTRODUCTION

Two-dimensional grammars (or array grammars) play important roles in image processing and pattern recognition. In such areas, there exist some cases where the relationships between several separated objects are very important. To generate some separated patterns from a connected pattern, it is convenient that symbols have their own coordinates. In a "coordinate grammar", each symbol has coordinates (e.g. d-tuples of integers) associated with it. A rewriting rule in the grammar replaces a tuple of symbols, e.g. $A_1, \ldots, A_m$, by another tuple of symbols, $B_1, \ldots, B_n$, where the coordinates of the Bs are computed from those of the As by a set of partial functions associated with the given rule. It was shown in Milgram and Rosenfeld[1] that such grammars are "too powerful", in the sense that even if the form of the rules and the nature of the coordinate-computing functions are greatly restricted, they already have the power of a Turing machine. It was suggested in the same paper that coordinate grammars might be made more interesting by imposing a boundedness constraint on the coordinate computing functions, i.e. requiring that the new symbols are all within a bounded distance of the old symbols. In Rosenfeld,[2] boundedness-constrained coordinate grammars are shown to be closely related to isometric grammars, which have a hierarchy very similar to that of conventional grammars.

On the other hand, many models for graph grammars have been proposed as a kind of hyper-dimensional generating system (see e.g. Refs. 3–6). The basic primitive in a graph grammar is a directed (or non-directed) graph which is a set of labeled vertices and labeled edges. Thus, most of the graph grammars have some kind of the "embedding" rules as

167

well as the "production" rules to embed the newly replaced graph in its host graph. One of the reasons why graph generating systems were proposed is to generalize the (one-dimensional or string) formal grammars to two-dimensional or more complex structures. However, few have known about the relationships between graph grammars and two-dimensional formal grammars. It is obvious that the graph grammars with no restrictions are more powerful than or incomparable with the two-dimensional formal grammars since there exist many graphs which cannot be embedded in any two-dimensional structures. Thus, in order to investigate such relationships, the graph grammars are restricted such that they can generate planar graphs only. In the two-dimensional formal grammars, the "array" is used as an implicit structure of the generated patterns (i.e. two-dimensional words). Even if restricted to planar graphs, almost all structures, on the other hand, can be formed in the graph grammars by making use of various "embedding" rules. Therefore, it is necessary to restrict the array grammars within the graphs having the two-dimensional array structure. It has been shown in Ref. 7, however, that such restriction may bring sufficient generative power as an isometric array grammar into a graph grammar having production rules of the context-free style.

In this paper, we will define a graph grammar called node-replacement graph grammar with path controlled embedding (nPCE grammar) which uses a sequence of edges instead of the single edge to embed a newly replaced graph into the host graph. Then we will show some relationships between two-dimensional coordinate grammars and nPCE grammars. We also suggest an extension of PCE grammars to describe "disconnected coordinate languages".

We assume that readers are familiar with the theories of two-dimensional grammars and graph grammars (see e.g. Refs. 8 and 9). The following notations will be used in the rest of this paper.

(1) Let X and Y be sets. By 2^X we denote the set of subsets of X and by $X \backslash Y$ we denote the set $\{x \mid x \in X, \ x \notin Y\}$. If X is finite, then $\#X$ denotes the cardinality of X.

(2) Let X, Y, Z be sets, let f be a mapping from X into Y and let g be a mapping from Y into Z. By $g \circ f$ we denote the composition of f and g (first f, then g).

(3) A *graph* is a system $H = (V, E, \Sigma_V, \Sigma_E, \phi_V, \phi_E)$, where V is a finite nonempty set called the *set of nodes*, E is a set of pairs of two elements from V called the *set of edges*, Σ_V is a finite nonempty set called the *set of node labels*, Σ_E is a finite nonempty set called the *set of edge labels*, ϕ_V is a mapping from V into Σ_V called the *nodes labeling function*, and ϕ_E is a mapping from E into Σ_E called the *edges labeling function*. H is called a graph over (Σ_V, Σ_E). Throughout this paper, $V(H)$ and $E(H)$ denote the set of nodes and the set of edges of H respectively.

(4) Let $H = (V, E, \Sigma_V, \Sigma_E, \phi_V, \phi_E)$ be a graph and let (x, y) be an edge of H. We say that the edge (x, y) is *incident with* the nodes x and y, and the nodes x, y are *neighbors*.

(5) Let $H = (V, E, \Sigma_V, \Sigma_E, \phi_V, \phi_E)$ be a graph and let x be a node of H. Then the *degree of* x, denoted as $\deg(x)$, is the number of edges incident with x.

(6) Let $A = (V, E, \Sigma_V, \Sigma_E, \phi_V, \phi_E)$ and $B = (V', E', \Sigma_V', \Sigma_E', \phi_V', \phi_E')$ be graphs.

A is a *subgraph* of B of $V' \supseteq V$, $E' \cap \{(x, y) \mid x, y \in V\} \supseteq E$, $\Sigma_{V'} \supseteq \Sigma_V$, $\Sigma_{E'} \supseteq \Sigma_E$, $\phi_{V'}(x) = \phi_V(x)$ for $\forall x \in V$, $\phi_{E'}((x, y)) = \phi_E((x, y))$ for $\forall(x, y) \in E$. In this case, we call A the subgraph *spanned by V in B*. By $B\text{-}A$ we denote the subgraph spanned by $V'\backslash V$ in B.

(7) Let $A = (V, E, \Sigma_V, \Sigma_E, \phi_V, \phi_E)$ and $B = (V', E', \Sigma_V, \Sigma_E, \phi_{V'}, \phi_{E'})$ over (Σ_V, Σ_E). An *isomorphism from A into B* is a bijective mapping h from V into V' such that $\phi_{V'}h = \phi_V$ and $E' = \{(h(x), h(y)) \mid (x, y) \in E\}$. We say that A *is isomorphic to B*.

(8) A graph $A = (V, E, \Sigma_V, \Sigma_E, \phi_V, \phi_E)$ is connected if for every x, y in V, there exists a sequence $x_1, x_2, \ldots, x_n$ of nodes in V such that $x_1 = x$, $x_n = y$ and for $1 \leqslant i \leqslant n - 1$, x_i is a neighbor of x_{i+1}.

(9) Given a class X of rewriting systems, $\mathscr{F}(X)$ denotes the family of all languages generated by systems in X. We will use $\mathscr{F}(\text{CFAG})$ to denote the class of context-free array languages respectively. Definitions of context-free array grammars and their languages can be found, for example, in Ref. 8.

2. DEFINITIONS AND RESTRICTIONS FOR COORDINATE GRAMMARS

First, we will review the definitions of coordinate grammars and their languages. In the grammars, each symbol has a coordinate associated with it. We will use almost the same definitions and notations as that of the coordinate grammars in Refs. 1 and 2. In a general coordinate grammar, the coordinates can in principle be d-tuples of arbitrary real numbers ($d \geqslant 1$). However, since we are primarily interested in discrete two-dimensional arrays of symbols, it is reasonable to require that the coordinates be pairs of integers ($d = 2$).

Definition 2.1. A *coordinate grammar* is defined as a 6-tuple $G = \langle V, V_T, D, n, P, s \rangle$, where

V is a finite set of nonterminal symbols,
V_T is a set of terminal symbols, $V \cap V_T = \varnothing$,
D is a domain of coordinates,
n is a positive integer, the number of coordinates used (i.e. the dimension of the space in which symbols are to be placed).
P is a finite set of productions, each of which is a quadruple $\langle \Lambda, \Sigma, \pi, \Phi \rangle$, where
    Λ is a j-tuple of elements of $V \cup V_T$, for some $j \geqslant 1$.
    Σ is a k-tuple of elements of $V \cup V_T$, for some $k \geqslant 1$.
    π is a predicate with k arguments, each of which is an n-tuple of coordinates,
    Φ is a j-tuple of functions, each having k arguments; the arguments and function values are n-tuple of coordinates.
$s \in V$ is a special symbol called the initial symbol.

Definition 2.2. A set S_{i+1} of symbols and associated n-tuples of coordinates is said to *directly reduce* to a set S_i if there exists a production $\langle \Lambda, \Sigma, \pi, \Phi \rangle$, for which Σ is a subset of S_{i+1}; its coordinates satisfy π, the coordinates of the symbols of Λ are obtained from those in Σ by applying the functions in Φ, and $S_{i+1} - \Sigma \cup \Lambda = S_i$. Similarly, S'' is said to *reduce* into S' if there exists $S'' = S_n, S_{n-1}, \ldots, S_1, S_0 = S'$ such that S_i directly reduces into S_{i-1}, $1 \leq i \leq n$. S is said to be a *sentence* of G if it reduces to s. the set of all sentences whose symbols are all terminals is called the *language of G*.

As stated in Refs. 1 and 2, the grammars defined above are "too powerful", in the sense that even if the forms of the rules and the nature of the coordinate-computing functions are greatly restricted, they already have the power of a Turing machine. In fact, the following example shows that even if the productions are all "right linear" and their associated functions are all computable by finite automata, the resulting language need not be context-free.

Example 1.   Let $G = \langle \{g, A, B\}, \{t\}, D, l, P, g \rangle$, where D is the set of integers, and P contains the following productions:

$g^{(0)} \rightarrow A^{(1)}$ $(f(0) = 1$; undefined otherwise$)$

$A^{(i)} \rightarrow A^{(2i)}$ $(f(x) = 2x)$

$A^{(i)} \rightarrow B^{(i)}$ $(f(x) = x)$

$B^{(i)} \rightarrow B^{(i-1)}t^{(i)}$ $(f_1(x) = x - 1$ if $x > 1$; $f_2(x) = x$ if $x > 1$; f_1 and f_2 are undefined otherwise$)$

$B^{(1)} \rightarrow t^{(1)}$ $(f(1) = 1$; undefined otherwise$)$.

These functions are evidently all computable by finite automata. However, each sentence of G has lengths which are powers of 2; by Parikh's theorem, the language of G is not context-free.

We review here some restrictions on coordinate grammars introduced in Ref. 2

Definition 2.3.   For any given coordinate grammar G, P of G is of *bounded-diameter* if there exists a positive integer k such that, in any production of P, all symbols are within a distance k of one another. P of G is *shift-invariant* if the applicability of any rule depends only on the relative position of A rather than on the absolute position.

When we require that all rules be shift-invariant and of bounded diameter, it is no longer necessary to explicitly associate coordinates with each symbol, or to explicitly compute coordinates when rules are applied. So the definition of P is changed as follows: P is a finite set of productions, each of which is a pair $\langle \alpha, \beta \rangle$, where α is a j-tuple of elements of $V \cup V_T$, for some $j \geq 1$, β is a k-tuple of elements of $V \cup V_T$, for some $k \geq 1$, each symbol of α and β is located in a specified relative position. In more detail, the relative positions in a rule are specified by writing the rule in the form

$$\alpha \equiv \langle A_1, A_2, \ldots, A_m \mid h_1, h_2, \ldots, h_j \rangle, \text{ where } h_m = (p, q), 0 \leq p, q \leq d$$

$$\beta \equiv \langle B_1, B_2, \ldots, B_m \mid i_1, i_2, \ldots, i_k \rangle, \text{ where } i_n = (p, q), -d \leq p, q \leq d.$$

Here d defines the bounds on the rule diameters and is the same for all rules.

In the rest of this paper, we will treat only the coordinate grammar with productions which are shift-invariant and of bounded diameter.

Definition 2.4.   A coordinate grammar is in *standard form* if for any rule $\alpha \rightarrow \beta$

$$\alpha \equiv \langle A_1, A_2, \ldots, A_m \mid h_1, h_2, \ldots, h_m \rangle$$

$$\beta \equiv \langle B_1, B_2, \ldots, B_m \mid h_1, h_2, \ldots, h_m \rangle.$$

Proposition 2.5.[2]   For any coordinate grammar G, there exists a coordinate grammar in standard form G' such that $L(G) = L(G')$.

A relationship between ordinary array languages and coordinate grammars has been discussed in Ref. 2.

Proposition 2.6.[2]   For any array language L, there exists a coordinate grammar G such that $L(G) = L$.

For a given rule $\alpha \rightarrow \beta$, let $S = \{h_i \mid A_i = \# \text{ and } B_i \neq \#\}$ and $T = \{h_i \mid A_i \neq \# \text{ and } B_i = \#\}$. Then consider the following conditions:

(a) For each $h_i \in S$, B_i is connected in β to some non-# B_j such that $h_i \notin S$.

(b) For each $h_i \in T$, any pair of neighbors of h_i that are non-# in α or that are not hs must be connected in α by a path not containing any symbol in T (except possibly for its end points)

Proposition 2.7.[2]   Every coordinate grammar which satisfies the conditions (a) and (b) generates a connected array language.

Definition 2.8.   A coordinate grammar is *monotonic* if no rule creates #s, i.e. if $B_i = \#$ implies $A_i = \#$, $1 \leqslant i \leqslant m$. A coordinate grammar is *context-free* if the left side of each rule consists of a single element of V together with #s, and the right side consists of non-#s.

For the context-free coordinate grammars, the normal form presented in Definition 2.4 is a kind of "Greibach normal form". It is not so difficult for the context-free coordinate grammars to define "Chomsky normal form", i.e. the right hand side of each production rule has at most two nonterminal symbols or one terminal symbol.

3.   PCE GRAMMARS AND COORDINATE GRAMMARS

In this section, we will show some relationships between coordinate grammars and PCE grammars. First, we will define PCE grammars which use sequences of edges to embed replaced graphs into the host graph.

Definition 3.1.   For any given graph H, its node P, and a string $\pi = \{c_1 c_2 \ldots c_i\}$ of its edge labels, $P\pi$ is *realizable on* H if and only if there exists a set of nodes $\{P_0, P_1, \ldots, P_i\}$ such that $P_0 = P$ and P_j is the unique neighbor of P_{j-1} joined by an edge labeled with c_j $(1 \leqslant j \leqslant i)$.

Definition 3.2.   *A node-replacement graph grammar with path controlled embedding*, denoted as nPCE grammar, is a construction
$G = \langle \Sigma_N, \Sigma_E, P, Z, \Delta_N, \Delta_E \rangle$, where

Σ_N is a finite nonempty set of node labels,
Σ_E is a finite nonempty set of edge labels,

Δ_N is a finite nonempty subset of Σ_N, called terminal node labels,

Δ_E is a finite nonempty subset of Σ_E, called terminal edge labels,

P is a finite set of productions of form (a, β, ψ), where a is a node, $\beta = (V, E, \Sigma_V,$ $\Sigma_E, \phi_V, \phi_E)$ is a connected graph and y is a mapping from Σ_E^+ into $2^{(V(\beta) \times \Sigma_E)}$; ψ is called the *embedding function*.

Z is a connected graph over (Σ_N, Σ_E) called *the axiom*.

The derivation steps in an nPCE grammar is defined as follows:

Definition 3.3. Let $G = \langle \Sigma_N, \Sigma_E, P, Z, \Delta_N, \Delta_E \rangle$ be an nPCE grammar and let H, H' be graphs over (Σ_V, Σ_E).

(1) H *directly derives* H' in G, denoted as $H \underset{G}{\Rightarrow} H'$, if there exists a production $p = (a, \beta, \psi)$ in P, a graph β' with $V(\beta') \cap V(H - a) = \varnothing$ and an isomorphism h from β' into β such that H' is isomorphic to the graph X constructed as follows:

$X = (V, E, \Sigma_V, \Sigma_E, \phi_V, \phi_E)$, where
$V = V(H - a) \cup V(\beta')$,
$E = \{(x, y) \mid x, y \in V(H - a)$ and $(x, y) \in E(H)\} \cup \{(x, y) \mid x, y \in V(b')$ and $(h(x), h(y)) \in E(\beta)\} \cup \{(x, y) \mid x \in V(b'), y \in V(H - a)$, there exists a path $p \in \text{dom}(y)$ with $y = a\pi$ and $\langle h(x), e \rangle \in y(p)$ for some e in $\Sigma_E\}$,
ϕ_V is equal to the node labeling function of H for nodes in $V(H - a)$ and to the node labeling function of β' for nodes in $V(\beta')$,
ϕ_E is equal to the edge labeling function of H for edges between the nodes of H and to the edge labeling function of β' for nodes in $V(\beta')$.

We also say that H' is derived from H by replacing a using the production p.

(2) We will denote the reflexive and the transitive closure of $\underset{G}{\Rightarrow}$ by $\underset{G}{\overset{*}{\Rightarrow}}$ and the transitive closure of $\underset{G}{\Rightarrow}$ by $\underset{G}{\overset{+}{\Rightarrow}}$.

(3) The language of G, denoted as $L(G)$, is defined by $L(G) = \{H \mid H$ is a graph over (Σ_V, Σ_E) and $Z \underset{G}{\overset{*}{\Rightarrow}} H\}$.

We present here an example of the derivations of nPCE grammars.

Example 2. The application of the production in Fig. 1(a) to the graph in Fig. 1(b) results in the graph in Fig. 1(c).

To characterize coordinate grammars by classes of nPCE grammars, we need a stipulation to regard a two-dimensional array as a graph.

Stipulation 3.4.

(1) A symbol in an array is regarded as a label of the corresponding node of a graph.

(2) A horizontal connection of two points is regarded as an edge labeled with h or h'. These two labels appear alternately along a row.

(3) A vertical connection of two points is regarded as an edge labeled with v or v'. These two labels appear alternately along a column.

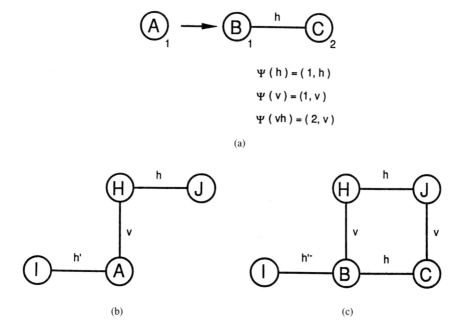

(a)

(b)   (c)

Fig. 1.   An example of derivations of nPCE grammar.

Example 3.   An array in Fig. 2(a) is regarded as a graph in Fig. 2(b) in the sense of Stipulation 3.4.

Let L be a set of arrays. Let L' be a set of graphs such that for each element a of L' there exists one and only one element of L which is regarded as the graph a in the sense of Stipulation 3.4. Then we will use a notation $L = {}_1L'$ to represent the above relation.

Now, we have sufficient tools for characterizing context-free coordinate grammars by a class of PCE grammars. Describing the PCE grammars generating array langues, however, needs somewhat clumsy production rules especially in path descriptions. So, we will discuss PCE grammars using partial path groups to describe paths in the embedding functions. The partial path groups seem to be useful tools to introduce structures into graph grammars.

We review here the definitions of the partial path groups. For more precise definitions of the partial path groups, see Refs. 10 and 11.

Definition 3.5.   Let H be a connected graph of degree d, i.e. no more than d edges emanate from any node. By an *edge coloring* of H we mean an assignment of colors to the edges of H such that the edges emanating from any given node will have different colors.

Definition 3.6.   Let p be a node of a graph H and let π be a string of colors. Then $p\pi$ is defined as the terminal node of the path defined by π starting from p, provided this path is realizable. For convenience, let us define a fictitious "blank" color representing "no

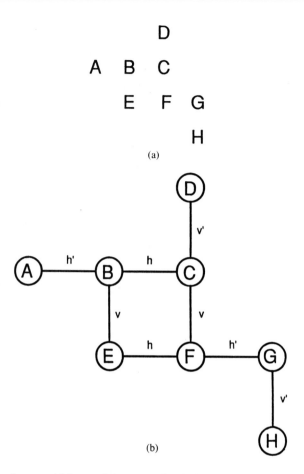

Fig. 2.   An array (a) is regarded as a graph   (b) in the sense of Stipulation 3.4.

move''. It is obvious that the structure defined above resembles a group structure called ''partial'' group''. From now on we shall refer to this partial group as the *partial path group* of *H* defined by given coloring, and denote it by $\Pi(H)$.

Note that the partial path groups can be defined on a graph generated by a graph grammar by relating the edge labels of the generated graph to the colors mentioned in the above definitions.

Definition 3.7.   A partial path group $\Pi(H)$ is called *near-abelian* if each color except a blank color commutes with all but one of the other colors, and does not commute with the remaining one.

It is shown in Ref. 10 that the near-abelian partial path groups with four colors correspond to a subgraph of a two-dimensional array.

We define nPCE grammars using embedding functions with near-abelian partial path groups to describe paths.

Definition 3.8. An *nPCE grammar with near-abelian partial path groups*, denoted as nPCE$_\Pi$ grammar, is a construction: $G = \langle \Sigma_N, \Sigma_E, P, Z, \Delta_N, \Delta_E \rangle$, where $\Sigma_N, \Sigma_E, Z, \Delta_N$, Δ_E are the same as in the definition of nPCE grammars. P is a finite set of productions of forms (a, β, ψ) or (a, β, ψ_Π), where a, β, ψ are the same as in the definition of nPCE grammars. ψ_Π is a mapping from Σ_E^+ into $2^{(V(\beta) \times \Sigma_E)}$; ψ_Π is called an embedding function with near-abelian partial path groups. For a path π, $\psi_\Pi(\pi)$ implies the shortest realizable path equivalent to π under near-abelian partial path groups instead of π itself.

In the nPCE$_\Pi$ grammars, we use ψ_Π instead of the embedding function ψ of nPCE grammars. In this case, arbitrarily long paths can be used to embed the newly replaced graphs. We state here a relationship between connected context-free coordinate grammars and nPCE$_\Pi$ grammars.

Lemma 3.9. For every connected context-free coordinate grammar T, there exists an nPCE grammar G such that $L(G) = {}_1L(T)$.

Proof. Let $T = \langle V, V_T, D, n, P, s \rangle$. Without loss of generality, we can assume that T has the normal form and the right hand side of each production rule has at most two nonterminal symbols or one terminal symbol. Since T generates connected array languages, these two symbols must be directly connected to each other. Then we construct the following nPCE$_\Pi$ grammar:

$$G = \langle \Sigma_N, \Sigma_E, \mathcal{P}, Z, \Delta_N, \Delta_E \rangle,$$

where $\Sigma_N = V$, $\Sigma_E = \{h, h', v, v'\}$, $\Delta_N = V_T$, $\Delta_E = \Sigma_E$, $\mathcal{P}$ is defined as follows:

For every production rule $\langle A, \quad \# \mid (p_1, q_1), \quad (p_2, q_2) \rangle \to \langle B, \quad C \mid (p_1, q_1),$ $(p_2, q_2) \rangle$,

$(\textcircled{A}_1, \textcircled{B} \underset{r}{\text{—}} \textcircled{C}_2, \; \psi_\Pi(r') = (1, r'), \quad \psi_\Pi(s) = (1, s),$
$\psi_\Pi(s') = (1, s'), \quad \psi_\Pi(sr) = (2, s),$
$\psi_\Pi(s'r) = (2, s'), \quad \psi_\Pi(srr's) = (2, r')$
if $p_1 = p_2$ and $q_1 = q_2 - 1$ then $r = h, r' = h', s = v, s = v'$
if $p_1 = p_2$ and $q_1 = q_2 + 1$ then $r = h', r' = h, s = v', s = v$
if $p_1 = p_2 - 1$ and $q_1 = q_2$ then $r = v, r' = v', s = h, s = h'$
if $p_1 = p_2 + 1$ and $q_1 = q_2$ then $r = v', r' = v, s = h', s = h$
where $A, B, C \in \Sigma_N \backslash \Delta_N$).

For every production rule $\langle A \mid (p_1, q_1) \rangle \to \langle a \mid (p_1, q_1) \rangle$,

$(\textcircled{A}_1, \textcircled{a}_1, \; \psi(h) = (1, h), \quad \psi(v) = (1, v),$
$\psi(h') = (1, h'), \quad \psi(v') = (1, v'),$
where $A \in \Sigma_N \backslash \Delta_N$ and $a \in \Delta_N$).

and Z is a graph having only one node labeled with s.

175

Starting with the graph Z, G simulates the derivation of T. In general, each single step of T is corresponding to the single step of G. For each node labeled with a symbol from Σ_N, G replaces the node with a graph by applying a production rule. Then, the newly replaced graph is embedded by making use of the embedding function attached to the used production rule. If there is sufficient space to embed such replaced graphs, then each node of the embedded graph is connected with appropriate nodes of the host graph by the edges labeled with the symbols from Δ_E. If not (this case can happen since G cannot use #s in its production rules), the nodes of the embedded graph form at least one adjacent relation connected with two or more edges having the same label (see Fig. 3). The nodes having such adjacency cannot be replaced by any nodes labeled with the elements of Δ_N since no production rule which rewrites Σ_Ns to Δ_Ns can define a realizable path between such neighbors (note such production rules have Ψ as their embedding functions). This procedure is repeated to simulate the generating steps of T.

From this result, since isometric array grammars can be regarded as connected coordinate grammars, it is easy to see that we can show almost the same lemma for CFAGs.

Lemma 3.10. There exists a subclass of nPCE$_\Pi$ grammars such that for every element G of the class, there exists an equivalent context-free array grammar G' under Stipulation 3.4.

Proof. Define a subclass $\mathcal{L}$ of PCE$_\Pi$ grammars as the set of all PCE$_\Pi$ grammars having embedding function with four colors free near-abelian partial path groups and production

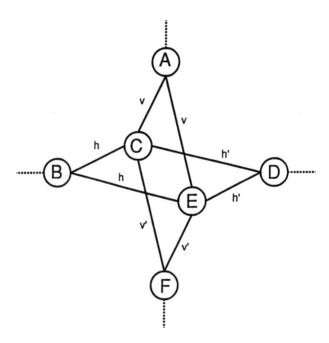

Fig. 3.   Nodes with more than one edge having the same label.

rules of the forms represented in the proof of Lemma 3.9. Then, from the definition of PCE$_\Pi$ grammars, it is not so difficult to see that $\mathscr{F}$(CFAG) $\supseteq \mathscr{L}$.

In Definition 3.8, if we allow β in P to be a set of connected graphs connected by sequences of edge labels, nPCE grammars have the capability of generating disconnected languages. For such cases, we add a special node label, $*$, to connect disconnected graphs. This special label is a kind of terminal node label and is never rewritten to any other symbols in the course of derivation steps. We will call them n*PCE grammars. They are defined as follows:

Definition 3.11. An *n*PCE grammar with near-abelian partial path groups*, denoted as n*PCE$_\Pi$ grammar, is a construction: $G = \langle \Sigma_N, \Sigma_E, P, Z, \Delta_N, \Delta_E, * \rangle$, where Σ_N, Σ_E, Z, Δ_N, Δ_E are the same as in the definition of nPCE grammars. P is a finite set of productions of forms (a, β, ψ), (a, β, ψ_Π), or (a, β', ψ_Π), where a, β, ψ, ψ_Π are the same as in the definition of nPCE grammars. β' is a set of connected graphs which are connected by sequences of edge labels (see Fig. 4(a)). $*$ is a distinguished symbol of Δ_N. The sequences of edge labels in β' are regarded as the connecting paths between disconnected graphs. If there are some parts of the sequence which cannot be realized on the host graph, the necessary numbers of the symbol $*$ are inserted as padding. The embedding functions for such padding are defined implicitly as the connections to four neighbors.

We present an example of the derivation steps of n*PCE grammars.

Example 4. The application of the production in Fig. 4(a) to the graph in Fig. 4(b) results in the graph in Fig. 4(c).

At this point, we need one more stipulation to regard a two-dimensional disconnected array as a graph having nodes labeled with $*$.

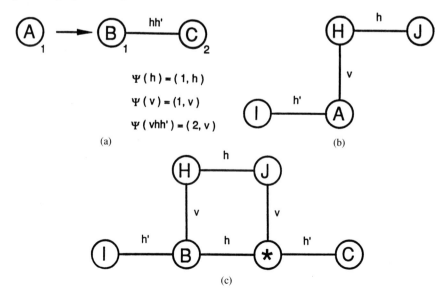

Fig. 4.   An example of derivations of n*PCE$_\Pi$ grammar.

Stipulation 3.12. An array is regarded as a graph which is of the form that if all nodes labeled with ∗s are ignored, then the array is regarded as the graph in the sense of Stipulation 3.4.

As in the case of Stipulation 3.4, we will use a notation $L = {}_2L'$.

Similar to Lemma 3.9, we will show that there exists an n∗PCE$_\Pi$ grammar which generates the language of given context-free coordinate grammar.

Lemma 3.13. For every context-free coordinate grammar T, there exists an n∗PCE$_\Pi$ grammar G such that $L(G) = {}_2L(T)$.

Proof. For given T, the construction of n∗PCE$_\Pi$ grammar G is similar to that of Lemma 3.9 with the exception of disconnectivity. G places ∗s to fill in the blanks when it meets a part where no realizable path exists. At this time, there are some possibilities that there exist, in fact, some connecting edges there (i.e. almost the same as the case in Fig. 3). We, however, can ignore such cases since the graphs containing such parts cannot be elements of the language of G. So the remaining problem is to ensure the unrewritability of the symbol ∗ since there are some possibilities that the newly replaced graphs override ∗s. To do so, we prove the following claim:

Claim. For every CFAG G', there exists CFAG G'' having the following properties:
(1) $L(G') = L(G'')$
(2) For each element g'' of $L(G'')$ and a border position p of g'', there exists at least one derivation process which starts at p and generates g''.

Proof of Claim. For every element g' of G', there exists at least one spanning tree which represents the derivation process of g' and is rooted at the position of the starting symbol. Thus, for every border point of g', there exists at least one path which leads to the derivation starting point. Therefore we get G'' by introducing new alphabets obtained by dotting original alphabets and adding production rules to trace the path. So, G'' starts its derivation at a border point then traces the path nondeterministically. When G'' guesses the derivation starting point of G', it starts normal derivation of G'.

By making use of the climb, we can construct G to ensure the unrewritability of the symbol ∗ since the derivation processes of T for the connecting part started by a nonterminal symbol is the same as that of CFAG.

The proof of the next lemma is almost the same as that of Lemma 3.10.

Lemma 3.14. There exists a subclass of n∗PCE$_\Pi$ grammars such that for every element G of the class, there exists an equivalent context-free array grammar G' under Stipulation 3.12.

The results in this paper are summarized by the following theorem:

Theorem 3.15. There exists a subclass of nPCE$_\Pi$ grammars which is equal to the class of two-dimensional *connected* context-free coordinate grammars under Stipulation 3.4. There also exists a subclass of n∗PCE$_\Pi$ grammars which is equal to the class of two-dimensional *disconnected* context-free coordinate grammars under Stipulation 3.12.

4. CONCLUDING REMARKS

In this paper, we have shown some relationships between two-dimensional context-free coordinate grammars and nPCE grammars in both connected and disconnected cases. The coordinate grammars can be regarded as generalized isometric array grammars. They seem to be useful for generating patterns such that some disconnected shapes on array are related to each other. Therefore it seems to be of interest to define two-dimensional multiple context-free array grammars by making use of coordinate grammars.

REFERENCES

1. D. L. Milgram and A. Rosenfeld, "A note on 'grammars with coordinates'", in *Graphic Languages*, Eds. F. Nake and A. Rosenfeld, North-Holland, Amsterdam, 1972, pp. 187–191.
2. A. Rosenfeld, "Coordinate grammars revisited: Generalized isometric grammars", *Int. J. Pattern Recognition and Artificial Intelligence* **3 & 4** (1989) 435–444.
3. D. Janssens and G. Rozenberg, "On the structure of node label controlled graph languages", *Information Sciences* **20** (1980) 191–216.
4. D. Janssens and G. Rozenberg, "Restrictions, extensions, and variations of NLC grammars", *Information Sciences* **20** (1980) 217–244.
5. D. Janssens and G. Rozenberg, "Graph grammars with neighborhood-controlled embedding", *Theoretical Computer Science* **21** (1982) 55–74.
6. S. H. von Solms, "Node-label controlled graph grammars with context conditions", *Int. J. Computer Mathematics* **15** (1984) 39–49.
7. A. Nakamura and K. Aizawa, "On a relationship between graph L-systems and picture languages", *Theoretical Computer Science* **24** (1983) 161–177.
8. A. Rosenfeld, *Picture Languages*, Academic Press, 1979.
9. M. Nagl, "A tutorial and bibliographical survey on graph grammars", *Lecture Notes in Computer Science* **73**, Springer-Verlag, 1979.
10. A. Rosenfeld, "Partial path groups and parallel graph contractions", in *The Book of L*, Eds. G. Rozenberg and A. Salomaa, Springer-Verlag, 1985, pp. 369–382.
11. R. A. Melter, "Tessellation graph characterization using rosettas", *Pattern Recognition Letters* **4** (1986) 79–85.

Akira Nakamura received the B.A. degree from Hiroshima University in 1953 and the Doctor of Science degree in mathematics from Nagoya University in 1963. From 1959 to 1964, he was an Assistant Professor and from 1965 to 1970 an Associate Professor of Applied Mathematics at Nihon University. Between 1966 to 1968 he was also a Visiting Assistant Professor at the Department of Information Science of the University of North Carolina at Chapel Hill.

Since 1970, he has been a Professor of Applied Mathematics at Hiroshima University. He was a Visiting Professor at the Computer Science Center, University of Maryland from November 1977 to January 1978, and at the Tata Institute of Fundamental Research, Bombay, in September 1980. He was also a Visiting Scientist of the Division of Mathematics and Statistics, CSIRO, Australia, in September 1985. He is working in the theory of picture languages and non-standard logics for artificial intelligence.

Kunio Aizawa received the M.A. degree from Hiroshima University in 1982.

He is currently a Research Associate in the Department of Applied Mathematics at Hiroshima University. His research interests include the theory of picture languages and digital image understanding.

FINITE IMAGES GENERATED BY GL-SYSTEMS

A. SAOUDI, K. RANGARAJAN* and V. R. DARE*

*Université Paris VII, Laboratoire d'Informatique Théorique et Programmation
2, Place Jussieu, 75221 Paris Cedex 5, France*

Received 6 May 1988
Revised 1 May 1989

In this paper, we introduce a new device called GL-systems (i.e. Grammar-Lindenmayer systems) for generating finite images. GL-systems are sequential/parallel systems in which the horizontal rules form a Chomskian grammar and the vertical rules form a DTOL system. We obtain hierarchical results of various types of GL-systems. We study some properties like, closure properties, combinatorial results, pumping lemma and decidability results. An algebraic characterization for GL-systems (with variation) is presented.

Keywords: Grammars; Images; L-systems.

1. INTRODUCTION

There have been several studies on theoretical models for generating two dimensional objects. These studies adapt the techniques and utilize the existing results of formal string language theory.[1,2] These can be viewed as a generalization of the classical theory of languages studied by Chomsky and Schützenberger[3] and also as a syntactic approach to pattern recognition.

In the literature, various array grammars and picture grammars have been studied. Rosenfeld[4,5] has proposed array grammars having array rewriting rules. The research group of Siromoney has introduced many array models.[6-9] Wang[10-14] has made a study of matrix grammars and array grammars. A survey of most of the array models can be found in Refs. 4, 15 and 16.

The Lindenmayer systems known as L-systems[2] have been studied extensively. Incorporating the L-system type of generation, several array models were introduced. All these models are either parallel/sequential in nature or having array rewriting rules. In Refs. 17 and 18, the notion of tables borrowed from L-systems is considered and the rules of the vertical generation are given in the form of tables. Parallel OL-systems[19] are parallel/sequential matrix grammars in which horizontal rules form an L-system and vertical rules are right-linear rules. An extended controlled table L-array model[8,20] which reflects the growth along the four edges of a rectangular array is found useful in the construction of public key crypto-systems for picture languages. To reflect internal growth, array languages incorporating parallel rewriting of every symbol in a rectangular array are introduced in Refs. 21 and 22.

---

* On leave from Department of Mathematics, Madras Christian College, Madras, India.

181

International Journal of Pattern Recognition and Artificial Intelligence Vol. 3 No. 3 & 4 (1989) 459–467
© World Scientific Publishing Company

It has been the pattern to obtain two dimensional models of different types by considering various families of Chomskian/L-system string languages. In this paper, we define a GL-system (i.e. Grammar-Lindenmayer system) to be a sequential/parallel model in which the horizontal rules are classical Chomskian rules which are used for generating the horizontal language and the vertical rules are given by DTOL systems, for generating images from horizontal words. These systems also exhibit lack of closure properties similar to L-systems. We also present a variation of GL-systems, the language of which can be characterized in terms of L-substitution and Chomskian languages.

The organization of the paper is as follows. Section 2 deals with the preliminaries needed for this paper. Undefined terms and notions not in this section can be found in Refs. 1 and 2. In the third section, we present GL-systems, hierarchical results and examples. We study various properties like closure properties, combinatorial lemma, pumping lemma and decidability results in the fourth section. A variation of GL-systems and its characterization is given in the last section.

2. PRELIMINARIES

Let Σ be a finite alphabet. Then a word is a mapping from $[n]$ to Σ where $[n] = \{1, 2, \ldots, n\}$. We denote by Σ^* the set of all finite words on Σ. An image is a mapping from $[n] \times [m]$ to Σ. We denote by Σ^{**} the set of all finite images on Σ. $\Sigma^{++} = \Sigma^{**} - \{\square\}$ where $\square$ is the empty image. If $x \in \Sigma^{**}$, then dom $(x) = \{(k, 1) : k \in [n] \text{ and } 1 \in [m]\}$. If $x \in \Sigma^{**}$, the column size of x is the number of columns of x and it is denoted by $|x|_v$. If $x \in \Sigma^{**}$, then the row size of x is the number of rows of x and it is denoted by $|x|_h$. We denote by column (I), the set of columns occuring in I.

A pseudo-image I on Σ is a mapping from $[n] \times N$ to Σ such that
(i) $I : [n] \times N \rightarrow \Sigma \cup \{\#\}$
(ii) if $I(i, j) = \# \Rightarrow I(k, j) = \#$ for all $k \geq i$.
The symbol $\#$ represents a blank symbol.

We now define two kinds of operations on images.
Let $\textcircled{1}$ be a partial operation, called column catenation defined from $(\Sigma^{**})^2$ to Σ^{**} by

$$x \textcircled{1} y = (x \, y) \text{ if } |x|_h = |y|_h$$

undefined otherwise.

Let $\ominus$ be a partial operation, called row catenation defined from $(\Sigma^{**})^2$ to Σ^{**} by

$$x \ominus y = \begin{matrix} x \\ y \end{matrix} \text{ if } |x|_v = |y|_v$$

undefined otherwise

Let $X = \begin{matrix} x_1 \\ \cdot \\ \cdot \\ \cdot \\ x_n \end{matrix}$ or $X = (y_1 \ldots y_m)$ be an image such that $x_i \in \Sigma^+$ and $y_i \in \Sigma_+$, then $X_v(i) = x_i$ and $x_h(i) = y_i$.

Let I and I' be subsets of Σ^{**} then we denote by

$$I \oplus I' = \{x \oplus y : x \in I \text{ and } y \in I'\} \text{ where } \oplus \in \{\ominus, \oplus\}.$$

Let $I_0 = I^0 = \{\Box\}$ where $\Box$ is the empty image, i.e. dom $(\Box) = \varnothing$. Then $I_{n+1} = I \ominus I_n$, and we denote by $I_* = \cup I_n(n \geqslant 0)$ and $I_+ = \cup I_n(n > 0)$.

Let $I^{n+1} = I \oplus I^n$ and $I^* = \cup I^n(n \geqslant 0)$ and $I^+ = \cup I^n(n > 0)$.

Let $x \in \Sigma^{**}$, then x^T is the image defined as follows:

(i) dom $(x^T) = \{(j, i) : (i, j) \in \text{dom } (x)\}$,

(ii) for all $(i, j) \in$ dom (x^T), $x^T(i, j) = x(j, i)$.

Let $x = (x_1 \ldots x_n) \in \Sigma^{++}$ then column $(x) = \{x_1, \ldots, x_n\}$.

Let h : $\Sigma \to \Sigma^+$ be a homomorphism then h is said to be a U-morphism (i.e. Uniform morphism)

if $|h(a)| = |h(b)|$ for each $a, b \in \Sigma$. If $x = a_1 \ldots a_n \in \Sigma^+$ then $x^T = \begin{matrix} a_1. \\ . \\ . \\ . \\ a_n. \end{matrix}$

3. GL-SYSTEMS AND IMAGES

In this section we will define GL-systems, where G represents Grammar and L represents Lindenmayer.[2] Examples and hierarchical results are also given.

Definition 3.1. A GL-system is a structure $S = \langle V, \Sigma, s, R, \Phi \rangle$, where

(i) Base $(S) = \langle V, \Sigma, s, R \rangle$ is a context-sensitive grammar, and

(ii) Φ is a finite set of U-morphisms.

Let H = Base (S), then we define the horizontal language of S (i.e. H(S)) as the language generated by H.

$$H(S) = \{u \in \Sigma^+ : s \Rightarrow_h^+ u\}.$$

Let $\phi \in \Phi$ be a U-morphism, then we extend ϕ to Σ^{++} by $\bar{\phi}$ which is defined inductively by:

(i) if $I = (a_1 \ldots a_n) \in \Sigma^+$ then $\bar{\phi}(I) = \phi(a_1)^T \oplus \ldots \oplus \phi(a_n)^T$

(ii) if $I = I_1 \ominus I_2$ then $\bar{\phi}(I) = \bar{\phi}(I_1) \ominus \bar{\phi}(I_2)$.

The language generated by the GL-system S is defined as $I(S) = \{I \in \Sigma^{++} :$ there exists $f \in \Phi^*$ and there exists $u \in H(S)$ such that $\bar{f}(u) = I$, where $\bar{f} = \bar{f}_1 \ldots \bar{f}_n$ and $f = f_1 \ldots f_n\}$. We give an example to illustrate the definitions.

Example 1.   (Checkers)

Let $R = \{s \rightarrow abs + ab\}$.

$$f : a \rightarrow aba, \; b \rightarrow bab \text{ then } H(S) = (ab)^+$$

$$I(S) = (ab)^+ \cup \left\{ \left(\left(\binom{a}{b}_n \oplus a \right) \oplus \left(\binom{b}{a}_m \oplus b \right) \right)^m : 2n + 1 = 3^k \text{ and } m \geq 1 \text{ and } k \geq 0 \right\}.$$

By interpreting a as white cell and b as black cell, one can generate by S the following checkers.

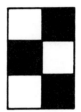 

Let $X = \{CS, CF, R\}$, then we define by an XGL-system a GL-system having a base which is an X-grammar.

Let XGL be a family of sets of images generated by XGL-systems, then we have:

$$RGL \subset CFGL \subset CSGL.$$

4.   PROPERTIES OF GL-SYSTEMS

In this section, we will study some properties of GL-systems such as closure properties, combinatorial property and pumping lemma.

Lemma 4.1.   (Combinatorial lemma)

For each GL-SYSTEM $S = \langle V, \Sigma, s, R, \Phi \rangle$, and I belongs to I(S), we have:

$$\text{Card (column (I))} \leq \text{Card } (\Sigma).$$

This combinatorial lemma follows from the fact that the rewriting process is deterministic.

Theorem 4.2.   For $X \in \{CS, CF, R\}$, the family XGL is not closed under union, intersection and complementation.

Proof.   Let S_1 and S_2 be two GL-systems such that:

$H(S_1) = a$, $H(S_2) = a^+$ with $\Phi_1 = \{a \rightarrow a^2\}$ and $\Phi_2 = \{a \rightarrow a\}$ then
$I(S_1) = \{(a)_k : k = 2^n, \, n \geq 0\} = I_1$ and
$I(S_2) = (a)^+ = I_2$.

I_1 and I_2 are generated by GL-systems but $I_1 \cup I_2$ is not generated by any GL-system.

Let $H(S_3) = ab$ and $\Phi_3 = \{a \to a,\ b \to b]$ then

$$I_3 = I(S_3) = ab \text{ and } \bar{I}_3 = \{x \in \Sigma^{**} : x \neq ab\}.$$

By combinatorial lemma, $\bar{I}_3$ cannot be generated by any GL-system; hence the proof. ∎

Consider $H(S_4) = \{a, b, c\}$, $H(S_5) = \{a\}$, where:

$$\Phi_4 : a \to c^2;\ b \to a^2;\ c \to c^2$$
$$\Phi_5 : a \to a^2$$

then

$$I = I(S_4) \cap I(S_5) = \left\{a,\ \frac{a}{a}\right\}.$$

I cannot be generated by any GL-system.

Lemma 4.3. (Pumping lemma)

For each set of finite images I over Σ generated by a context-free GL-system S, there is an integer N such that for each $X \in I$ and $|X|_h > N$, we have:
(i) $X = X_1 \oplus X_2 \oplus X_3 \oplus X_4 \oplus X_5$, where $|X_2 \oplus X_3 \oplus X_4| > 1$, and
(ii) for each $i \geq 1$, $X_1 \oplus (X_2)^i \oplus X_3 \oplus (X_4)^i \oplus X_5 \in I(S)$.
The proof is the same as in the string language case.

Corollary 4.4.   The emptiness and finiteness problems for context-free GL-systems are decidable because of pumping lemma.

Remark.   In defining GL-systems, we use Φ as a set of U-morphisms. We observe that all results will carry over even if we use Φ as a set of morphisms, in such case the sentential forms of the generation are pseudo-images.

5.   GENERATING IMAGES BY VGL-SYSTEMS

In this section, we define a variation of GL-systems by specifying morphisms to be applied to some column rather than the array itself. This variation allows us to obtain an algebraic characterization of the families defined by GL-systems in terms of L-substitution and Chomskian languages.

A VGL-system (i.e. Vertical GL-system) is a structure $S = \langle V, \Sigma, s, R,$ $\Phi = \{\Phi_a\}\ (a \in \Sigma)\rangle$, where V, Σ, s and R are defined as for a GL-system, and Φ_a is a set of U-morphisms from Σ to Σ^+. Let $u \in H(S)$ such that $u = a_1 a_2 \ldots a_n$, then we define the vertical rewriting rule as follows:

$$I_1 \oplus I_2 \oplus \ldots \oplus I_n \Rightarrow_v^{(f,i)} J_1 \oplus J_2 \oplus \ldots \oplus J_n \text{ iff}$$

(i) $J_i = (f(I_i^T))^T$,
(ii) $J_k = I_k$ for $k \neq i$ where $I_i, J_i \in (\Sigma \cup \#)_+$; $1 \leq i \leq n$ and $f \in \Phi_{a_i}$.
Let $\Rightarrow_v$ be $\cup \Rightarrow_v^{f,i}$, where $i \in N$, $f \in \Phi_{a_i}$ and $\Rightarrow_v^*$ be the reflexive closure of $\Rightarrow_v$.

We denote by $I_v(S)$ the set of images generated by the GL-system with variation, where $I_v(S) = \{I \in \Sigma^{++} : \text{there exist } u \in H(S) \text{ and } u \Rightarrow_v^* I\}$.

Let $X = \{CS, CF, R\}$ then we define by XVGL the family of sets of images generated by GL-systems with variation, then we have

$$RVGL \subset CFVGL \subset CSVGL$$

We give an example which clarifies the process of vertical derivations in GL-systems.

Example 2. Let S be a GL-system such that $H(S) = ab$, and $\Phi = \{f_1, f_2, f_3\}$.

$$f_1 : \{a \to ab, \; b \to ab\}$$
$$f_2 : \{a \to aa, \; b \to bb\}$$
$$f_3 : \{a \to bb, \; b \to aa\}$$

Through GL-systems, we can have the following derivations:

$$
ab \Rightarrow^{f_1} \begin{matrix} a & a \\ b & b \end{matrix} \Rightarrow^{f_1} \begin{matrix} a & a \\ b & b \\ a & a \\ b & b \end{matrix}
$$

$$
\Rightarrow^{f_2} \begin{matrix} a & a \\ a & a \\ b & b \\ b & b \end{matrix}
$$

$$
\Rightarrow^{f_3} \begin{matrix} b & b \\ b & b \\ a & a \\ a & a \end{matrix}
$$

Definition 5.1. A GL-system $S = \langle V, \Sigma, s, R, \Phi \rangle$ is said to be simple if Φ contains only one U-morphism (i.e. $Card(\Phi) = 1$).

A VGL-system is said to be simple if and only if for each $a, b \in \Sigma$ we have $Card(\Phi_a) = 1$ and $\Phi_a = \Phi_b$. Let SXGL (respectively SXVGL) be the family of sets of images generated by a simple GL-system (respectively VGL-system).

Proposition 5.2. For each $X \in \{CS, CF, R\}$ the family SXGL is equal to the family of SXVGL.

Remark.
(1) A GL-system is a sequential/parallel system in which the horizontal rules form a Chomskian grammar and the vertical rules form a DTOL system.

(2) A simple GL-system is a sequential/parallel system in which the horizontal rules form a Chomskian grammar but the vertical rules form a DOL system.

From the above remarks, it follows that SXGL $\subset$ XGL, for each X $\in$ {CS, CF, R}.

Definition 5.3. An image L-substitution is a mapping from Σ to 2^{Δ^*}, where $(\sigma(a))^T$ is a DTOL language for each $a \in \Sigma$. ∎

σ is called simple if $(\sigma(a))^T$ is a DOL language for each $a \in \Sigma$. Each L-substitution can be given as a sequence $\sigma = (L_a)(a \in \Sigma)$ where $\sigma(a) = L_a$. If $x = a_1 \ldots a_n \in \Sigma^+$ then $\sigma(x) = \sigma(a_1) \oplus \ldots \oplus \sigma(a_n)$.

Now we give a characterization of XVGL in terms of L-substitutions and Chomskian languages.

Theorem 5.4. For each X $\in$ {CS, CF, R} and for each set I of images the following conditions are equivalent:
(i) I is generated by an XVGL system, and
(ii) there is a language L $\in$ X and an L-substitution σ such that I = σ(L).

Proof. (i) $\Rightarrow$ (ii)

Let S = $\langle V, \Sigma, s, R, \Phi = \{\Phi_a\}(a \in \Sigma)\rangle$ be an XVGL system. We shall exhibit an L-substitution $\sigma = L_a$ and a language L $\in$ X such that I(S) = σ(L).

Let L = L(G) where G = Base (S) and L $(G_a) = L_a = \sigma(a)$ where $G_a = \langle \Sigma, \Phi_a, a\rangle$ is a DTOL system, then I(S) = σ(L). ∎

To prove (ii) $\Rightarrow$ (i).

Let L = L(G) and $\sigma = L_a (a \in \Sigma)$ where G = $\langle V, \Sigma, s, R\rangle$, L $\in$ X, $L_a = L (G_a)$ and $G_a = \langle \Sigma, \bar{\Phi}_a, u_a\rangle$ is a DTOL system.

Construction:

(i) $\bar{\Sigma} = \{(\bar{a} : a \in \Sigma\} = \{\bar{a}_1, \cdots \bar{a}_n\}$.
(ii) $\bar{h} : \bar{\Sigma} \rightarrow \Sigma^+$ where $\bar{h}(a) = u_a$ for each $a \in \bar{\Sigma}$.
(iii) $\zeta : \Sigma \rightarrow \bar{\Sigma}$ where $\zeta(a) = \bar{a}$ for each $a \in \Sigma$.
(iv) $\Phi_a = \bar{\Phi}_a \cup \{\bar{h}\}$.
(v) Let $\bar{G} = \langle \bar{V}, \bar{\Sigma}, \bar{s}, \bar{R}\rangle$ be a grammar generating ζ(L).
(vi) S = $\langle \bar{V}, \Sigma \cup \bar{\Sigma}, \bar{s}, \bar{R}, \Phi = \{\Phi_{\bar{a}}\}\rangle$.
It is easy to prove that I(S) = σ(L).

We give an example to illustrate the above construction.

Example 3. $G_a : f_1 = \{a \rightarrow a^2, b \rightarrow b^2\}; u_a = ab; L_a = \{a^{2n}b^{2n} : n \geq 0\}$.

$G_b : \{f_2 = \{a \rightarrow a^2, b \rightarrow b\}, f_3 = \{a \rightarrow a, b \rightarrow b^2\}\} u_b = aba;$
$L_b = \{a^{2n}b^{2m}a^{2n} : n, m \geq 0\}$.
$G : s \rightarrow asb + ab.$
$\bar{\Sigma} = \{\bar{a}, \bar{b}\}.$
$\bar{h} : \bar{a} \rightarrow ab, \bar{b} \rightarrow aba.$
$\bar{V} = \{s\}; \bar{R} = \{s \rightarrow \bar{a} s \bar{b} + \bar{a}\bar{b}\}.$
$\Phi_{\bar{a}} = \{f_1, \bar{h}\}; \Phi_{\bar{b}} = \{\bar{h}, f_2, f_3\}.$

Corollary 5.5. For each X ∈ {CS, CR, R} and for each set I of images the following conditions are equivalent:

(i) I is generated by a simple XVGL system, and

(ii) there is a language L ∈ X and a simple L-substitution such that I = σ(L).

Now we study the closure properties of XVGL-systems under union and intersection.

Theorem 5.6. For each X ∈ {(CS, CF, R} the family SXVGL is not closed under union and intersection.

The proof uses the same examples as in the XGL-systems.

Note that the above theorem is also valid for XVGL-systems.

Theorem 5.7.

(1) The pumping lemma stated for CFGL-systems also holds good for CFVGL systems.

(2) The emptiness and finiteness problems for CFVGL-systems are decidable.

(3) The combinatorial lemma is not true for XVGL-systems.

ACKNOWLEDGEMENT

It is a pleasure to acknowledge the kind encouragement of Prof. M. Nivat, Prof. R. Siromoney and Prof. R. Narasimhan.

REFERENCES

1. J. E. Hopcroft and J. D. Ullman, *Introduction to Automata Theory, Languages and Computation*, Addison Wesley, 1979.
2. G. Rozenberg and A. Salomaa, *The Mathematical Theory of L-systems*, Academic Press, 1980.
3. N. Chomsky and M. P. Schützenberger, "The algebraic theory of context free languages", in *Computer Programming and Formal Systems*, Eds. P. Bradfford and D. Hirschberg, North-Holland, Amsterdam, 1963, pp. 118–161.
4. A. Rosenfeld, *Picture Languages—Formal Models for Picture Recognition*, Academic Press, 1979.
5. A. Rosenfeld, "Array grammar normal forms", *Inf. and Control* **23** (1973) 173–182.
6. G. Siromoney, R. Siromoney and K. Krithivasan, "Abstract families of matrices and picture languages", *Computer Graphics and Image Processing* **3** (1972) 284–307.
7. G. Siromoney, R. Siromoney and K. Krithivasan, "Picture languages with array rewriting rules", *Inf. and Control* **22** (1973) 447–470.
8. R. Siromoney, K. G. Subramanian and V. R. Dare, "On infinite arrays obtained by deterministic controlled table L-array systems", *Theoret. Comp. Sci.* **33** (1984) 3–11.
9. K. G. Subramanian, Studies in Array Languages, Ph. D Thesis, Madras University, 1979.
10. P. S. Wang, "Sequential/Parallel matrix array languages", *J. Cybernetics* **5** (1975) 19–36.
11. P. S. Wang, "Hierarchical structures and complexities of isometric patterns", *IEEE-PAMI* **5**, 1 (1983) 92–99.
12. P. S. Wang and C. Cook, "A Chomsky hierarchy of isotonic array grammars and languages", *Computer Graphics and Image Processing* **8**, (1978) 144–152.
13. P. S. Wang, "Finite turn repetitive checking automaton and sequential/parallel matrix languages", *IEEE Computers* **30**, 5 (1981) 366–390.
14. H. J. Lin and P. S. P. Wang, "Pushdown recognizers for array patterns", *Int. of Pattern Recognition and Artificial Intelligence* **3 & 4** (1989) 377–392.
15. R. Siromoney, "Array languages and Lindenmayer systems—a survey" in *The Book of L*, Eds. G. Rozenberg and A. Salomaa, Springer-Verlag, Berlin, 1985.

16. R. Siromoney, "Advances in array languages", *LNCS* **291**, Springer-Verlag, Berlin, 1987, pp. 549–563.
17. M. Nivat, A. Saoudi and V. R. Dare, "Parallel generation of finite images", *Int. J. Pattern Recognition and Artificial Intelligence* **3** (1989).
18. R. Siromoney, K. G. Subramanian and K. Rangarajan, "Parallel/Sequential rectangular arrays with tables", *Int. J. Computer Mathematics* **6** (1977) 43–58.
19. R. Siromoney and G. Siromoney, "Parallel OL-languages", *Int. J. Computer Mathematics* **5**, Sec. A (1975) 109–123.
20. R. Siromoney and G. Siromoney, "Extended controlled table L-arrays", *Inf. and Control* **35** (1977) 119–138.
21. K. Krithivasan and N. Nirmal, "OL and TOL array languages", *J. Indian Inst. Sc.* **62A** (1980) 101–110.
22. N. Nirmal and K. Krithivasan, "Table matrix L-systems", *Int. J. Computer Mathematics* **10** (1982) 247–265.

Ahmed Saoudi has been an Associate Professor since 1985 at the University of Paris XIII. He received the Master degree in computer science from the University of Louis Pasteur (Strasbourg) in 1979, the doctorat of 3rd cycle from the University of Paris VII in 1972, and the doctorat d'Etat in computer science from the University of Paris VII in 1987. In 1984 he was an Assistant Professor in Computer Science at the University of Orsay.

Pro. Saoudi is a member of LITP (Laboratory of Theoretical Computer Science and Programming) since 1980 and a member of EATCS (European Association of Theoretical Computer Science). His areas of research are automata and grammars on trees, logic and programming, parallel algorithms, syntactic pattern recognition and image processing.

year 1988–89. His research interests include formal languages and automata theory, Petri nets and concurrency.

V. R. Dare received his M.Sc. and M.Phil. in mathematics from Madurai University in 1976 and 1977 respectively. His Ph.D. degree is from Madras University (1986). He is at present on the faculty of the Department of Mathematics, Madras Christian College, Tambaram, Madras. He was a post-doctoral fellow at LITP (Laboratory of Theoretical Computer Science and Programming), University of Paris VII, during the year 1987–88. His research interests include topological studies of formal languages and studies on infinite words and infinite arrays.

K. Rangarajan received his M.Sc., M.Phil. and Ph.D. in mathematics from Madras University. He is at present on the faculty of the Department of Mathematics, Madras Christian College, Tambaram, Madras. He is a member of the Special Interest Group in Petri nets. He was a post-doctoral fellow at LITP (Laboratory of Theoretical Computer Science and Programming), University of Paris VII, during the

GRAMMARS ON THE HEXAGONAL ARRAY

KUNIO AIZAWA and AKIRA NAKAMURA

Department of Applied Mathematics, Hiroshima University
Higashi-Hiroshima, 724 Japan

Received 20 April 1989

In this paper, we will define array grammars on the hexagonal grid. One of the advantages obtained from using the hexagonal grid is that each point has only one kind of neighbor. It is shown that the class of the context-free array grammars on the hexagonal grid includes the class of the rectangular ones even if their languages are restricted to the pictures connected on the rectangular grid. It is also shown that, in the monotonic case, they own the same class of languages jointly.

Keywords: Array grammars; Discrete spaces; Hexagonal array; Turing array acceptors.

1. INTRODUCTION

Array grammars are defined as the two-dimensional extensions of usual string grammars. The languages of these array grammars are embedded in the rectangular grid. In the processes to generate these languages, there is a shearing effect as the rows or columns of the host array must be stretched or shrunk by varying amounts in order to accommodate the array rewriting rules. To avoid the problem, a restriction called ''isometric'' is usually inserted to each production rule. Both sides of an ''isometric'' production rule are geometrically identical. So the growth of an array can only happen along the border of the array by replacing the blank symbols (i.e. #s) with other symbols.

In this paper, we will define array grammars on the hexagonal grid. Since the definitions of the isometric array grammars are independent from the structures of arrays in which they are embedded, the isometric grammars on the hexagonal array can be defined almost in the same way as in the case of the rectangular grid. The hexagonal grid was defined formally in Mylopoulos and Pavlidis[1] and Rosenfeld[2] by making use of abelian groups. For example, in Ref. 1, the rectangular grid is defined as a free abelian group with two generators ''go left'', ''go above'', and their inverses ''go right'', ''go below''. The hexagonal grid is defined as an abelian group with three generators and their inverses. One of the advantages obtained from using the hexagonal grid is that each point has only one kind of neighbor. This property is very useful to study topological properties of digital pictures. So introducing array grammars on the hexagonal array may shed light on the relationships between array grammars and digital pictures.

International Journal of Pattern Recognition and Artificial Intelligence Vol. 3 No. 3 & 4 (1989) 469–477
© World Scientific Publishing Company

In Sect. 3 of this paper, we will compare the generative powers of the grammars on the hexagonal grid and the rectangular grid. It is shown that the class of the context-free array grammars on the hexagonal grid includes the class of the rectangular ones even if their languages are restricted to the pictures connected on the rectangular grid. It is also shown that, in the monotonic case, they own the same class of languages jointly.

We assume the reader is familiar with the theory of two-dimensional languages (otherwise please see, e.g. Ref. 3).

2. DEFINITIONS AND NOTATIONS

We will here review some definitions and notations of the hexagonal grid. Then we will define two-dimensional grammars on the hexagonal array. At first, we review the definitions of discrete space and hexagonal array. We will use almost the same definitions and notations as in Ref. 1.

Definition 2.1. A *discrete space* is a finitely presented abelian group $\Gamma = (X/D)$, where X has $2n$ generators $s_1, s_2, \ldots, s_n, s_1^{-1}, s_2^{-1}, \ldots, s_n^{-1}$, and D contains all relations other than the commutativity $(s_i s_j s_i^{-1} s_j^{-1} = 1)$ and the inverse iterations $(s_i s_i^{-1} = 1)$.

Definition 2.2. The *hexagonal array* is a discrete space described by a group Γ generated by the following relative directions: $s_1 =$ (right), $s_2 =$ (above right), $s_3 =$ (above left), $s_1^{-1} =$ (left), $s_2^{-1} =$ (below left), $s_3^{-1} =$ (below right), and $D = \{s_1 s_3 s_2^{-1} = 1\}$.

Note that Γ defined above is not a free group because (right) (above left) (below left) returns one to the original point. Hence D contains the relation $s_1 s_3 s_2^{-1} = 1$. See Fig. 1 for a graphical image of the hexagonal grid and its generators.

Now, we review the definitions of some basic notions of discrete space. Let $X' = X \cup \{s_0\}$, where s_0 is the group identity.

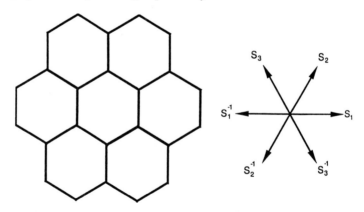

Fig. 1. The hexagonal array and its generators.

Definition 2.3. For a given point x of $\Gamma = (X/D)$, a *direct neighbor* of x is any point $y \in \Gamma$ such that $y = xg$ for some $g \in X'$. The set of all direct neighbors of x is denoted by $ND(x)$, i.e. $ND(x) = \{xg \mid g \in X'\}$.

Note here that $ND(x)$ contains x itself. The set of direct neighbors of x excluding x is denoted as $ND^*(x)$, i.e. $ND^*(x) = ND(x) - \{x\}$.

Definition 2.4. The *neighborhood* of a point x, denoted as $N(x)$, consists of
(1) $ND(x)$ and
(2) all points z such that there exist y, $y' \in ND^*(x)$ with the property that the shortest path from y to y' not passing through z passes through z.

Again $N^*(x) = N(x) - \{x\}$.

Definition 2.5. A *direct-path* (d-path) between two points w_1 and w_2 of Γ is an ordered sequence of points $w_1 = x_1, x_2, \ldots, x_{n-1}, x_n = w_2$ such that $x_{i+1} \in ND^*(x_i)$, for $1 \le i \le n-1$. A path is an ordered sequence of points such that $x_{i+1} \in N^*(x_i)$, for $1 \le i \le n - 1$. The *length of a (d-)path* is defined as the number of points in the path. A *shortest (d-)path* between two points is a (d-)path with minimum length.

Definition 2.6. Two points w_1 and w_2 of a finite subset F of Γ are *(d-) connected in F* if and only if there exists a (d-)path between them in F.

The relation "connected" defined above is obviously an equivalence relation. Thus it partitions Γ into equivalence classes.

Definition 2.7. The *(d-)components* of Γ are the equivalence classes of "(d-)connected" relations.

The isometric grammars on the hexagonal array can be defined almost in the same way as in the case of the rectangular array since their definitions are independent from the structures of the arrays in which they are embedded.

Definition 2.8. An isometric grammar on the hexagonal array, denoted as IAG_h, is a construct $G = \langle V, T, P, S, \# \rangle$, where V is a finite nonempty set of nonterminals, T is a finite nonempty set of terminals ($V \cap T = \varnothing$), S is an element of V (the starting symbol), $\#$ is a symbol not contained in $V \cup T$ (the blank symbol), and P is a finite nonempty set of productions each of which is of the form $x \to y$. These x and y are geometrically identical arrays over $V \cup T \cup \{\#\}$ and satisfy the following conditions:
(1) If the non-$\#$s of x do not touch the border of x, then the non-$\#$s of y must be connected (and nonempty).
(2) Otherwise,
   (a) every connected component of non-$\#$s in y must contain the intersection of some component of non-$\#$s in x with the border of x;
   (b) conversely, every such intersection must be contained in some component of non-$\#$s in y.

For the case of the rectangular array, it is shown in Ref. 3 that if conditions (1) and (2) defined above hold, applying the rule $x \to y$ does not disconnect or eliminate the non-$\#$s. For the case of the hexagonal array, the same property can be shown in a similar way.

Definition 2.9. Let W and Z be arrays over $V \cup T \cup \{\#\}$. For a given IAG_h, the array W directly derives array Z in G, denoted as $W \underset{G}{\Rightarrow} Z$, if there exists a production $x \to y$ in P, W contains x as a subarray, and Z is identical to W except that the subarray x is replaced with the array y. $\underset{G}{\overset{*}{\Rightarrow}}$ is defined as the reflexive and transitive closure of $\underset{G}{\Rightarrow}$. The *language* of G, denoted as $L(G)$, is defined by $L(G) = \{W | W$ is an array over T and $S \underset{G}{\overset{*}{\Rightarrow}} W\}$.

An IAG_h is called *monotonic*, denoted as MAG_h, if #s are never created by any rule. We can also define a *context-free* array grammar on the hexagonal array, denoted as $CFAG_h$, if G is an MAG_h and, for all rules $x \to y$ of G, x consists of a single nonterminal symbol and (possibly) of #s. Note here that all grammars defined above have 6-connectedness instead of 4-connectedness since each point of the hexagonal array has at most six direct neighbors.

3. GENERATIVE POWER OF GRAMMARS ON THE HEXAGONAL ARRAY

In this section, we will compare the generative power of grammars on the hexagonal and on the usual rectangular arrays. Because of the differences between the hexagonal and the rectangular arrays, it is difficult to compare these grammars directly. Thus we need an interpretative transformation between these two different arrays. Intuitively, if we regard the hexagonal array as a kind of brick array (see Fig. 2) and slide each row to the left (see Fig. 3), then we get a rectangular array. Namely the generator $s_2 = $ (above right) is regarded as $s_2' = $ (above).

Stipulation 3.1. An array Σ on the hexagonal array, described by $\Gamma = (s_1, s_2, s_3, s_1^{-1}, s_2^{-1}, s_3^{-1}/s_1 s_3 s_2^{-1} = 1)$, and an array Σ' on the discrete space $\Gamma' = (s_1, s_2', s_3, s_1^{-1}, s_2'^{-1}, s_3^{-1}/s_1 s_3 s_2'^{-1} = 1)$ are said to be *equivalent under Stipulation 3.1*, denoted as $\Sigma = {}_1\Sigma'$, if $\Sigma = \Sigma'$ when the generators $s_2 = $ (above right) and $s_2 = $ (below left) of Γ are regarded as $s_2' = $ (above) and $s_2' = $ (below) respectively.

Note that the discrete space $\Gamma' = (s_1, s_2', s_3, s_1^{-1}, s_2'^{-1}, s_3^{-1}/s_1 s_3 s_2'^{-1} = 1)$ defines a slightly different array from the usual rectangular array, i.e. the discrete

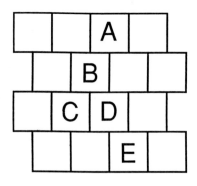

Fig. 2. The blick array.

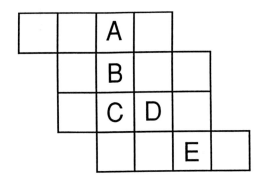

Fig. 3. The rectangular array.

space Ξ generated by $s_1 = $ (right), $s_2 = $ (above), $s_1^{-1} = $ (left), $s_2'^{-1} = $ (below), since each point of Γ' has six (not four) direct neighbours other than itself (see Fig. 4). Moreover it is different from the original hexagonal array since each point of Γ' has eight neighbors other than itself.

The class of IAG_h is obviously not equal to that of IAG even if we use the stipulation for there exist the languages of IAG_h whose elements are not d-connected under Ξ. In fact, even if we consider only the languages whose elements are d-connected under the discrete space Ξ, there exists $CFAG_h$ G *such that* $L(G)$ is not contained in $\mathscr{F}(CFAG)$.

Lemma 3.2. There exists a language of $CFAG_h$ which is d-connected under the discrete space Ξ and is not contained in $\mathscr{F}(CFAG)$.

Proof. Let $G = \langle \{S, A, B, C\}, \{a\}, P, S, \# \rangle$ be a $CFAG_h$, where P consists of the following production rules on the hexagonal array:

$$\begin{array}{c} {}^{\#}{}^{S} \\ {}_{\#}{}^{\#} \\ {}_{\#}{}^{\#} \\ \#{}^{\#}\# \end{array} \rightarrow a{}^{a}_{a}{}^{a}_{a}A$$

$$A\#{}^{\#}\# \rightarrow aa{}^{a}A$$

$$A\#{}^{\#} \rightarrow aa{}^{B}_{a}$$

$$\begin{array}{c} \# \\ B \end{array} \rightarrow {}^{C}_{a}$$

$$\#{}^{\#C} \rightarrow a{}^{aa}$$

$$\#\#C \rightarrow Caa$$

195

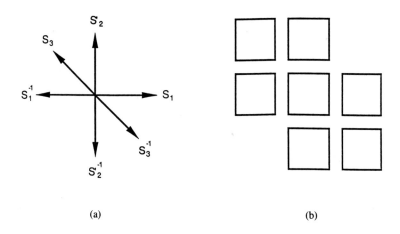

          (a)   (b)

Fig. 4.   (a) Generators of Γ',   (b) the direct neighbors of an arbitrary point in Γ'.

An example of the derivation steps of G is shown in Fig. 5. It is not so difficult to see that each element of $L(G)$ is d-connected under the discrete space Ξ. Assume here that there exists a CFAG G' which generates the language of G. Since G' generates arrays embedded in the discrete space Ξ, each element of $L(G')$ is of the form represented in Fig. 6. The top horizontal part of an element of $L(G')$ must be generated independently from the rightmost vertical run (see Fig. 7). In general, the top horizontal part can be arbitrarily long, then G' must use at least one nonterminal symbol more than once (see Fig. 8(a)). Thus, if G' generates the elements of $L(G)$, G' also generates arrays which are not contained in $L(G)$ (see Fig. 8(b)). It is a contradiction. ∎

On the other hand, we will show that tape-bounded array acceptors accept the class of languages of MAG_h which are d-connected under Ξ. A Turing array acceptor is a Turing machine defined on two-dimensional input tapes. If it "bounces off" #s, it is called tape-bounded (denoted as TBAA). It is known that the languages generated by MAGs are the same as the languages accepted by TBAA. For detailed definitions and proofs, see, e.g. Ref. 3.

Lemma 3.3.   For any MAG_h G generating hexagonal arrays which are d-connected under the discrete space Ξ, there exists a tape-bounded Turing array acceptor A such that $L(A) = L(G)$.

Proof.   Given an MAG_h, the definition of a TBAA that accepts exactly $L(G)$ is almost the same as that of TBAAs for the languages of MAGs. So, given an array Σ in the terminal alphabet T of G, embedded in an infinite array of #s, A moves around nondeterministically, starting at some point of Σ, and rewrites each non-# symbol p into $(p, \#)$. Finally, at some step, A rewrites some p as (p, S); this can happen only once. After it happens, A begins to stimulate rules of G on the second terms of pairs. A problem arises with the TBAA if G has a rule $x \rightarrow y$ whose non-#s of right-hand sides are not d-connected under Ξ. These disconnected productions may raise

```
       a        a          a
      a        a          a
S ⇒  a    ⇒   a     ⇒    a
    a        a   a      a   a   a
    a A     a a a A    a a a a a A

       a
      a
*⇒   a                 B
    a   a   a   a   a
   a a a a a a a a a

       a
      a          C a a
*⇒   a                 a
    a   a   a   a   a
   a a a a a a a a a

       a
      a          a a a a
⇒    a         a       a
    a   a   a   a   a
   a a a a a a a a a
```

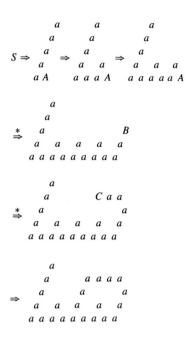

Fig. 5. An example of derivations of G.

```
a
a      a a a a
a      a       a
a   a  a   a   a
a a a a a a a a a
```

Fig. 6. An example of elements of $L(G')$.

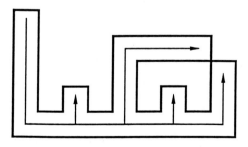

Fig. 7. An example of generation of G'.

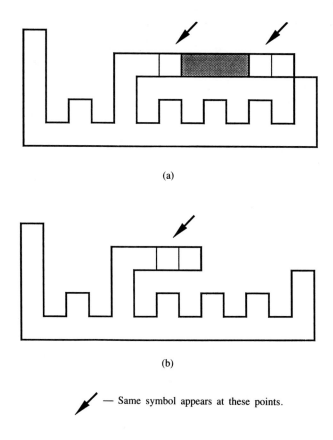

(a)

(b)

✔ — Same symbol appears at these points.

Fig. 8.   (a) An element of $L(G')$ which is also in $L(G)$, and   (b) an element of $L(G')$ which is not in $L(G)$.

disconnected parts on Σ (from the assumption, of course, Σ is d-connected as a whole). A must cross the disconnected part in order to apply the rule. Suppose that A is located at position (i, j) and wants to cross the position (i', j'), then the absolute values of the differences $|i-i'|$ and $|j-j'|$ are equal to 1 and both points are on the same border of Σ. To find the point (i', j'), A marks (i, j), follows the border of Σ, and keeps track of its net up, down, left and right moves. If A returns to (i, j) without finding the point (i', j'), the rule $x \to y$ cannot apply to the part. Otherwise A can continue its simulation. ∎

It is obvious that the class of the languages of $CFAG_h$ (MAG_h) includes the class of the languages of CFAG (MAG, respectively) in the sense of Stipulation 3.1. So it is not so difficult to see the following theorem:

Theorem 3.4.

(1) The class of the languages of $CFAG_h$s which are d-connected under the discrete space Ξ includes the class of the languages of CFAGs properly in the sense of Stipulation 3.1.

(2) The class of the language of MAG_hs which are d-connected under the discrete space Ξ is equal to the class of the languages of MAGs in the sense of Stipulation 3.1.

5. CONCLUDING REMARKS

In this paper, we have shown the generative powers of some array grammars generating hexagonal patterns. The hexagonal array used in this paper is also defined as a near abelian partial path group of degree 6 (see Ref. 2). Graph grammars using path controlled embedding, PCE grammars, can define the structure of their language by making use of partial path groups. So it seems to be of interest to consider the PCE grammars which generate hexagonal array languages.

REFERENCES
1. J. P. Mylopoulos and T. Pavlidis, "On the topological properties of quantized spaces", *J. ACM* **18** (1971) 239 − 254.
2. A. Rosenfeld, "Partial path groups and parallel graphs constructions", in *The Book of L,* Eds. G. Rozenberg and A. Salomaa, Springer-Verlag, 1986, pp. 369 − 382.
3. A. Rosenfeld, *Picture Languages,* Academic Press, 1979.

Kunio Aizawa received the M.A. degree from Hiroshima University in 1982.

He is currently a Research Associate in the Department of Applied Mathematics at Hiroshima University. His research interests include the theory of picture languages and digital image understanding.

Akira Nakamura received the B.A. degree from Hiroshima University in 1953 and the Doctor of Science degree in mathematics from Nagoya University in 1963. From 1959 to 1964, he was an Assistant Professor and from 1965 to 1970 an Associate Professor of Applied Mathematics at Nihon University. Between 1966 to 1968 he was also a Visiting Assistant Professor at the Department of Information Science of the University of North Carolina at Chapel Hill.

Since 1970, he has been a Professor of Applied Mathematics at Hiroshima University. He was a Visiting Professor at the Computer Science Center, University of Maryland from November 1977 to January 1978, and at the Tata Institute of Fundamental Research, Bombay, in September 1980. He was also a Visiting Scientist of the Division of Mathematics and Statistics, CSIRO, Australia, in September 1985. He is working in the theory of picture languages and non-standard logics for artificial intelligence.

REPRESENTATION OF ITERATIVE PATTERNS[†]

HIROTOMO ASO

Department of Information Engineering, Tohoku University
Sendai 980, Japan

and

NAMIO HONDA

Toyohashi University of Technology
Toyohashi 440, Japan

Received 1 May 1989

Iterative patterns can be described by the component pattern of iteration and their way of connection for iteration. It is shown that the shape of the component pattern can be a rectangle for any iterative pattern, which is called a tile. The tile is related to the basis of the parallel translation group of the iterative pattern. The component pattern itself is identified by a "tessera" which is defined by a non-degenerate colored tile. The tessera is a compact representation of iterative patterns. Some natures of tesseras and tiles are also discussed. The number of the kinds of distinct iterative patterns for each way of iteration is evaluated.

Keywords: Iterative pattern; Parallel translation group; Tile; Tessera; Enumeration of patterns.

1. INTRODUCTION

Iterative patterns can be described by the component pattern of iteration and the way of its connection for iteration. Usually the shape of the component pattern seems to be complicated and involves the way of iteration. The complicated shape may require much superfluous area for it to be stored in a computer memory and complicated operations for it to reproduce an iterative pattern from a component pattern.

This paper gives a compact and simple representation of iterative patterns. We shall show that for any iterative pattern whose component pattern seems to have a complicated shape at a glance, we can choose a rectangular pattern as a component, called a tessera or a colored tile.

The ways to create artistic iterative patterns like Escher's works are shown in Ref. 1. The key point of the methods seems to be a design of a component pattern with a complicated shape. In contrast with this, the representation shown in this paper may not be appropriate to create any artistic iterative patterns but it is suitable to store them in order to use or to reproduce the patterns. Furthermore, the representation induces a systematic enumeration of all kinds of iterative patterns in principle. The number increases exponentially with the size of the component patterns.

[†] This paper is a minor revision of Ref. 5.

International Journal of Pattern Recognition and Artificial Intelligence Vol. 3 No. 3 & 4 (1989) 479–495
© World Scientific Publishing Company

The symmetry of iterative patterns was discussed in Refs. 2 and 3. It may be regarded as the theory of two-dimensional crystallographic groups. It is known that there are seventeen kinds of symmetries which include rotative symmetry. With the crystallographic terminology, it may be said that the object of this paper is to determine a simple way of representing a lattice group, or a parallel translation subgroup of a crystallographic group. We find a simple way of representation, or appropriate generators of the lattice group, to describe iterative patterns. The generators correspond to the shape of the component pattern. The component pattern of our representation may consist of several component patterns defined by rotative symmetry.

Sections 2 to 5 give the main discussion on the representation of iterative patterns. The new concepts of tile and tessera are introduced and the validities are discussed. In Sect. 6, some natures of iterative patterns are shown. In Sect. 7, we evaluate the number of the kinds of iterative patterns for each shape of component patterns. This discussion is an interesting application of the theory of arithmetic functions.

2.   ITERATIVE PATTERNS

Let Z be the set of integers, $Z(0) = Z$ and $Z(k) = \{0, 1, \ldots, k - 1\}$ for each $k > 0$. Let $Z^2 = \{(i, j) \mid i, j \in Z\}$ be the set of two-dimensional lattice points. The elements are regarded as row vectors and denoted by α, β, etc. $(0, 0) \in Z^2$ is simply denoted by 0.

Definition 2.1.

(1) A mapping c from Z^2 into Q is called a configuration. The set of configurations is denoted by C, i.e.

$$C = \{c \mid c : Z^2 \to Q\}$$

(2) Let Q be a finite set of symbols (or colors). For each $\beta \in Z^2$, a mapping s^β on C is defined as

$$s^\beta(c)(\alpha) = c(\alpha - \beta)$$

for any $\alpha \in Z^2$, and it is called a translation map.

Thus "pattern" which is used informally is called "configuration" formally. (In Sect. 5, "pattern" is defined formally.) A configuration c may be regarded as an infinite matrix, i.e. $c(i, j)$ is an (i, j)th entry of the matrix. A translation map translates a configuration in parallel to the direction of β.

Lemma 2.2.   The set of translation maps is a commutative group with composition operation, which is isomorphic to Z^2 with vector addition.

Note that $s^{\beta + \gamma}(c) = s^\beta(s^\gamma(c))$ and $s^{-\beta}$ is a unique inverse of s^β.

Definition 2.3.   A configuration $c \in C$ is iterative if there exists a $\beta \in Z^2$ such that $\beta \neq 0$ and $s^\beta(c) = c$. Otherwise c is called uniterative.

Definition 2.4.   For each $c \in C$, the following subset $S(c)$ of Z^2 is called a parallel translation group of c.

$$S(c) = \{\beta \mid s^\beta(c) = c\}.$$

Clearly, $0 \in S(c)$ for any $c \in C$. The next proposition is immediate from the definitions.

Proposition 2.5. $c \in C$ is iterative if and only if $S(c) \neq \{0\}$. Equivalently, $c \in C$ is uniterative if and only if $S(c) = \{0\}$.

To represent an iterative configuration, we need to know that something like a period or its component pattern appeared iteratively in it. Such a period or component pattern will be expressed in a tractable form by the investigation of the parallel translation group of configuration.

The next proposition is obvious by Definition 2.4 and Lemma 2.2.

Proposition 2.6. A parallel translation group $S(c)$ of any $c \in C$ is a Z-module and a submodule of the free module Z^2.

3. Z-MODULE AND TILE

We will consider a finite description of a Z-module and introduce the concept of "tile".

Note that a module is an additive commutative group and that a Z-module is a module for which scalar multiples by integers is defined. The free module Z^2 is also a Z-module and has a finite basis (a set of elements which are linearly independent and generate Z^2), and the number of elements of the basis is equal to the dimension or is two. Any submodule of the free module is also a free module and there exists a basis. The basis of a submodule of Z^2 may be represented by such a $b \times 2$ matrix that its rows are elements of the basis and b is equal to the number of elements of the basis ($b = 1$ or 2).

Now let B be a $b \times 2$ matrix on Z, that is, any entry of B is an integer. And let $G(B)$ be a Z-module generated by B, that is,

$$G(B) = \{\beta \mid \beta = zB, \ z \in Z^b\} \subset Z^2.$$

Definition 3.1. Two matrices B_0 and B_1 on Z are equivalent, which is denoted by $B_0 \equiv B_1$, if $G(B_0) = G(B_1)$.

Lemma 3.2. For two $b \times 2$ matrices B_0 and B_1, $G(B_0) \subset G(B_1)$ if and only if there exists a $b \times b$ matrix U on Z such that $B_0 = UB_1$.

Lemma 3.3. Suppose that the rows of the $b \times 2$ matrices B_0 and B_1 are linearly independent, respectively. $B_0 \equiv B_1$ if and only if there exists a $b \times b$ matrix U on Z such that $|\det U| = 1$ and $B_0 = UB_1$, where $\det U$ is the determinant of a square matrix U.

This is immediately seen from Lemma 3.2. By this lemma, U^{-1} is also a matrix on Z and $B_1 = U^{-1}B_0$.

Now we will define a kind of canonical form of a basis of a Z-module.

Definition 3.4. Let S be a Z-module which is a submodule of Z^2. The matrix B defined below is called the basic matrix of S.
(i) $B = [0, 0]$ if $S = \{0\}$.
(ii) For the case of $S \neq \{0\}$, B is a basis of S and

(ii-a) if $B = [i, k]$ then $i = 0$ and $k > 0$, or $i > 0$ and $k \in Z$,

(ii-b) if $B = \begin{bmatrix} i & k \\ k' & j \end{bmatrix}$ then $i, j > 0$, $k' = 0$ and $0 \leqq k < j$.

Let $gcd(a, b)$ be the greatest common divisor of integers a and b. Particularly, $gcd(0, a) = gcd(a, 0) = a$.

Lemma 3.5. For any Z-module $S \subset Z^2$, there exists a basic matrix of S.

Proof. Assume $S \neq \{0\}$. Let B be a basis of S.

Case 1: $B = [i, k]$. Let

$$U = \begin{cases} -1 & \text{if } i < 0 \text{ or } i = 0 \text{ and } k < 0 \\ 1 & \text{otherwise.} \end{cases}$$

Then $B \equiv UB$ by Lemma 3.3 and UB is a basic matrix.

Case 2: B is a 2×2 matrix. There exists a matrix U_1 such that $|\det U_1| = 1$ and $i_1 \geqq k'_1 \geqq 0$, where $(U_1 B)_{11} = i_1$, $(U_1 B)_{21} = k'_1$. (Note U_1 exchanges rows and/or changes signs of rows of B.) If $k'_1 \neq 0$ then let $\delta = gcd(i_1, k'_1)$ and let μ and ν be integers such that $\mu i_1 + \nu k'_1 = \delta$. Now let

$$U_2 = \begin{bmatrix} \mu & \nu \\ -k'_1/\delta & i_1/\delta \end{bmatrix}.$$

If $k'_1 = 0$, then let U_2 be an identity matrix. By the definition of U_2, U_2 is a matrix on Z and $\det U_2 = 1$ for any cases of k'_1. Now we have $(U_2 U_1 B)_{21} = 0$ and $(U_2 U_1 B)_{11} = \delta > 0$. Let U_3 be a diagonal matrix such that $U_{3,11} = 1$ and $U_{3,22} = sgn((U_2 U_1 B)_{22})$. Then $|\det U_3| = 1$. Let $B' = U_3 U_2 U_1 B$ then $B'_{11} > 0$, $B'_{21} = 0$ and $B'_{22} > 0$. Let p and q be integers such that

$$B'_{12} = pB'_{22} + q \text{ and } 0 \leqq q < B'_{22}.$$

Let U_4 be a matrix like an identity matrix but $U_{4,21} = -p$. Then $U_4 B'$ is a matrix of which $(2, 1)$-entry is $q \geqq 0$ and the others are the same as the corresponding entries of B'. Thus, $B_0 = U_4 U_3 U_2 U_1 B$ has a form defined in (ii-b) of Definition 3.4. Furthermore $B_0 \equiv B$ by Lemma 3.3. Hence B_0 is a basic matrix of S. ■

Proposition 3.6. For any Z-module $S \subset Z^2$, there exists a basic matrix B of S uniquely. And $S = G(B)$.

Proof. The existence has been proved in Lemma 3.5. The proof of uniqueness is straightforward so details are omitted. ■

This proposition tells us that the basic matrix is a suitable candidate to describe a Z-module. To make it sure and reasonable, we will extract a meaning from the basic matrix as a tile, which will be shown to correspond to a kind of period of an iterative configuration.

Definition 3.7.

(1) A triple (i_0, j_0, k_0) of such integers that $i_0, j_0 \geq 0$, $0 \leq k_0 < j_0$ if $j_0 > 0$, and $k_0 = 0$ if $i_0 = 0$, is called a tile index.
(2) A tile corresponding to a tile index (i_0, j_0, k_0) is defined as a pair $\langle T(i_0, j_0), k_0 \rangle$, where $T(i_0, j_0) = Z(i_0) \times Z(j_0)$. $T(i_0, j_0)$ is sometimes denoted by T only. (Remember the convention for $Z(i)$). (i_0, j_0, k_0) is also called a tile index of the tile.
(3) A basic matrix corresponding to a tile index (i_0, j_0, k_0) is a 2×2 matrix B_0 such that

$$B_0 = \begin{bmatrix} i_0 & k_0 \\ 0 & j_0 \end{bmatrix}.$$

$G(B_0)$ is called a Z-module generated by tile $\langle T(i_0, j_0), k_0 \rangle$ and denoted by $G(i_0, j_0, k_0)$ also.
(4) If $i_0 \cdot j_0 > 0$ then the corresponding tile is called finite and $i_0 \cdot j_0$ is called a size of the tile; otherwise, it is called infinite. (These correspond to the cardinality of $T(i_0, j_0)$.)

Note that the set $T(i_0, j_0)$ in the above definition is a subset of Z^2 and may be regarded as a rectangle if $i_0 \cdot j_0 > 0$, and $i_0 \cdot j_0$ is the area size of the rectangle, which is also equal to det B_0. If $i_0 = 0$ or $j_0 = 0$, then $T(i_0, j_0)$ has a shape of an infinite belt of width j_0 or i_0 respectively. If $i_0 = 0 = j_0$ then $T(0, 0) = Z^2$.

It is obvious by the definition that the basic matrix of a tile is not necessarily equal but is equivalent to the basic matrix of the Z-module generated by the tile. For finite tiles, however, they are identical. But otherwise the former consists of linearly dependent rows and the latter of a single row.

Theorem 3.8. For any Z-module $S \subset Z^2$, there exists a unique tile $\langle T(i_0, j_0), k_0 \rangle$ such that S is generated by the tile. (This tile is called the tile of S).

Proof. Let B be a basic matrix of S. The tile corresponding to the following tile index (i_0, j_0, k_0) is the desired one. If $B = [0, j]$ then $(i_0, j_0, k_0) = (0, j, 0)$. If $B = [i, k]$ and $i \neq 0$ then $(i_0, j_0, k_0) = (i, 0, k)$. And if $B = \begin{bmatrix} i & k \\ 0 & j \end{bmatrix}$ then $(i_0, j_0, k_0) = (i, j, k)$. ∎

Thus we know that if one of a Z-module S, a tile index (i_0, j_0, k_0) and a tile $\langle T(i_0, j_0), k_0 \rangle$ is given, then the others corresponding to it can be identified. In order to state a close relation between a Z-module S and its tile, we introduce mappings on Z^2.

Definition 3.9. Corresponding to a tile index (i_0, j_0, k_0), the mappings $h_0 : Z^2 \rightarrow T(i_0, j_0)$ and $g_0 : Z^2 \rightarrow Z^2$ are defined as follows and called a reducing map and a relative position map of a tile respectively. For any $(i, j) \in Z^2$,

$$h_0(i, j) = (i \bmod i_0, (j - \lfloor i/i_0 \rfloor \cdot k_0) \bmod j_0) \text{ and}$$

$$g_0(i, j) = (\lfloor i/i_0 \rfloor, \lfloor (j - \lfloor i/i_0 \rfloor \cdot k_0)/j_0 \rfloor).$$

Theorem 3.10. Let S be a Z-module which is a submodule of Z^2 and $\langle T(i_0, j_0), k_0 \rangle$ be the tile of S. Let $T = T(i_0, j_0)$. Then $S \cap T = \{0\}$ and $Z^2 = S + T = \{(r, s) + (p, q) \mid (r, s) \in S, (p, q) \in T\}$. Furthermore, there exists a unique decomposition of any $(i, j) \in Z^2$ into the sum of elements of S and T. The decomposition is given by $g_0(i, j)B_0$ and $h_0(i, j)$, where g_0, h_0 and B_0 are a position map, a reducing map, and the basic matrix corresponding to the tile index (i_0, j_0, k_0) respectively.

Proof. It is clear that $Z^2 \supset S + T$. If it is proved that $(i, j) = g_0(i, j)B_0 + h_0(i, j)$ for any $(i, j) \in Z^2$, then the proof is completed. Now let $g_0(i, j) = (r', s')$ and $h_0(i, j) = (p, q)$. Then we have $i = r'i_0 + p$ and $j - r'k_0 = s'j_0 + q$, by the definition. Hence we have

$$(i, j) = (r'i_0, \ r'k_0 + s'j_0) + (p, q) = (r', s')B_0 + (p, q).$$

Clearly $(r', s')B_0 \in S$ and $(p, q) \in T$. ∎

The meaning of this theorem can be illustrated in Fig. 1. Remember that the coordinates of Z^2 are taken as matrix-like. From Fig. 1, we know that a finite tile may be regarded as a real rectangular tile; putting them side by side forms a belt and placing the belts upward and downward sliding by k_0 covers the whole space. Also we know that the infinite tile may be regarded as a special case of the finite one. The set $\beta + T(i_0, j_0)$ for each $\beta \in S$ may be said to be the tile at β. Since $g_0(\beta)B_0 = \beta$ for any $\beta \in S$, $g_0(\beta)$ is a relative coordinate of β with respect to the basis B_0 and is regarded as a relative position of the tile at β. And $h_0(\beta)$ is regarded as a position of point β in the tile at β. These are the meanings of g_0 and h_0.

Note that tile $\langle T, k_0 \rangle$ with addition $\alpha \oplus \beta = h_0(\alpha + \beta)$ is isomorphic to the difference group $Z^2 - S$ (or the quotient group Z^2/S).

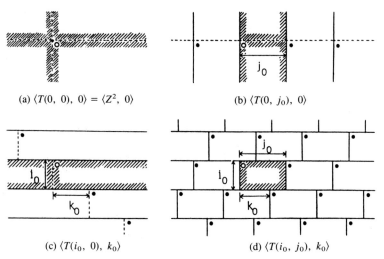

(a) $\langle T(0, 0), 0 \rangle = \langle Z^2, 0 \rangle$

(b) $\langle T(0, j_0), 0 \rangle$

(c) $\langle T(i_0, 0), k_0 \rangle$

(d) $\langle T(i_0, j_0), k_0 \rangle$

Fig. 1. Z-module S and its tile, where circle represents $(0, 0)$, dot represents element of S and hatched area represents tile.

4. CONFIGURATION AND TESSERA

For any configuration c, the tile index of $S(c)$ is called the tile index of the configuration c. Theorem 3.10 or Fig. 1 tells us that the tile of iterative configuration c can be regarded as a period of c.

Now let $\langle T, k_0 \rangle$ be the tile of c and ϕ be a mapping from T to Q such that $\phi = c|T$, i.e. a restriction of c to the domain T. (Note that c is a mapping from the domain Z^2 to Q.) Thus any configuration may correspond to a pair of $\langle T, k_0 \rangle$ and ϕ. We will formulate this fact.

Definition 4.1. For a tile $\langle T(i_0, j_0), k_0 \rangle$, a mapping $\phi : T(i_0, i_0) \to Q$ is called a coloring. The triple of $\langle T(i_0, j_0), k_0, \phi \rangle$ is called a colored tile and denoted sometimes by $\phi[i_0, j_0, k_0]$ or by ϕ for the sake of simplicity. A configuration c by a colored tile $\langle T(i_0, j_0), k_0, \phi \rangle$ is defined such that

$$c(\alpha) = \phi(h_0(\alpha)) \text{ for any } \alpha \in Z^2,$$

where h_0 is a reducing map of the tile. The configuration is sometimes denoted by $c[\phi]$ or $c[\phi; i_0, j_0, k_0]$.

The following lemma is obvious.

Lemma 4.2. For any colored tiles $\phi[i_0, j_0, k_0]$ and $\phi'[i_0, j_0, k_0]$, $c[\phi] = c[\phi']$ if and only if $\phi = \phi'$.

Proposition 4.3. For any configuration $c[\phi]$ by a colored tile $\phi[i_0, j_0, k_0]$, $S(c[\phi]) \supset G(i_0, j_0, k_0)$. ∎

Proof. By the definition of h_0, we have $h_0(\alpha - \beta) = h_0(\alpha)$ for any $\alpha \in Z^2$ and $\beta \in G(i_0, j_0, k_0)$. Therefore we have $s^\beta(c[\phi]) = c[\phi]$ for any $\beta \in G(i_0, j_0, k_0)$. ∎

Definition 4.4. A colored tile $\phi[i_0, j_0, k_0]$ is called degenerate if $S(c[\phi]) \neq G(i_0, j_0, k_0)$. Otherwise the tile is called non-degenerate. And a non-degenerate colored tile is called a tessera. The set of all tesseras is denoted by T_{es}.

Proposition 4.5. Let $\langle T(i_0, j_0), k_0 \rangle$ be the tile of a configuration c and a coloring ϕ be $c \mid T(i_0, j_0)$. Then the configuration $c[\phi]$ by the colored tile $\phi[i_0, j_0, k_0]$ is identical with c. And the colored tile is a tessera. (Hence it is called a tessera of c).

This is proved by straightforward calculation using the fact that $\alpha - h_0(\alpha) = \beta \in S(c)$ for any $\alpha \in Z^2$ by Theorem 3.10.

Thus the following theorem is followed.

Theorem 4.6. There is a one-to-one correspondence between configurations and tesseras.

Remember that $T(i_0, j_0)$ is a rectangle for a finite tile $\langle T(i_0, j_0), k_0 \rangle$. Therefore a coloring ϕ on $T(i_0, j_0)$ can be represented by an $i_0 \times j_0$ matrix whose entries are the elements of Q. The indices of the entries vary in integers from 0 to $i_0 - 1$ and 0 to $j_0 - 1$ respectively. A colored tile $\phi[i_0, j_0, k_0]$ can be represented by a coloring matrix with a dot under the $(i_0 - 1, k_0)$th entry. For the sake of clarity, a dot may be placed on the right side of the $((0, j_0) - 1)$th entry, too. For example, a colored tile

$$\phi[2,\ 4,\ 2] = \left\langle T(2,\ 4),\ 2,\ \begin{bmatrix} 1 & 1 & 1 & 0 \\ 0 & 1 & 0 & 1 \end{bmatrix} \right\rangle$$

is represented by $\begin{bmatrix} 1 & 1 & 1 & 0 \\ 0 & 1 & 0 & 1 \end{bmatrix} \cdot$

The dots correspond to the relative positions to put the real colored tile side by side in the two-dimensional space like in Fig. 2(b). It is easily known that the above colored tile is a tessera of a configuration in Fig. 2(a). That is, if the above colored tiles are placed side by side according to the indication of the dots, we have the iterative configuration in Fig. 2(a).

Thus given a finite tessera as a coloring matrix, we can easily construct a corresponding iterative configuration. Conversely, we can identify a tessera for a given iterative configuration. Therefore, we advocate that a tessera or its matrix form is a suitable representation of an iterative configuration in order for it to be stored into computer memory.

Whether or not a given colored tile is a tessera is not explicit in the definition. The following gives a condition to distinguish tesseras from degenerate colored tiles.

Theorem 4.7. For any colored tile $\phi_0[i_0, j_0, k_0]$, let ϕ_β be a coloring for each $\beta \in T(i_0, j_0)$ such that

$$\phi_\beta = s^\beta(c[\phi_0]) \mid T(i_0, j_0).$$

Then $\phi_0[i_0, j_0, k_0]$ is a tessera if and only if $\phi_0 \neq \phi_\beta$ for any $\beta \neq 0$.

Proof. It is easily shown that $c[\phi_\beta] = s^\beta(c[\phi_0])$ by the fact that $h_0(\alpha + \beta) = h_0(h_0(\alpha) + h_0(\beta))$ for any $\alpha, \beta \in Z^2$, which is proved straightforwardly by the definition of the reducing map h_0 for the tile $\langle T(i_0, j_0), k_0 \rangle$.

Sufficiency: Since $\beta \notin S(c[\phi_0]) = G(i_0, j_0, k_0)$ if $\beta \in T(i_0, j_0)$ and $\beta \neq 0$ by Theorem 3.10, we have $c[\phi_\beta] = s^\beta(c[\phi_0]) \neq c[\phi_0]$. Therefore by Lemma 4.2, $\phi_\beta \neq \phi_0$.

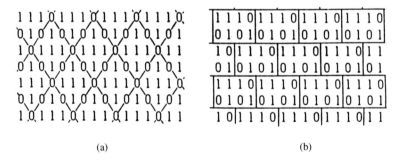

(a)   (b)

Fig. 2.   (a) An iterative pattern and   (b) decomposition by its tessera.

Necessity: Assume that $S(c[\phi_0]) \neq G(i_0, j_0, k_0)$. Then there is some $\gamma \in Z^2$ such that $\gamma \in S(c[\phi_0])$ and $\gamma \notin G(i_0, j_0, k_0)$ by Proposition 4.3. By using the notation of Theorem 3.10, we have $\gamma = h_0(\gamma) + g_0(\gamma)B_0$. Now let $\beta = h_0(\gamma)$, then by Theorem 3.10 we have $\beta \neq 0$ and $\beta \in T(i_0, j_0)$. And $\beta = \gamma - g_0(\gamma)B_0 \in S(c[\phi_0])$, since $g_0(\gamma)B_0 \in G(i_0, j_0, k_0) \subset S(c[\phi_0])$ and $S(c[\phi_0])$ is closed under addition. Thus we have $c[\phi_\beta] = s^\beta(c[\phi_0]) = c[\phi_0]$ or $c_\beta = c_0$. This completes the proof. ∎

Since ϕ_β is equal to $c[\phi_0] \mid (\beta + T(i_0, j_0))$ as an $i_0 \times j_0$ matrix, whether or not $\phi[i_0, j_0, k_0]$ is a tessera is checked by the investigation of all kinds of $i_0 \times j_0$ submatrices of a $2i_0 \times 2j_0$ matrix of coloring $c[\phi_0] \mid T(2i_0, 2j_0)$.

5. PATTERNS

Any configuration has an absolute coordinate. But sometimes, especially in considering a so-called pattern, the coordinate has little significance. So we abstract a pattern from the configuration.

Definition 5.1.

(1) A relation $\parallel$, called a parallel relation, between configurations is defined such that for any $c, c' \in C$, $c \parallel c'$ if $s^\gamma(c) = c'$ for some $\gamma \in Z^2$.
(2) For each $c \in C$, a subset $\langle c \rangle = \{c' \mid c \parallel c'\}$ is called a pattern. The set of patterns is denoted by C_P. Patterns are denoted by X, Y and so on, as elements of C_P.
(3) A pattern X is (un)iterative if $c \in X$ also.

Note that the parallel relation is an equivalence relation and the partition of C by it is C_P.

Definition 5.2. Colored tiles (or tesseras) $\phi_0[i_0, j_0, k_0]$ and $\phi_1[i_1, j_1, k_1]$ are equivalent, or $\phi_0 \equiv \phi_1$, if $c[\phi_0] \parallel c[\phi_1]$. The equivalence class of a tessera ϕ_0 with respect to the relation $\equiv$ in T_{es} is denoted by $\langle \phi_0 \rangle$.

Obviously the relation $\equiv$ is well-defined as an equivalence relation.

Theorem 5.3. For any pattern X, tiles of $c \in X$ are identical. And tesseras of $c \in X$ are equivalent to each other. Conversely, any configurations by equivalent tesseras belong to a single pattern.

Proof. For $c_0, c_1 \in X$, there is $\gamma \in Z^2$ such that $c_0 = s^\gamma(c_1)$. Since $c_1 = s^\beta(c_1)$ for any $\beta \in S(c_1)$, we have $c_0 = s^\gamma(c_1) = s^\gamma s^\beta(c_1) = s^\gamma s^\beta s^{-\gamma}(c_0) = s^\beta(c_0)$ for any $\beta \in S(c_1)$. Therefore $S(c_0) \supset S(c_1)$. Similarly, we have $S(c_0) \subset S(c_1)$. Hence $S(c_0) = S(c_1)$. By Theorem 3.8, it has been shown that tiles of c_0 and c_1 are identical. The latter part is obvious by the definitions and the above. ∎

Hence the tile is called the tile of pattern.

Corollary 5.4. The set C_P of patterns corresponds one-to-one to the partition $T_{es}/\equiv$ of the set T_{es} of tesseras, with respect to the equivalence relation $\equiv$.

Thus any pattern corresponds to an equivalence class of a tessera. The appropriate representative of the class may be regarded as a tessera of the pattern. Since a practical iterative pattern may have a finite tessera, tesseras of matrix form may be compact and simple representations of iterative patterns.

Proposition 5.5. For any tessera $\phi_0[i_0, j_0, k_0]$,

$$\langle \phi_0 \rangle = \{\langle T(i_0, j_0), k_0, \phi_\beta \rangle \mid \beta \in T(i_0, j_0)\},$$

where ϕ_β is the one defined in Theorem 4.7. And for any finite tessera $\phi_0[i_0, j_0, k_0]$, $|\langle \phi_0 \rangle| = i_0 \cdot j_0$.

Proof. The former is obvious by Theorem 5.3 and the definition of $\langle \phi_0 \rangle$. The latter is known by the fact that $\phi_\beta \neq \phi_\gamma$ for any β and γ such that $\beta \neq \gamma$, which is the immediate consequence of Theorem 4.7. ∎

This proposition tells us that an iterative pattern with finite tessera contains a finite number of configurations and the number is the determinant of the basic matrix of the title of the pattern.

6. FINITE COLORED TILE

Now we will investigate the natures of finite colored tiles with a fixed tile index.

Definition 6.1.

(1) A relation $\ll$ between tile indices is defined as follows: for two tile indices (i_0, j_0, k_0) and (i_1, j_1, k_1),

$$(i_1, j_1, k_1) \ll (i_0, j_0, k_0)$$

if and only if $G(i_1, j_1, k_1) \supset G(i_0, j_0, k_0)$. For this case the tile of (i_1, j_1, k_1) is called a small tile of (i_0, j_0, k_0).

(2) $D(i_0, j_0, k_0) = \{(i_1, j_1, k_1) \mid (i_1, j_1, k_1) \ll (i_0, j_0, k_0)\}$.

By Propositions 4.3 and 4.5, the tessera of the configuration by a given colored tile has a small tile of the given tile index.

Lemma 6.2. For tile indices (i_0, j_0, k_0) and (i_1, j_1, k_1), $(i_1, j_1, k_1) \ll (i_0, j_0, k_0)$ if and only if there exist integers a, b and e such that $i_0 = ai_1$, $j_0 = bj_1$ and $k_0 = ak_1 + ej_1$. Furthermore if $i_0 j_0 > 0$ then $1 \leq i_1 \leq i_0$ and $1 \leq j_1 \leq j_0$.

Proof. Assume that $i_0 j_0 > 0$. Let B_0 and B_1 be the basic matrices corresponding to the tile indices, respectively. By Lemma 2.2, $B_0 = UB_1$ for some matrix U. Let

$$U = \begin{bmatrix} a & e \\ e' & b \end{bmatrix},$$

then we have $e' = 0$ and the desired equations. The latter part is obvious. For the case of $i_0 j_0 = 0$, the proof is similar and omitted here. ∎

Although we discuss hereafter the case of $i_0 j_0 > 0$, we state here some obvious results related to Lemma 6.2 for the case of $i_0 j_0 = 0$. If $i_0 > 0$ and $j_0 = 0$ then b must be zero and the constraint for j_1 is the only third equation. If $i_0 = 0$ and $j_0 > 0$ (in this case

$k_0 = 0$), then a and e must be zero and hence i_1 and k_1 may take arbitrary values. Lastly if $i_0 = j_0 = 0$ then a, b and e must be all zero and hence i_1, j_1 and k_1 are all arbitrary.

From the above, the corresponding results for the case of $i_0 j_0 = 0$ may be understood with little modifications for the results for $i_0 j_0 > 0$. In the following, we will be concerned with the case of $i_0 j_0 > 0$ or the finite tile without the notice. The next lemma is obvious by the definition of reducing maps.

Lemma 6.3. Let h_0 and h_1 be reducing maps for tile indices of (i_0, j_0, k_0) and (i_1, j_1, k_1) respectively. If $(i_1, j_1, k_1) \ll (i_0, j_0, k_0)$ then $h_1(h_0(\beta)) = h_1(\beta)$ for any $\beta \in Z^2$.

Theorem 6.4. For any colored tile $\langle T(i_0, j_0), k_0, \phi_0 \rangle$, there exists a unique tessera $\langle T(i_1, j_1), k_1, \phi_1 \rangle$ such that $c[\phi_0] = c[\phi_1]$. And for the tile indices, $(i_1, j_1, k_1) \ll (i_0, j_0, k_0)$. Conversely, if $(i_1, j_1, k_1) \ll (i_0, j_0, k_0)$ and $\langle T(j_1, j_1), k_1, \phi_1 \rangle$ is a tessera, then there exists a unique colored tile $\langle T(i_0, j_0), k_0, \phi_0 \rangle$ such that $c[\phi_0] = c[\phi_1]$.

Proof. The first part is obvious by Theorem 4.6 and Proposition 4.3. For the converse, let $\phi_0 = c[\phi_1] \mid T(i_0, j_0)$. Then for any $\alpha \in Z^2$,

$$
\begin{aligned}
c[\phi_0](\alpha) &= \phi_0(h_0(\alpha)) \text{ by definition,} \\
&= (c[\phi_1] \mid T(i_0, j_0))(h_0(\alpha)) \text{ by definition of } \phi_0, \\
&= c[\phi_1](h_0(\alpha)) \text{ by } h_0(\alpha) \in T(i_0, j_0), \\
&= \phi_1(h_1(h_0(\alpha))) = \phi_1(h_1(\alpha)) \text{ by Lemma 6.3,} \\
&= c[\phi_1](\alpha).
\end{aligned}
$$

Thus $c[\phi_0] = c[\phi_1]$. The uniqueness is obvious by Lemma 4.2. ∎

This theorem tells us that the set of all colorings for a tile $\langle T(i_0, j_0), k_0 \rangle$ corresponds one-to-one to the set of all tesseras with small tiles of (i_0, j_0, k_0).

Next we discuss what kinds of small tiles of a tile (i_0, j_0, k_0) exist. The next lemma is well known in the theory of integers.

Lemma 6.5. For any integers a, b and c, the necessary and sufficient condition that there exists a solution for an equation: $a\mu + b\nu = c$ with indeterminate integers μ and ν is that $\delta = gcd(a, b)$ is a divisor of c. And if the condition holds then the general solution is given as $\mu = \mu_0 c_0 + q b_0$ and $\nu = \nu_0 c_0 - q a_0$, where q is arbitrary, $a = a_0 \delta$, $b = b_0 \delta$, $c = c_0 \delta$, and μ_0 and ν_0 are particular solutions of the equation: $a_0 \mu_0 + b_0 \nu_0 = 1$.

Note that the existence of μ_0 and ν_0 is assured by the fact that $gcd(a_0, b_0) = 1$. Let $\mu(a, b)$ be a solution μ of equation: $a\mu + b\nu = gcd(a, b)$. Lemma 6.5 says $\mu(a, b) = \mu(a_0, b_0) = \mu_0$.

Proposition 6.6. Let (i_0, j_0, k_0) be a tile index and i_1 and j_1 be divisors of i_0 and j_0 respectively. There exists an integer k_1 such that (i_1, j_1, k_1) is a tile index and $(i_1, j_1, k_1) \ll (i_0, j_0, k_0)$ if and only if $\delta = gcd(i_0/i_1, j_1)$ is a divisor of k_0. If this condition holds then there exist exactly δ kinds of k_1's satisfying $(i_1, j_1, k_1) \ll (i_0, j_0, k_0)$ and they are given as

$$
k_1 = (\mu_0 k_0 / \delta \mod (j_1/\delta)) + \kappa j_1/\delta,
$$

where $\kappa = 0, 1, \ldots, \delta - 1$ and $\mu_0 = \mu(i_0/i_1, j_1)$. (Note that a, b and e in Lemma 6.2 are expressed as $a = i_0/i_1$, $b = j_0/j_1$, and $e = (|\mu_0 k_0/j_1| - \kappa)(i_0/i_1)/\delta + \nu_0 k_0/\delta$.

Proof. The former part is obvious by Lemmas 6.2 and 6.5, since given k_0, $a = i_0/i_1$, and given j_1, there must exist k_1 and e satifying the equation:

$$k_0 = ak_1 + ej_1. \tag{*}$$

For the latter part, by Lemma 6.5, we have

$$k_1 = \mu_0 k_0/\delta + qj_1/\delta$$

as a solution of equation (*). Since (i_1, j_1, k_1) must be a tile index, it holds that $0 \leq k_1 < j_1$. Hence we have $-q_0 \leq q < \delta - q_0$ where $q_0 = |\mu_0 k_0/\delta|$. Letting $\kappa = q_0 + q$, we have $0 \leq \kappa < \delta$ and $k_1 = \mu_0 k_0/\delta - q_0 j_1/\delta + \kappa j_1/\delta$. And the first two terms equal to $\mu_0 k_0/\delta \bmod j_1/\delta$, since $q_0 = |(\mu_0 k_0/\delta)/(j_1/\delta)|$. ∎

The set $D(i_0, j_0, k_0)$ of tile indices of all of the small tiles of a tile index (i_0, j_0, k_0) is identified for some particular cases. The proof of the next proposition is a straightforward application of Proposition 6.6.

Proposition 6.7.

(1) If i_0 and j_0 are relatively prime, then for any k_0 such that $0 \leq k_0 < j_0$,

$$D(i_0, j_0, k_0) = \{(i, j, k) \mid i|i_0, \ j|j_0, \ k = k_0\mu(i_0/i, j) \bmod j\}.$$

(2) For any i_0 and j_0,

$$D(i_0, j_0, 0) = \{(i, j, k) \mid i|i_0, \ j|j_0, \ k = \kappa j/\delta, \ \kappa = 0, 1, \ldots, \delta - 1,$$
$$\text{and } \delta = gcd(i_0/i, j)\}.$$

For the other case of i_0, j_0 and k_0, it seems to be difficult to express $D(i_0, j_0, k_0)$ in an explicit form.

To illustrate a small tile of (i_0, j_0, k_0), we will show all kinds of sufficient conditions for $i_1 = 1$ or i_0 and $j_1 = 1$ or j_0 satisfying $(i_1, j_1, k_1) \ll (i_0, j_0, k_0)$. The proof is again omitted since it is the immediate consequence of Proposition 6.6.

Proposition 6.8. The following holds for any tile index (i_0, j_0, k_0).

(i) $(1, 1, 0) \ll (i_0, j_0, k_0)$ and $(i_0, 1, 0) \ll (i_0, j_0, k_0)$.

(ii) If i_0 and j_0 are relatively prime then $(1, j_0, k_0\mu(i_0, j_0) \bmod j_0) \ll (i_0, j_0, k_0)$.

(iii) Assume that i_0 and j_0 are not relatively prime. Let $\delta_0 = gcd(i_0, j_0)$ $(\delta_0 \geq 2)$.

(iii-a) If $\delta_0|k_0$ then for each κ $(0 \leq \kappa < \delta_0 - 1)$, $(1, j_0, k + \kappa j_0/\delta_0) \ll (i_0, j_0, k_0)$, where $k = (\mu(i_0, j_0)k_0/\delta_0) \bmod (j_0/\delta_0)$.

(iii-b) If $\delta_0 k_0$ then there exists no k such that $(1, j_0, k) \ll (i_0, j_0, k_0)$.

(iv) Particularly, if $i_0 = j_0$, then for the only case of $k_0 = 0$, $(1, j_0, \kappa) \ll (j_0, j_0, 0)$ for each $\kappa = 0, 1, \ldots, j_0 - 1$.

Examples of these are illustrated in Fig. 3.

(i-a) $(1, 1, 0) \ll (3, 4, 2)$ (i-b) $(3, 1, 0) \ll (3, 4, 2)$

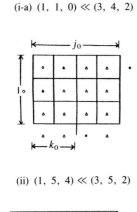
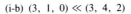
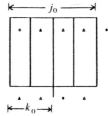
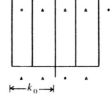

(ii) $(1, 5, 4) \ll (3, 5, 2)$ (iii-b) No small tile: $(3, 6, 4)$ etc.

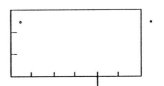

(iii-a) $(1, 6, 1 + 2\kappa) \ll (3, 6, 3)$ $\kappa = 0, 1, 2$

$k_i = 1$ $k_i = 3$ $k_i = 5$

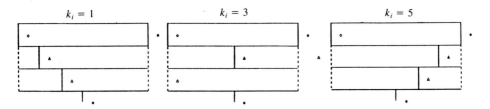
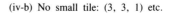

(iv-a) $(1, 3, \kappa) \ll (3, 3, 0)$ (iv-b) No small tile: $(3, 3, 1)$ etc.

$\kappa = 0$ $\kappa = 1$ $\kappa = 2$

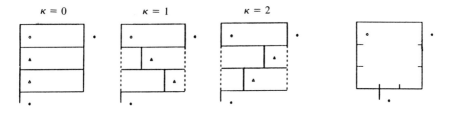

Key: $\circ$—$(0, 0)$, $\bullet$—(i_0, k_0), $(0, j_0)$, $\blacktriangle$—(i_1, k_1), $(0, j_1)$
     $\triangle$—points of $G(i_1, j_1, k_1)$

Fig. 3. Small tiles $((i_1, j_1, k_1) \ll (i_0, j_0, k_0),$ i_1 or $j_1 = 1)$.

7. THE NUMBER OF FINITE TESSERAS

Let $|Q| = s$ and $f(i_0, j_0, k_0)$ be the number of tesseras with finite tiles of a tile index (i_0, j_0, k_0).

Lemma 7.1.

$$\sum_{(i,j,k) \in D(i_0, j_0, k_0)} f(i, j, k) = s^{i_0 j_0} \qquad (*)$$

Proof. The right side is the number of all possible colorings for the tile $\langle T(i_0, j_0), k_0 \rangle$, since there are s kinds of assignments of colors to each element of $T(i_0, j_0)$. The left side is the sum of the numbers of tesseras with small tiles of (i_0, j_0, k_0). The identity holds by Theorem 6.4. ∎

This equation (*) gives a straightforward recursive algorithm to calculate the value of $f(i_0, j_0, k_0)$, while $f(i, j, k)$ will be estimated recursively by a similar equation for each $(i, j, k) \in D(i_0, j_0, k_0) - \{(i_0, j_0, k_0)\}$.

Now we will show an explicit form for $f(i_0, j_0, k_0)$. To apply Proposition 6.6, we introduce a function $P_{\mathrm{div}} : Z^2 \to \{0, 1\}$ such that

$$P_{\mathrm{div}}(a, b) = \begin{cases} 1 & \text{if } a \mid b. \\ 0 & \text{otherwise} \end{cases}$$

Using this function, we have the next equation equivalent to (*).

$$\Sigma_{j \mid j_0} \Sigma_{a \mid i_0} P_{\mathrm{div}}(\delta_{aj}, k_0) \cdot$$

$$\sum_{\kappa=0}^{\delta_{aj}-1} f(i_0/a, j, (\mu_{aj} k_0/\delta_{aj}) \bmod (j/\delta_{aj}) + \kappa j/\delta_{aj})$$

$$= s^{i_0 j_0}, \qquad (**)$$

where $\delta_{aj} = \gcd(a, j)$ and $\mu_{aj} = \mu(a, j)$.

To simplify the equation, we need some functions. Let M be the Möbius' function, i.e. $M(1) = 1$, and for $n > 1$,

$$M(n) = \begin{cases} (-1)^r & \text{if } n = p_1 \cdots p_r \ (p_k\text{'s are distinct primes}), \\ 0 & \text{if } n = p^2 n' \text{ for some prime } p. \end{cases}$$

The next lemma is well-known.

Lemma 7.2. For integer functions F and G,

$$\Sigma_{d \mid n} F(d) = G(n) \text{ if and only if } F(n) = \Sigma_{d \mid n} M(d) G(n/d).$$

Note that $F(d)$ of Lemma 7.2 must not depend on both d and n/d. So the next lemma is not trivial but the proof is similar to Lemma 7.2.

Lemma 7.3   For integer functions F and G,

$$\Sigma_{d|n}(n/d)F(d) = G(n) \text{ if and only if } F(n) = \Sigma_{d|n} dM(d)G(n/d).$$

Let r be a function from Z^2 to Z such that $r(a, b)$ is the product of all prime factors of a which are not any prime factors of b. Hence $r(a, b)$ and b are relatively prime and $r(a, b)$ is a divisor of a. If $b|a$ then $r(a, b) = r(a/b, b)$.

Lemma 7.4.   Let i_0, j_0 and k_0 be arbitrary non-negative integers. For any integer a, $a|i_0$, $b = gcd(a, j_0)$ and $b|k_0$ if and only if $d|d_0$, $e|r(i_1^*, d)$, $b = d_0/d$ and $a = ed_0/d$ for some integers d and e, where $\delta_0 = gcd(i_0, j_0) = gcd(\delta_0, k_0) = gcd(i_0, j_0, k_0)$, and $i_1^* = r(i_0/\delta_0, \delta_0/d_0)$.

Furthermore, a solution μ of the equation: $a\mu + j_0\nu = b$ is expressed as $\mu = \mu_1 i_1^*/e + mj_0/d_0$, where μ_1 is a solution of the equation: $i_1^*\mu_1 + (j_0/d_0)\nu_1 = 1$ and m is an arbitrary integer.

The proof is straightforward and omitted. Note that $gcd(i_1^*, j_0/d_0) = 1$, since i_0/δ and j_0/δ_0 are relatively prime, $i_1^* \mid (i_0/\delta_0)$, $j_0/d_0 = (j_0/\delta_0)(\delta_0/d_0))$, and i_1^* and δ_0/d_0 are relatively prime. And notice that δ_0, d_0, i_1^* and μ_1 are determined by i_0, j_0 and k_0 and do not depend on a, b, d or e.

Applying Lemma 7.2 for (**) as it is the summation with respect to $j|j_0$, and then applying Lemma 7.4, we have the next equation.

$$\Sigma_{d|d_0} \Sigma_{e|r(i_1^*,d)} \Sigma_{\kappa=0}^{d_0/d-1}$$

$$f(di_0/(d_0e),\ j_0,\ d((i_1^*/e)\mu_1 k_0/d_0 \bmod(j_0/d_0) + \kappa\ j_0/d_0))$$

$$= \Sigma_{j|j_0}M(j)s^{i_0j_0/j}. \tag{***}$$

Using this equation, we have the next proposition, which is proved by mathematical induction on the number of prime factors of i_0.

Proposition 7.5.   For each of the integers i_0 and j_0, let $\delta_0 = gcd(i_0, j_0)$ and d_0 be any divisor of δ_0. Then

$$f(i_0,\ j_0,\ d_0k_1) = f(i_0,\ j_0,\ d_0)$$

for any integer k_1 such that k_1 is relatively prime to δ_0/d_0. Hence for any k_0, such that $0 \le k_0 < j_0$, $f(i_0, j_0, k_0) = f(i_0, j_0, gcd(i_0, j_0, k_0))$.

By this fact, equation (***) and Lemma 7.3, we have the last main result after a rather lengthy and tedious proof[4] of induction on the number (the sum of all exponents) of prime factors of i_0, so that we cannot help but omit it.

Theorem 7.6.   Let i_0 and j_0 be positive integers and k_0 be an integer such that $0 \le k_0 < j_0$. Let $d_0 = gcd(i_0, j_0, k_0)$ and $i_1 = r(i_0, gcd(i_0, j_0))$. The number of tessera with (i_0, j_0, k_0) is given as follows.

$$f(i_0, j_0, k_0) = \sum_{d \mid d_0} \sum_{j \mid i_1 j_0} d M(d) M(j) s^{i_0 j_0 / (dj)}.$$

Note that i_1 comes from the fact that $i_1 = r(i_1^*, d_0)$, $r(i_1^*, d) = r(i_1^*/i_1, d) \cdot i_1$. And note that $r(i_1^*/i_1, d)$ and i_1 are relatively prime.

8. CONCLUSION

To represent iterative patterns, the new concepts of tile and tessera are introduced and their validity is shown. It is shown that the tessera is a compact description of iterative patterns.

It is easy to extend the results to three-dimensional iterative patterns. But the enumeration of tesseras may require further consideration.

ACKNOWLEDGEMENT

The authors would like to thank Professor Y. Inagaki of Nagoya University for his helpful advice and comments.

REFERENCES

1. K. Husimi and G. Nakamura, "Unraveling of the mystery of the Escher's art of drawing", *Asahi J. of Sciences*, May 1979.
2. G. Nakamura, "Iterative patterns and Escher's drawings", *Mathematical Sciences*, May 1981.
3. H. S. M. Coxeter and W. O. J. Moser, *Generators and Relations for Discrete Groups*, Springer-Verlag, Berlin, 1965.
4. H. Aso and N. Honda, "The number of iterative patterns with a fixed iteration", Tech. Res. Rep. of Inf. Sci. No. 8212, Nagoya University, 1982.
5. H. Aso and N. Honda, "A description method of iterative patterns", *Trans. IECEJ* **E66** 4 (1983) 234–240.

Hirotomo Aso received the B.E., M.E. and D.E. degrees in electrical engineering from Tohoku University, Sendai, Japan in 1968, 1970 and 1974 respectively. He was with the Department of Information Engineering, Tohoku University in 1973. He joined the Faculty of Engineering, Nagoya University from 1979 to 1986. He is now an Associate Professor at Tohoku University.

He has engaged in research in the fields of learning and adaptive automata, neural networks, cellular automata, concurrent program schema and parallel processing.

Dr. Aso is a member of the Institute of Electronics, Information and Communication Engineers of Japan, the Information Processing Society of Japan, IEEE, EATCS and ACM.

Namio Honda received the B.E. and D.E. degrees in electrical communication engineering from Tohoku University, Sendai, Japan, in 1944 and 1959 respectively. He joined the Faculty of the Research Institute of Electrical Communication, Tohoku University in 1946. He was a Professor of Tohoku University from 1960 and was President of the Research Institute from 1972 to 1975. He was Professor of Nagoya University from 1976 to 1981. He then joined Toyohashi University of Technology, where he was Vice-President from 1982 to 1984. He has now been President of the university since 1984.

He has engaged in research on information theory and automata theory. He is the author of the books *Introduction to Information Theory* and *Theory of Automata and Languages*.

Dr. Honda is a member of IEE Japan, IEICE Japan and IEEE.

ENCRYPTION-DECRYPTION TECHNIQUES FOR PICTURES

RANI SIROMONEY, K. G. SUBRAMANIAN and P. J. ABISHA

Department of Mathematics, Madras Christian College
Tambaram, Madras 600 059, India

Received 30 May 1989

Language theoretic public key cryptosystems for strings and pictures are discussed. Two methods of constructing public key cryptosystems for the safe transmission or storage of chain code pictures are presented; the first one encrypts a chain code picture as a string and the second one as a two-dimensional array.

Keywords: Cryptosystems; L-systems; Array grammars.

1. INTRODUCTION

During recent years, cryptography has been a major field of study with researchers having different backgrounds contributing to the explosive growth of this area. One of the main reasons for the interest has been the need for ensuring secrecy and security of data.

Messages to be sent through an insecure channel are called plain texts. The sender encrypts the plain text and sends the resulting cryptotext through the channel. The receiver decrypts the cryptotext and obtains the plain text. The encryption and decryption are carried out in terms of a specific cryptosystem.

There has been a lot of interest in the construction of safe and effective public key cryptosystems (PKC). The basic idea of a PKC is due to Diffie and Hellman.[1] For a PKC to be safe and effective, encryption and decryption are to be easy but cryptanalysis or breaking the code is to be difficult. The secret information in the trapdoor enables the legal recipient to decrypt the cryptotext easily. Without the trapdoor information, decoding the message is difficult.

Salomaa[2] has discussed the general technique for the construction of a PKC. Choose a difficult (undecidable or intractable) problem Q and a subproblem P which is solvable, preferably in linear time. Shuffle P to obtain $\bar{P}$, which looks like Q. The manner of shuffling is the trapdoor which keeps the information secret. Use $\bar{P}$ to encrypt and P to decrypt.

Several PKCs based on different principles are known. The RSA system[3] and the knapsack system[4] are two well-known PKCs. Recently, PKCs based on formal language theory have been proposed and investigated.[5-9] In this note, we discuss the language theoretic methods of encryption and decryption of words and pictures and introduce suitable modified cryptosystems for pictures.

International Journal of Pattern Recognition and Artificial Intelligence Vol. 3 No. 3 & 4 (1989) 497–503
© World Scientific Publishing Company

2. LANGUAGE THEORETIC PKCS FOR STRINGS

The earliest PKC[2,5,10] based on language theory or more specifically on the theory of L-systems was constructed using a TOL system for public encryption key. This TOL system was obtained from a much simpler underlying system, namely a DTOL system. The trapdoor information kept secret is concerned with how the DTOL system can be recovered from the TOL system. It was pointed out that without this information, cryptanalysis leads to the membership problem for TOL systems, which is NP-complete, whereas for the DTOL systems the membership problem is solvable in polynomial time. This PKC is an interesting application of formal language theory to cryptography. Recently, Kari[11] has made a cryptanalytic attack on this PKC, which might reveal the plain text.

Motivated by the PKC outlined above another PKC based on L-systems has been proposed in Ref. 12. Here the public encryption key involves a TOL system obtained from a DOL system making use of a morphism. The advantage is that the decryption based on the trapdoor information is very straightforward and simpler than that of Ref. 5. Again cryptanalysis depends on an NP-complete problem, namely, the membership problem for TOL system. The cryptanalytic attack of Kari[11] is not suitable here due to the fact that the plain text does not control the application of TOL tables and, in addition, the axiom for encryption keeps changing depending on the plain text.

PKCs based on word problems have also been proposed.[8,9,13,14] Salomaa points out[10] a method for breaking the PKC given in Ref. 9 by preprocessing. In Ref. 13 we have proposed a PKC based on word problems for Thue systems and using the concept of codes. The technique is to use a Church-Rosser Thue system T satisfying certain conditions and using a morphism, construct another Thue system $\bar{T}$. The morphism is the trapdoor function. Encryption of a plain text is done using $\bar{T}$ and decryption with the help of T. It is known that the word problem for a Thue system is undecidable, whereas, for a Church-Rosser Thue system, it is solvable in linear time. This fact enables us to make decryption easy but cryptanalysis hard. As a special case, we can take a finitely presented group G for encryption and a free group with certain code conditions for decryption. Besides these, in Ref. 6 a PKC is discussed based on the undecidability of the word problem for a special Thue system. Decryption depends on the solvability of word problems in linear time for the restricted Dyck set.

Among the various techniques developed so far the methods introduced in Refs. 12 and 13 seem to work better with respect to encryption and decryption, and cryptanalysis seems to be difficult.

3. PKCS FOR PICTURES

A picture is treated as a composition of simple subpictures whose structure is described by linguistic tools. Pictures whose components are cells or unit lines from a rectangular grid are suitable for a formal approach and are very close to many situations in digital image processing. Sets of pictures composed of cells are referred to as array languages. A survey of various array models that generate or parse sets of pictures is given in Ref. 15.

A very simple model for line pictures has been investigated in Ref. 16. A line picture is described by a word over the alphabets $\{l, r, u, d\}$ where "u" means go (and draw) one unit line "up" from the current point and d, r, l are interpreted similarly. Sets of such pictures are called "chain code pictures".

In Ref. 7, we have constructed PKCs for picture languages. Two kinds of systems are proposed. In the first system, pictures to be encrypted are taken in the form of chain code pictures and are described using the alphabet $\{l, r, u, d\}$. The deterministic tabled OL array system[17] is found useful since four tables namely, left, right, up and down are used in the generation, which will reflect the four letter alphabet. A nondeterministic OL array system is constructed from the deterministic model and it is used to encrypt a chain code picture as a two-dimensional array. This system is an extension of the system constructed in Ref. 5 and as such is vulnerable to the kind of cryptanalytic attack envisaged in Ref. 11.

In the second type of PKC for pictures, the picture is considered as a digitized array and array morphisms and substitutions are used for decryption and encryption. This system is an extension of the method proposed in Ref. 12. The uniform size of the arrays in the array substitutions used for encryption might give a clue to a possible cryptanalytic method for this kind of PKC.

4.   ENCRYPTION AND DECRYPTION OF PICTURES

Having discussed PKCs for pictures, and having pointed out the advantages and disadvantages of the systems, in this section we modify suitably the methods for encryption and decryption of pictures and introduce a DOL/TOL based PKC for chain code pictures.

4.1.   DOL/TOL PKC for Chain Code Pictures

In Ref. 7, a PKC has been given to encrypt chain code pictures as two-dimensional arrays, using the technique given by Salomaa.[5] The system in Ref. 7 is vulnerable to the cryptanalytic attack suggested by Kari in Ref. 11. We now describe a method for encrypting chain code pictures as strings using the technique of the system in Ref. 12.

The PKC is constructed as follows: Choose four words x_l, x_r, x_u, x_d over $\Sigma = \{0, 1\}$, corresponding to the plain text alphabet $\{l, r, u, d\}$ such that $\{x_l, x_r, x_u, x_d\}$ forms a code, that is, any word over $\{0, 1\}$ has at most one decomposition over $\{x_l, x_r, x_u, x_d\}$. Let h be a homomorphism on $\{0, 1\}$ such that $\{x_l, x_r, x_u, x_d, h(0), h(1)\}$ is again a code.

Choose another alphabet Δ whose cardinality is much greater than that of Σ and define $g: \Delta \rightarrow \Sigma \cup \{\lambda\}$ as in Ref. 12. Choose words w_l, w_r, w_u, w_d in $g^{-1}(x_l)$, $g^{-1}(x_r)$, $g^{-1}(x_u)$, $g^{-1}(x_d)$ respectively. Define substitutions t_i, $i = 1, 2, \ldots, m$ for some $m > 1$ on Δ^* such that $t_i(d)$ is a finite nonempty subset of $g^{-1}(h(g(d)))$ for all d in Δ.

221

The encryption key is $(\Delta, t_1, \ldots, t_m, w_l, w_r, w_u, w_d)$ and it is publicized. The encryption of a plain text $w = p_1 p_2 \ldots p_r, p_j \in \{l, r, u, d\}, j = 1, \ldots, r$ is done as follows: A word z is obtained from w by replacing each p_j by w_l (w_r, w_u, w_d) according to $p_j = l$ (r, u, d). The cryptotext is obtained by choosing an arbitrary word c from $t_{j_k} (t_{j_2} (t_{j_1} (z))) \ldots), k \geq 1$ where $j_1, j_2, \ldots, j_k \in \{1, 2, \ldots, m\}$.

Decryption is done as follows: If c is the cryptotext, $g(c)$ is found first and then parsed using the homomorphism h. Since $\{x_l, x_r, x_u, x_d, h(0), h(1)\}$ is a code, the plain text can be obtained uniquely.

We illustrate with a toy example.

Let $x_l = 01$, $x_r = 10$, $x_u = 110$, $x_d = 111$, $h(0) = 001$, $h(1) = 000$
$\Delta = \{c_1, c_2, c_3, c_4, c_5\}$. Define $g : \Delta \to \Sigma \cup \{\lambda\}$ by
$g(c_1) = g(c_2) = 0$, $g(c_3) = 1$, $g(c_4) = g(c_5) = \lambda$.

Let $w_l = c_1 c_4 c_3$, $w_r = c_5 c_3 c_2$, $w_u = c_3 c_4 c_3 c_5 c_1$, $w_d = c_4 c_3 c_5 c_4 c_3 c_3$.
$t_1 = \{c_1 \to c_1 c_2 c_3, c_1 \to c_1 c_2 c_3 c_4, c_2 \to c_2 c_2 c_3, c_3 \to c_2 c_1 c_2,$
$\qquad c_4 \to c_4 c_5, c_5 \to c_5 c_4 c_5\}$
$t_2 = \{c_1 \to c_1 c_1 c_4 c_3, c_2 \to c_1 c_1 c_3 c_4, c_3 \to c_1 c_5 c_2 c_2, c_4 \to c_4, c_5 \to c_5 c_5\}$

Let *ruld* be the plain text. Then *ruld* is replaced by $w_r w_u w_l w_d$ which is equal to

$$c_5 c_3 c_2 c_3 c_4 c_3 c_5 c_1 c_1 c_4 c_3 c_4 c_3 c_5 c_4 c_3 c_3$$

which derives

$$c_5 c_4 c_5 c_2 c_1 c_2 c_2 c_2 c_3 c_2 c_1 c_2 c_4 c_5 c_2 c_1 c_2 c_5 c_4 c_5 c_1 c_2 c_3 c_1 c_2 c_3 c_4 c_4 c_5 c_2 c_1 c_2 c_4 c_5$$

$$\times \; c_2 c_1 c_2 c_5 c_4 c_5 c_4 c_5 c_2 c_1 c_2 c_2 c_1 c_2 .$$

For decryption, applying g to this we get

$$000001000000001001000000000000,$$

from which we get 1011001111. Hence the plain text is *ruld*.

In Ref. 7, a PKC for chain code pictures is given where the plain text is used as a control word which provides the order in which the substitutions should be applied on a given axiom word. Hence it is vulnerable to the attack given in Ref. 12. But in this PKC, the plain text corresponds to the axiom and we require the set $\{x_l, x_r, x_u, x_d, h(0), h(1)\}$ to be a code. This makes the decryption possible and at the same time the attack described in Ref. 11 fails to break this PKC.

4.2. Encryption of Pictures as Pictures

In Sect. 4.1, a method of encrypting a chain code picture as a string is discussed. In this section, we describe another method which encrypts a chain code picture as a two-dimensional picture. Encryption is done using a tabled OL array system[17] and the decryption is done using a deterministic tabled OL array system. Since the membership problem for TOL systems is NP-complete and for DTOL systems it takes polynomial time, cryptanalysis for this PKC is hard while encryption and decryption are easy.

A tabled OL array system (TOLAS) consists of an alphabet Σ and four complete tables of rewriting rules for the letters of Σ corresponding to the four letters l, r, u, d of the chain code alphabet. The lengths of the right sides of any two rules in the same table are equal. A derivation is done by applying the rules of the left (right, up or down) table in parallel, to the left side (right side, top row or bottom row) of an array respectively. A TOLAS is said to be a deterministic TOLAS (DTOLAS) if each of the four tables is deterministic.

The PKC is constructed as follows: Choose four arrays L_0, R_0, U_0, D_0 over $\Sigma = \{0, 1\}$ corresponding to the alphabet $\{l, r, u, d\}$ satisfying the following conditions:

(i) all of them have the same number of rows.

(ii) the set Y of rows and columns of these arrays forms a code.

Consider four homomorphisms h_l, h_r, h_u, h_d on $\Sigma = \{0, 1\}$ corresponding to the letters l, r, u, d respectively, satisfying the following conditions:

(iii) $|h_j(0)| = |h_j(1)|, j \in \{l, r, u, d\}$

(iv) the set $X = Y \cup \{h_j(0), h_j(1)/j \in \{l, r, u, d\}\}$ forms a code.

Conditions (i) and (iii) assert that the array operations performed will be well-defined. Conditions (ii) and (iv) help to parse a given array over the homomorphisms h_l, h_r, h_u, h_d.

As in the earlier cases, an alphabet Δ whose cardinality is much greater than that of Σ, is chosen and a morphism $g: \Delta \rightarrow \Sigma \cup \{x\}$ is defined where x is a new symbol. The homomorphisms h_l, h_r, h_u, h_d are extended to h_l', h_r', h_u', h_d' by introducing junk rules of the type $h_j'(x) = x \ldots x$ such that $|h_j'(x)| = |h_j(0)|, j \in \{l, r, u, d\}$. Define substitutions $t_l^i, t_r^i, t_u^i, t_d^i$ over Δ such that $t_j^i(d)$ is a finite, nonempty subset of $g^{-1}(h_j'(g(d))), j \in \{l, r, u, d\}$ for all d in Δ, $i = 1, \ldots, m$ for some finite m. For the sake of simplicity, we can even have two sets of four substitutions.

Consider four arrays L_0', R_0', U_0', D_0' by introducing columns and rows of x in L_0, R_0, U_0, D_0 such that the number of rows in L_0', R_0', U_0', D_0' are equal. Choose four arrays L_1, R_1, U_1, D_1 such that $g(L_1) = L_0', g(R_1) = R_0', g(U_1) = U_0', g(D) = D_0'$. The public encryption key is $(L_1, R_1, U_1, D_1, t_j'), j \in \{l, r, u, d\}$, $i = 1, \ldots, m$. Encryption is done by first replacing the occurrences of l, r, u, d by L_1, R_1, U_1, D_1 respectively and then the substitutions are applied. Decryption can be done easily by first applying "g", removing the xs, and then parsing the resultant array using h_l, h_r, h_u, h_d. This system is safe under the attack given in Ref. 11.

REFERENCES

1. W. Diffie and M. E. Hellman, "New directions in cryptography", *IEEE Trans. Information Theory* **22**, 6 (1976) 644 − 654.
2. A. Salomaa, "Public key cryptosystems and language theory" in *A Perspective in Theoretical Computer Science—Commemorative Volume for Gift Siromoney*, Ed. R. Narasimhan, World Scientific, 1989, pp. 257 − 266.

3. R. L. Rivest, A. Shamir and L. Adleman, "A method for obtaining digital signatures and public key cryptosystems", *Comm. ACM* **21**, 2 (1978) 120 – 126.
4. R. C. Merkle and M. E. Hellman, "Hiding information and signatures in trapdoor knapsacks", *IEEE Trans. Information Theory* **24**, 5 (1978) 525 – 530.
5. A. Salomaa, *Computation and Automata*, Cambridge University Press, 1986.
6. G. Siromoney and R. Siromoney, "A public key cryptosystem that defies cryptanalysis", *Bull. of EATCS* **28** (1986) 37 – 43.
7. R. Siromoney, K. G. Subraimanian and P. J. Abisha, "Cryptosystem for picture languages", in *Syntactic and Structural Pattern Recognition*, Eds. G. Ferrate, T. Pavlidis, A. Sanfeliu, H. Bunke, NATO ASI Series, Springer-Verlag, Berlin, 1988, pp. 315 – 332.
8. R. Siromoney, Do Long Van, P. J. Abisha and K. G. Subramanian, "Public key cryptosystem based on finitely presented groups" presented at the Int. Conf. on Mathematics in Developing Countries, Ho Chi Minh City, Vietnam, 1988.
9. N. R. Wagner and M. R. Magyarik, "A public key cryptosystem based on word problem" *Lecture Notes in Computer Science* **196**, Springer Verlag, 1985, pp. 19 – 35.
10. A. Salomaa and S. Yu, "On a public key cryptosystem based on iterated morphisms and substitutions", *Theoretical Computer Science* **48** (1986) 283 – 296.
11. J. Kari, "A cryptanalytic observation concerning systems based on language theory", *Discrete Applied Mathematics* **21** (1988) 265 – 268.
12. K. G. Subramanian, P. J. Abisha and R. Siromoney, "A DOL/TOL public key cryptosystem", *Information Processing Letters* **26** (1987/88) 95 – 97.
13. R. Siromoney, P. J. Abisha, Do Long Van and K. G. Subramanian "Public key cryptosystem based on word problems", Technical Report 17, Department of Mathematics, Madras Christian College, March 1987.
14. G. Siromoney, R. Siromoney, K. G. Subramanian, V. R. Dare and P. J. Abisha, "Generalized Parikh vector and public key cryptosystems" in *A Perspective in Theoretical Computer Science—Commemorative Volume for Gift Siromoney*, Ed. R. Narasimhan, World Scientific, 1989, pp. 301 – 323.
15. R. Siromoney, "Array languages and Lindenmayer systems—A survey" in *The Book of L*, Eds. G. Rozenberg and A. Salomaa, Springer-Verlag, Berlin, 1985 pp. 413 – 426.
16. H. A. Maurer, G. Rozenberg and E. Welzl, "Using string languages to describe picture languages", *Information and Control* **54** (1982) 155 – 185.
17. R. Siromoney and G. Siromoney, "Extended controlled table L-arrays", *Information and Control* **35** (1977) 119 – 138.

Rani Siromoney received the B.A. (Hons.) in mathematics from Madras University in 1950, the A.M. degree in 1960 from Columbia University, New York, where she was a Fulbright Smith-Mundt scholar and the Ph.D. degree from Madras University in 1970. From 1951 to 1979, she was on the teaching faculty of the Department of Mathematics, Madras Christian College, Tambaram, Madras. She was chairman of the department from 1979 to 1988. She is at present Professor Emeritus appointed by the University Grants Commission, Government of India and directs the research program at the Department of Mathematics, Madras Christian College, where she has built a strong and active research group in the areas of formal grammars and languages, automata, picture and graph languages, pattern recognition, cryptography, infinite words, codes, Thue systems and other related areas of theoretical computer science.

She is author or coauthor of more than fifty research papers and four books. She is on the editorial board of the journals *Theoretical Computer Science* and *International Journal of Foundations of Computer Science*. She was a member of the program committee for the conferences on Foundations of Software Technology and Theoretical Computer Science organized by the Tata Institute of Fundamental Research, Bombay, from 1980–88. She was a consultant at the University of Maryland in 1974 and has delivered special lectures and presented papers at various conferences at national and international levels. She is the recipient of awards such as "Distinguished Author", "Best Teacher" and "Outstanding Woman Professional", from different organizations in India.

K. G. Subramanian received the M.Sc. degree in mathematics in 1969 and the Ph.D. degree in 1980 from Madras University. Since 1970, he has been on the teaching faculty of the Department of Mathematics, Madras Christian College, Tambaram, Madras. In the academic year 1984–85, he visited the Institut National de Recherche en Informatique et Automatique and the University of Paris under a French government scholarship. He is author or coauthor of about thirty research papers in his fields of interest which include formal languages, automata, array and graph languages, cryptography, infinite words, codes and Thue systems. He has presented papers at several conferences in India.

P. Jeyanthi Abisha received the M.Sc. degree in mathematics from Madras University in 1983 and the M.Phil. degree from the same university in 1984. She is at present on the teaching faculty of the Department of Mathematics, Madras Christian College, Tambaram, Madras. She is doing research in the areas of cryptography, Thue systems and picture languages.

ABOUT THE EDITOR

Patrick S. P. Wang is a visting scientist at MIT Artificial Intelligence Laboratory, on leave from Northeastern University. He received his Ph. D. degree in computer science from Oregon State University, his M.S.I.C.S. degree from Georgia Institute of Technology, his M.S.E.E. degree from National Taiwan University and his B.S.E.E. degree from National Chiao Tung University.

Before joining Northeastern University as tenured full Professor of Computer Science, he had been with WANG Laboratories, GTE Laboratories, Boston University and University of Oregon as software engineering specialist, senior member of technical staff, adjunct Associate Professor and Assistant Professor, respectively. He is now also teaching part-time at Harvard University.

Prof. Wang has edited four books, and published over sixty technical papers in imaging technology, pattern recognition and artificial intelligence. One of his most recent inventions concerning Pattern Recognition Systems has been granted by the US Patent Bureau. He has attended and organized numerous international conferences for IEEE, ACM, ICS, AAAI, CLCS and the International Association for Pattern Recognition. He is also a reviewer for grants proposals of the NSF Intelligent Systems Division, and for several computer journals including *IEEE-PAMI, Computer Vision, Graphics, and Image Processing, Information Sciences,* and *Information Processing Letters.* Prof. Wang is now an editor-in-charge of the *International Journal of Pattern Recognition and Artificial Intelligence* (World Scientific Publishing Co.).

As a senior member of IEEE, Prof. Wang is also a member of ACM, AAAI, the Pattern Recognition Society and a governing board member and the newsletter editor of the Chinese Language Computer Society (CLCS), Washington, D.C. His research interests include software engineering, programming languages, pattern recognition, artificial intelligence, image technology, and automation.

Prof. Wang has also written several articles on the operas of Puccini and Wagner, and on Beethoven's and Mozart's symphonies.